GW00645256

5 v

947.00491714

TRURO
Tel: 79205

**15 NOV 1995**

15 SEP 1992 WITHDRAWN DEC 1995

2 9 FEB 1996

3 1 JAN 1994 − 8 JUN 1996

1 9 APR 1994
19 JUL 1994

1 1 FEB 1995

2 9 JUL 199

SEATON, ALBERT          N.F

The Horsemen of the Steppes
The story of the cossacks
0370305345

**CORNWALL COUNTY COUNCIL**
**LIBRARIES AND ARTS DEPARTMENT**

# THE HORSEMEN OF THE STEPPES
## *The Story of the Cossacks*

BY THE SAME AUTHOR

*The Russo-German War 1941–45*
*The Battle for Moscow 1941–42*
*Stalin as Military Commander*
*The Crimean War—A Russian Chronicle 1852–56*
*The Fall of Fortress Europe 1943–45*
*The German Army 1933–45*

# THE HORSEMEN OF THE STEPPES

## The Story of the Cossacks

## ALBERT SEATON

947.00491714

TRU

THE BODLEY HEAD
LONDON

947.00491714

British Library Cataloguing
in Publication Data
Seaton, Albert
The horsemen of the Steppes.
1. Cossacks—History
I. Title
947'.00491714       DK35
ISBN 0 370 30534 5

© Albert Seaton 1985
Printed in Great Britain for
The Bodley Head Ltd
9 Bow Street, London WC2E 7AL
by The Pitman Press Ltd, Bath
Set in Linotron 202 Sabon
by Rowland Phototypesetting Ltd
Bury St Edmunds, Suffolk
*First published 1985*

*The Russian Cossack did not exist while the Tatar
was lord of the steppe—Russian Cossacks only
came into being when the Tatar control was challenged—and they took on the ways of the Tatar
Cossacks.*

THE GEOGRAPHICAL DICTIONARY OF THE
RUSSIAN EMPIRE, 1804

# Contents

*Notes are gathered at the end of each chapter.*

# Acknowledgements

Grateful thanks are expressed to the Librairie Plon of Paris for their kind permission to quote (on pp. 118, 121 and 122) from Jean Hanoteau's translation of *The Memoirs of General de Caulaincourt*; and to Macmillan and Company of London for their generous agreement to the use of extracts from *1812*, edited by Anthony Brett-James. Acknowledgement is also made to Mr Andrew Gregorovich for the sight of an ancient map in his possession of the Don and Caucasian territories.

The full detail of the source of the illustrations can be found by reference to the bibliography at the end of this book. The sources are: Illustration No. 1 from Kargalov (artist E. Vaniukov); Nos. 2, 9, 10, 25, 26, 27 and 34 from Shcherbina; No. 3 (artist I. E. Repin), No. 4 (artist V. I. Surikov), No. 11 (artist A. O. Orlovsky), photos all from Cresson; Nos. 5 and 6 from Popov; Nos. 7 and 8 from *Istoricheskii Vestnik*, 1902; No. 12 (artist G. Doré) photo by courtesy of the BBC Hulton Picture Library, London; Nos. 13, 14 and 15 from Ackermann; Nos. 16, 18, 19, 33 are from Norman by courtesy of William Heinemann Ltd of London; Nos. 17, 20, 22 (artist Gorshel't), 23 (artist Gorshel't), 28, 29, 30, 31, 32, 35 (artist Gorshel't) all from Markov; No. 21 from the Harmsworth Universal Encyclopedia; Nos. 24 and 36 from Viskovatov; Nos. 39, 40, 41, 42, 43, 44 and 45 from d'Almeida and de Jongh; No. 37 from the Harmsworth Encyclopedia (courtesy Thomas Nelson and Sons Ltd of Walton on Thames); No. 38 (artist W. Kossak) photo from Cassell's Encyclopaedia (Children's Book of Knowledge); and Nos. 46 and 47 from *Piat'desiat Let Sovetskikh Vooruzhennykh Sil Foto-dokumenty*.

# List of Illustrations

# List of Maps

*Cartographer: Linda McFie*

# Foreword

I express my gratitude to the learned organizations and libraries in the United Kingdom and North America that have given me access to documents and printed material together with assistance in acquiring further sources. In particular the libraries of: the British Ministry of Defence and the Foreign Office; the Victoria and Albert Museum; the School of Slavonic and East European Studies of London University; Princeton University; Yale University; Harvard College; the Military Academy at West Point; the University of North Carolina; the University of Toronto; the University of Waterloo; McMaster University; the Royal Military College at Kingston; Carleton University; York University; McGill University; Queen's University at Kingston; and especially the D. B. Weldon Library of the University of Western Ontario.

I warm-heartedly thank Professors L. J. Shein and R. H. Johnston of McMaster University, Professor W. Shelest of Waterloo University and Mr D. R. Jones (of Dalhousie University Library) for their kindness in giving me information on possible further sources; and the librarians of the Bracebridge Library for their courtesy and enterprise in operating the international and inter library loan service that brought us old and sometimes rare books from sources throughout North America and Europe.

Lastly I thank my wife for typing and retyping the manuscript and for her invaluable collaboration on the production and on the Russian and German research. Without her work the book could not have been written.

A.S.
1984

# Introduction

To the general reader the name 'Cossack' probably conjures up a picture of a Don Cossack dance troupe, a picture of a community that was once homogeneous, with a close-knit cultural uniformity in custom, religion and in its Great Russian dialect. This is certainly a facet of Cossackdom, but the Don Cossacks were only one of eleven Russian and Ukrainian Cossack hosts; moreover these eleven Slav hosts, besides being late-comers on the Cossack scene, represented only a fragment of the Cossack peoples. There was no uniformity about the Cossacks for they were in no sense 'a nation', since they included tribes and subtribes of Mongols, Turkic-Tatars, Caucasians, Persians and Lithuanian-Tatars, as well as many splinter groups of Russians, Ukrainians and Poles, all independent of each other and all of different racial origin, speaking many languages and professing various faiths, Moslem, Christian, Lamaist or Shamanist, or having no religion at all. There was certainly no racial or cultural identity among them, for a Kalmyk had little affinity to a Ukrainian or a Circassian to a Kirghiz. The factor common to Cossacks was that they were usually steppe dwellers or steppe nomads organized into military communities of similar pattern, relying mainly on the horse for movement and for war: even so, there were exceptions in that some Kirghiz were camel-riders, some Caucasians were mountaineers, while some of the early Slav Cossack communities were without horses and were river pirates and sea-going mariners. Some eventually became agriculturists. Generally speaking, however, the Cossacks were horsemen-warriors who roamed the Asiatic or South-European steppes from the Carpathians to China and from the taiga to the Pamirs, their history, that dated back for thousands of years, being that of the nomad and resting on the keeping of cattle and the use of the horse.

Cossackdom's origins in Asia and its subsequent development in Siberia and in Europe cover a very wide area with a multitude of peoples, with names that may be new to the present-day reader in North America and in Western Europe. The story itself, however, is not complicated, and should be easily understood by reference, from time to time, to the two Appendices at the end of this book that show in diagram form the genealogy of the main hordes and hosts.

In transliterating Russian words the Library of Congress method has been used, except in place names where the earlier spelling of *The Times Atlas* of 1922 has been followed. This has occasionally given rise to inconsistencies such as the family name being spelt 'Iakovlev', while the place name on the Volga is spelt 'Krasnoiarsk' and that in Siberia 'Krasnoyarsk'. This, however, is relatively unimportant. Personal names such as 'Kerensky' and 'Budenny', well known in the west, have been given in the older and more familiar form. The less well-known Ukrainian names have been reproduced according to the Great Russian spelling, since the source material was taken largely from Russian language texts and maps. The general reader will have no difficulty in following the names as given. Foreign words and racial names are explained in the glossary included in the index.

1 Central Asia c.1200 A.D.

Russians

Bolgars

Turkic Nomads

Kipchaks

Kipchaks

Caucasians

Turks

Black Sea

Arabs

Caspian

L. Aral

KHWARIZMIAN EMPIRE

Persians

L. Balkhash

Turkic Nomads

L. Baikal

Merkits

Mongols

Tatars

Keraits

HSI-HSIA EMPIRE (Tanguts)

CHIN EMPIRE

SUNG EMPIRE

N

Steppe

1000 Miles
1600 Kms

0

# 1 Tatar Cossackdom

At the beginning of the Christian era the Eastern Slav tribal communities that were to form the Russian peoples had begun to move from the region that is now Poland and Belorussia, eastwards and south-eastwards through the great forest belt, so that eventually the new Slav settlements stretched over a great area, from present-day Novgorod in the north to the forest edge near the site of Kiev in the south. Beyond the limits of this forest belt down to the Black Sea shore lay the vast open steppe, several hundred miles in width, running westwards towards the Carpathians and eastwards for more than 2,000 miles to Lake Balkhash in Central Asia. These great plains had, from time immemorial, been the country of the nomad.

Across the broad southern steppes had come a succession of Asiatic horsemen, all moving from east to west. In recorded times the Scythians were displaced by the Sarmatian Alans; these were to be followed by the Asiatic Huns, a mixed Mongol-Turkic host of wandering peoples, sometimes identified with the earlier Hsiung-Nu of the Chinese annals, the marauding skin-clad mounted archers against whom the Chinese Wall had been built. Attila's Huns were horsemen from infancy and they virtually lived in the saddle; in war they relied on the mobility of their cavalry and mounted bowmen, terrorizing their enemies by the savagery with which they wiped out whole populations. After Attila's death, in A.D. 451, the hordes warred amongst themselves and the empire rapidly disintegrated.

The nomadic tribes and peoples that had once formed the framework of that empire remained, however, on the great steppes, unchanged in their way of life for the next thousand years, always on the move in search of new pasture, relying on the horse and the bow to hunt and protect their cattle and flocks, having no fixed homes and caring nothing for agriculture. They fought amongst themselves, increasing their wealth by cattle raiding and robbing and killing their weaker neighbours; the family and tribal feud was a part of their life and vengeance was very dear to them. And the South-European and mid-Asian steppe provided not only a vast pasture land and caravan route, but also the main invasion highway into Europe along which new Asiatic conquerors could swell the ranks of their warriors by forcing the tens of thousands of tribal horsemen they met on the way to fight for them.

By the twelfth century the East Slavs in the forest belt to the north of the steppe had come under the rule of the Varangian Vikings (the *Rus*) who had created the great Kievan empire that covered most of modern European Russia; this empire had prosperous trading links with Constantinople by way of the Dnieper, and with the Orient by way of the Volga and the Caspian. The Vikings took the religion of the Christian church at Constantinople, and it was a combination of this Greek religion and the foreign rule that the princes forced upon their subjects that cut off the mass of the Eastern Slavs (who had already taken the name of *Rus*) from their Slav cousins in Central Europe and the Balkans. The *Rus* were to become the Russian peoples that eventually assimilated their Norse conquerors.

The Kievan empire was severely weakened by an unworkable system of succession and partition and by the fratricidal strife of its princes, so that Russia splintered into a number of independent principalities, many of which were broken down again with each succeeding generation. When not at war amongst themselves the principalities were under attack, in the south by the Turkic Kipchak nomads and in the west by the growing power of the pagan and warlike Lithuanians. The Russian princes were, therefore, in no condition to withstand the terrible deluge that was about to overwhelm them from the east, a violent and massive onslaught that was to leave their peoples entirely subjugated by the most merciless of foes for the space of many centuries.

\*　\*　\*

The Chinese account of the Mongol Hsiung-Nu and Herodotus's picture of the Scythians are very similar and could probably be applied to most of the warlike nomads on the steppe of any age, for they certainly describe the Huns of the fifth and the Mongols of the thirteenth centuries A.D.[1]

Chengis Khan, born in 1162 as Temujen, the son of a Mongol tribal chieftain in the area east of Lake Baikal, conquered or absorbed all other Mongol peoples, including a Mongol tribe known as Tatars.[2] Then, at the head of these Mongol nomads, he rapidly won over the surrounding Turkic-speaking peoples, all of them herdsmen indistinguishable from the Mongols in their way of life. A Mongol-Turkic army overthrew the northern Hsi-Hsia empire in China, eighteen million people being slaughtered in China and Tangut in the course of a war that lasted only twelve years. In 1218, the Mongols picked a quarrel with the Moslem Khwarizmian empire (at the western end of the Asiatic steppe between the Caspian Sea and Lake Aral) that they destroyed with the greatest of savagery in a three-year war. In the city of Merv 700,000 people are said to have been massacred. As was their custom, the Mongols set out in pursuit of the fleeing enemy rulers and their armed remnants and allies; this brought them on to the Kipchak plain. In 1223 the Mongols crossed the lower Don near the Sea of Azov where, on the banks of the Kalka, a tributary of the Kalmius, they met a joint Russian force put into the field by several of the principalities together with the Kipchaks, and there they destroyed it; the captured Russian princes were crushed to death beneath a Tatar wooden banqueting floor. Nothing more was heard in Russia of this terrible enemy who made off, 'they knew not whither', as suddenly as he had appeared. No military preparations were made against his return.

Chengis Khan had started back for Mongolia, after an absence of six years, in order to reduce the rebellious Hsi-Hsia once more to vassaldom and to lay the foundation of an empire. This new empire was to be a Mongol great khanate resembling Attila's, in that it was to consist of a number of subordinate hordes, each being under a khan and each having a region allotted for its tribes. The successors to the great khan were to be elected by all the khans at a *kuriltai* assembled in Mongolia. Chengis's son Ogedei was nominated successor during his father's lifetime, and it was Ogedei who set up the first capital of the Mongol empire at Karakorum.

The original khanates were given to Chengis's sons; the largest, in the far west, went to Jochi the eldest, but on his early death this was divided among Jochi's three heirs, into Batu's Blue Horde that was to be based on the Kipchak plain on the lower Volga, Orda's White

2 The Mongol Empire
c.1280 A.D.

Khanate
of
Kubilai Khan

L. Baikal

• Karakorum

Peking

Sung
Empire

Khmer
Empire

Sheibanide Horde

L. Balkhash

White Horde

Chagatai Horde

Delhi Sultanate

L. Aral

Golden (Blue)
Horde

Caspian

Il-Khan Horde

Russian Vassals of the
Golden Horde

Black Sea

N

0        1000 Miles
         1600 Kms

Horde immediately to the east of the Blue Horde between Lake Aral and the upper Irtysh, and the Sheibanide Horde (mainly of Kirghiz) to the north-east of the White Horde. Chengis's son Chagatai received the horde that was to bear his name, to the south of the White Horde and with its capital at Kashgar in western Sinkiang, covering the region from the south of Lakes Aral and Balkhash to the Altai mountains and then southwards to Afghanistan and the borders of India. The portion of Chengis's fourth son Tolui came to be divided between Chengis's grandsons Hülegü and Kubilai, Hülegü's horde occupying the Il-Khanate still to be carved out, encompassing Iran, modern Iraq and much of Anatolia and Syria; Kubilai was to receive the sixth khanate in present-day China running from Tibet to the Amur river.[3]

Batu's Blue Horde, known to Europeans as the Golden Horde, was to be called the Kipchak Horde by the Mongols since it was given as its grazing area the Kipchak plain 'as far west as Mongol hoofs could beat'. The fate of Russia was to depend not only on the Golden Horde that was to engulf it, but, in varying degrees, on all of the Mongol hordes (except that of Kubilai Khan in China); each of these hordes at different times, directly or indirectly, influenced the course of Russian and East European history.

In the west the first Mongol task was to overrun the Kipchak steppe and secure Batu's flank by devastating Central Europe and reducing the Russian principalities to vassaldom. The great khan Ogedei ordered all the hordes to transfer troops to Batu for the new war; and, in the spring of 1236, a host variously estimated at being between 150,000 and 300,000 men left Asia on its way to Silesia and the Adriatic. No European troops could withstand them and, in the next five years, the cities of Russia and Central Europe were left in ruins, the inhabitants were massacred in hundreds of thousands, and the countryside laid waste in a series of campaigns that ended with the death of Ogedei. By then there was strife between the warring Mongol princes from the different hordes and all hastened back eastwards to Mongolia to safeguard themselves against an election that might threaten their interests and lives; for the election of a great khan was often followed by the murder of his princely opponents and their families.

The election of Küyük, Ogedei's successor, could indeed have been fatal to his enemy Batu, but Batu was saved by Küyük's early death. Möngke, the fourth great khan, was Batu's ally, but shortly afterwards, in 1260, the great khanate ended with the fifth great khan, Kubilai; for Kubilai was also khan of China and he was too busily engaged with his own eastern wars to be able to give any attention to the west, so that he chose to move the Mongolian capital from Karakorum to Peking. From this time onwards the five main western hordes (the Golden, the White, the Sheibanide, the Chagatai and Il-Khan) were independent and often at war with each other. Kubilai's failure to conquer Japan and the repeated defeats of the Il-Khan Mongols in Syria at the hands of the Egyptian Bahrite Mamelukes (who were themselves mainly Turks and Mongols) finally spelt the end of Mongol expansionism. Then, like Attila's conquerors of a thousand years before, the hordes began to destroy each other. In Persia and in China the Mongols did not last for very long beyond the thirteenth century because they were overwhelmed and absorbed by superior civilizations. The White, Sheibanide, Chagatai and Golden Hordes and their descendant khanates endured much longer because the nomadic khans and aristocracy ruled over populations that were, like themselves, pastoral and mainly Turkic in origin, living in lands with few towns and with little or no agriculture, that willingly provided armies trained and ready for war. The Golden Horde in particular depended for its existence almost entirely on war, plunder, regular tribute and taxes, and, above all, on the control of the east-west, north-south water and land caravan trade routes that centred on the north Caspian, and especially of the forty-mile wide land-bridge between the Don and the Volga, the same area that had once been the base for the wealth and power of the old Khazar empire and that would one day become the territories of the Don Cossacks.

* * *

The language of the horde aristocracy and some of the tribes was originally Mongol, but this language was not to survive outside the Mongolian motherland for it was soon supplanted by the tongue of the Turkic-speaking majority.[4] Chengis Khan spoke both Mongol and Turkic; Timurlane, who called himself a Mongol and who later claimed direct descent from Chengis, knew no word of the Mongol tongue. These Turco-Mongol peoples, speaking a variety of Turkic dialects, became known to the west as Tatars, although in truth they had no connection with the original Mongol Tatar tribe that had been crushed by Chengis Khan long ago.

The political and military organization of the Tatars was based on the family, the clan and the nomadic tribe, where every man from a very early age was a huntsman, a herdsman and a warrior. The ownership of land was foreign to these nomads since wealth was measured only by what the land would provide; the nomads had no fixed homes but housed their families in tents carried on ox- or horse-dråwn *kibitka* wagons, so that tribes and hordes were continually on the move. Raiding was the easiest way of acquiring wealth, and property consisted of herds and flocks, women, slaves, tents, carts, looted chattels and, above all, on tribute and taxes.[5] Weaker or smaller clans had their own leaders, social organization and cattle, and were generally left undisturbed except that they paid tribute to the more powerful tribes, and moved, pastured and fought under their orders; in return they wanted protection, and a head of a ruling people who failed to provide it or was defeated in the field might expect to lose the support of vassal tribes or clans, for these often transferred their allegiance to a more powerful warrior, even to the conqueror. On the other hand, a Tatar prince who broke away from a horde would frequently take his tribes with him, and these often numbered tens of thousands of fighting men. The density of the Tatar population thus fluctuated between feudal concentration for war and the tribal dispersion necessary to pasture the herds and spread the collection of plunder and tribute.

The Tatar military system resembled that of the earlier steppe conquerors and was probably thousands of years old, being based on the structure of the tens: ten men to the section or troop (the *arban*), one hundred to the squadron ( the *yaghun*) and a thousand to what would nowadays be a regiment (the *mingghan*), ten thousand to the equivalent of a division (a Tatar *tuman*), the whole force being based on cavalry and mounted archers. The Tatar trooper was the *kazak* or the *tovarishch* (the Tatar word for 'comrade'). The family and clan provided the *arban* and *yaghun*, while the tribe formed the *mingghan* and *tuman*. Any leader, whether of a section of ten men or of a great body of troops, was known as an *ataman*, his deputy being an *esaul*, and the choosing of leaders, at any rate at the lower levels, was done by election, a typical Mongol-Tatar procedure whereby the section leader was appointed by the common consent of the ten mounted archers, the squadron leader being selected not by the vote of the hundred rank and file but by the vote of the ten section leaders, so that the squadron ataman commanded the other nine section leaders together with the nine men of his own section who formed his immediate bodyguard and staff.[6] The leaders of the regiments (the thousands) might be similarly chosen by the squadron commanders, and, in theory at least, this process continued into the ten thousands and hundred thousands, even to the election of the khans and great khans through the *kuriltai*; in practice, however, it is doubtful whether the *tuman* or even all the regimental commanders were elected, since these more important appointments appear to have been held by the nobility or by professional soldier commanders designated by the khan or by his princes. For the Mongol aristocracy of 'the brave' (*ba'atur*) consisted almost exclusively of the chiefs (*noyan*) and the professional soldier class (*nuker*), and these, and members of the khan's privileged bodyguard, were usually given the higher commands. A Tatar prince was known as a *mirza* while a commander of the royal blood was an *ughlan* (from which the western 'uhlan'); an *ulus* was a people or collection of tribes, and their territory or pasture was a *yurt*, while a *kuren'* was a settlement or camp.[7] Nearly all of these words and many of the election practices were adopted by the Cossacks that were to follow.

The Mongol-Tatars disposed of great herds of ponies, partly feral and only partly broken to saddle, and these bore some resemblance to the original tarpan wild horse; in general the horses were small, rarely more than twelve or thirteen hands, the head and shoulders 'too heavy for elegance', the head being particularly large and coarse, the eyes none too full, the nose convex and the neck short and thick: the legs were good; the barrel was deep and long with no deficiency of bone. The hindquarters were low and muscular, and the tail and ears were long. Being reared on the open steppe, the ponies had dense coats and were used to the extremes of weather, and were not particular about what they ate. The commonest colours were bay, grey and red, although mouse occurred quite often. Tatar mounts were very hardy and handy under the saddle, could gallop an hour without stopping, and last out two days without drinking; their small hard hoofs could be used unshod all the year round. Movement at a trot, due to the straight shoulder, was uncomfortable and tiring to the rider, so that they were usually ridden at an amble, the only trotting pace at which they went really well. The horse was broken to the snaffle, a very light single-bridle jointed bit, and to a saddle made of wooden trees, padded leather cushions and surcingle, straw often being used in addition to a felt numnah. Stirrups were worn with very short leathers so that the Tatar rode, as it were, almost jockey-fashion with the lower leg at near right angles to the thigh.

The dress and equipment of the Tatar rider depended on his wealth. Generally he had no armour, though some wore iron casques together with chain mail or leather clothing on which small iron plates had been sewn in overlapping scales. Most wore a leather helmet with a back flap covering the nape of the neck, having in addition a fur cap with ear flaps; all wore felt stockings and felt and leather boots, and sometimes a cuirass of strips of black-lacquered leather. Pelisses, either with arm-holes or sleeves, were commonly worn, these reaching to below the knee, together with a rain-resistant felt cape known as a *burka*, made from sheep's wool, or camel or goat hair.[8]

Nearly all, whether rich or poor, higher commanders or simple archers, carried two quivers and often two bows, these being of laminated wood or bone of the short pattern used by mounted men, but capable, nonetheless, of firing an arrow to a range of about 200 paces. The arrows were long and heavy with a very broad knife-like blade of metal or bone, many of the blades having holes drilled in them that caused them to whistle in flight, presumably to disconcert the enemy; the arrow notches were so fine that they could not be fired from most European bows.[9] The Tatar had a lance with a broad head, very much like a boar spear but fitted with a large hook behind the blade for unseating enemy horsemen should the initial thrust be parried: he had, too, an iron or wooden mace hanging from the saddle, a small round shield and a curved sword, of the sabre or scimitar type; an axe and a horsehair lasso made up the rest of his equipment. Spurs were never worn, but the Tatar carried a long-lashed whip on a very short stock hung by a loop from his wrist, though this was rarely used on his own horse since, in the gallop, he was, according to Howorth, content to urge his excited mount forward with repeated cries of 'Hoida!'.[10]

In retrospect it is remarkable that these Mongol-Turkic nomads should have been able to overrun the larger part of Europe and of Asia in so short a time and have held most of Russia in subjugation for so many centuries. In the field the Tatars were rarely defeated by European or Asiatic troops, and the main cause of their eventual decline was that horde destroyed horde. Russia appeared defenceless against them; the reason for this lay not only in the lack of unity among the princes, but more particularly because the political and social structure of the principalities made them unfitted to combat even part of a Tatar horde.

Among the hordes there was no distinction between soldier and civilian, and every Tatar who was fit to sit a horse was a fully equipped and trained warrior, excelling in horsemanship and the use of weapons, who lived for campaigning and who depended on raiding and war to augment his wealth; the order of the khan or headman could not be denied under penalty of outlawing—even death. For such a people, as Howorth has said, the waging of war in far-flung campaigns was not an event out of the ordinary, for frequent moves were little change in the day-to-day habits of wandering people whose houses and provisions moved along with them.[11] The Russian peasant, on the other hand, was a man of peace, born to be a cultivator of the soil to which he was tied, who, in the main, got on well even with the minorities he assimilated; his village community taxed him, organized him, settled his disputes and allocated land. The Russian political and social structure was entirely unfitted for any form of defence; the possession of arms and the training in their use was reserved for nobles and their immediate dependants, and from the thirteenth to the seventeenth centuries the greater part of the Russian population was made up of peasants (many of whom became state peasants or serfs), slaves, artisans, tradesmen and monks. It is doubtful whether any of the Russian princes could call on more than a thousand regular troops, and those were mainly mercenary foot who formed little more than a body-guard. This mercenary foot and the untrained and ill-equipped peasant levies were unable to match the mobility and effectiveness of the disciplined and well-organized Tatar horse, or the fire-power of its bowmen.

It was moreover impossible for the Russian princes to keep large bodies of townsmen or peasantry under arms for long periods without paralysing the business of state and losing harvests; neither could they hastily concentrate a large force of levies from outlying towns or from the countryside should there be a sudden alarm. The Tatars, on the other hand, due to their tribal organization, their excellent intelligence and messenger service, and their mobility, could mount a campaign and strike anywhere, virtually unopposed, before the Russian princes knew of the danger: and these Tatar nomads could readily leave their herds for a summer, for a year if need be, in the care of the old men, the women, the children and the slaves; and so they would depart at the shortest of notice, each man leading spare horses, riding day and night, never lighting fires, eating in the saddle and not stopping for sup or bite.

Tatar warfare, as Grousset has said, was a perfected form of the old methods used 1,200 years before by the Hsiung-Nu—the eternal nomad tactics evolved from raiding and the great hunting drives on the steppes. The secret of success was implicit obedience, riding and archery, with hunting on horseback being regarded as the basis of training for war. The first requirement was for information, gained initially by sending forward silent and concealed scouts to observe the enemy; the second was to prepare to envelop the foe before he even knew that he was about to be attacked. For the Tatar's object was to frighten and confuse by surprise attacks in the enemy flanks and rear. The nomad regiments and squadrons manoeuvred rapidly, and usually in silence, directed by visual signals from the commanders' standard bearers who carried black and white yak-tails mounted on a short pole and topped by balls of wool. The Tatar was full of tricks and strategems and, when the enemy least expected it, would come in with a sudden dash, closing his ranks as he did so. More often, however, the Tatar would not press home his attacks on a strong unbroken enemy but would pour in flights of arrows on infantry or stationary cavalry, the object being to thin the enemy's ranks and shake his morale and judgement. In the event of an attack being made by formed bodies of enemy cavalry, the Tatars regarded it as no disgrace to flee, but would, as a matter of course, disperse into scattered groups, shooting from the saddle as they went, often leading the enemy into a trap. And the pursuing enemy who allowed himself to get strung out and scattered rarely had the training or discipline needed immediately to concentrate and reform.

The Tatar hordes were entirely horsed, and there was no Tatar foot. Even in later times they had no corps of infantry and little or no artillery except for sieges. But they sometimes forced their defeated enemies or vassals to provide bodies of foot, infantry that the Tatar regarded as expendable: these were obliged to undertake the dangerous work of making the first assault or of receiving the charge of enemy cavalry; meanwhile the Tatar mounted archers hung on the flanks and the rear, waiting until the enemy was sufficiently disorganized for the horsemen to decide the issue.

In the event of a Tatar force meeting a well-found body of enemy, it was likely to engage only by fire and harassment; this harrying, however, would continue by day and by night, with stragglers and detachments being cut off and destroyed. It was very difficult to bring a Tatar to battle until he himself was ready to fight; and it proved almost impossible to surprise these nomads, for they made very skilful use of vedettes and screens, could take good advantage of ground and cover, including darkness, sunken river beds, reeds, thickets and high grasses; their very horses were trained to lie and conceal themselves. Rivers were no obstacle, nor were they deterred by mountain or forest, though they naturally made poorer showing in fighting in those areas. And yet, although the Tatar was generally unwilling to engage strong forces in hand-to-hand combat, he was still much more determined in close-quarter fighting than the Russian cavalry of that time. For both Heberstein and Fletcher noted that whereas the Russian horse became speedily discouraged if the enemy did not break at the first onslaught, a Tatar would rarely give up, and once forced to fight would slash till he dropped. Tatars generally suffered the greatest losses when fighting Tatars. In June 1391 at Kandurcha on the Volga, in the land of the Bolgars near present-day Kuibyshev, when Tokhtamysh's and Timurlane's hordes clashed head-on, the battle lasted three days and 100,000 dead are said to have been left on the field.

The fighting in China had given the Mongol-Tatars much experience in sieges and they made use of both Chinese and Persian catapults, battering rams and other engines of war, though the dangerous work of manning these equipments, of filling ditches and moats and of scaling walls, was usually given to dismounted non-Turkic vassals, to prisoners and to rounded-up peasantry. In a land where there were virtually no maps and little literacy, the commanders relied on spies, the interrogation of the widely travelled caravan merchants and on the capture of prisoners. And just as Chengis Khan and his subordinate khans showed utter ruthlessness, breaking alliances, betraying loyalties and murdering their kinsfolk to further their ambitions, so could there be no faith in the word of any Tatar, for he was wilful and capricious and full of deceit, alternately disarming his opponents by fair words and promises or paralysing his enemies by mass terror. For the Tatars, no less than Attila and Chengis Khan, gloried in slaughter.

The early princelings and tribesmen of the Golden Horde lived as their forefathers had done, in the age-old custom of the steppe, wintering in one place and summering in another; the khan's summer capital was a tented court, continually on the move through-out his domain. Largely unlettered, the Tatars despised towns and agriculture, for civilization existed merely to provide them with plunder and tribute, while toil was fit only for slaves. They continued to live a nomadic life without education or culture, and, until 1272 when Möngke-Temür became a Moslem, with a very primitive Shamanist form of religion that was in the hands of the witch-doctors.[12]

When the Golden Horde embraced Islam, its peoples, like the Ottoman Turks, became, in Christian eyes, the infidels in Europe, and this served to isolate them and their Russian vassals from western civilization.[13] As Grousset has said, 'the Orient then began at Kiev'. Yet their khans were receptive to new ideas and to civilized methods that might bring them immediate gain, for they used foreign-born officials to organize the tax system, and encouraged, and taxed, international trade across their territories, escorting the caravans and policing the main routes with great efficiency. Genoese and Venetian merchants and shippers were licensed to set up depots on the coasts of the Black Sea, the Crimea and the Sea of Azov and were allowed to garrison and administer their own leased territories: these Italians provided many of the markets for the caravans and were the purchasers and shippers of Tatar booty and slaves.

\* \* \*

At the end of the thirteenth century what is now European Russia was divided into three distinctly separate territories: firstly, the vast and empty steppe and black-earth region to the south and south-east that provided the grazing grounds for the Tatar nomads and formed a cordon between the Russian principalities and the Golden Horde; secondly, the main Russian principalities that had once formed part of the old Kievan empire and were ruled by Russian princes in the name of the khan of the Golden Horde, princes who were the vassals of, and completely subservient to, the Tatar; and lastly, the former Russian principalities in the north-west, Polotsk, Turov-Pinsk and that part of Kiev that had been recently overrun and prised loose from the Tatar grasp by the fast expanding power of the Lithuanians.[14]

All the Russian principalities, except those occupied by Poland and Lithuania, remained for many centuries under the terrible Tatar yoke. The horde capital of Sarai had become the very centre of the

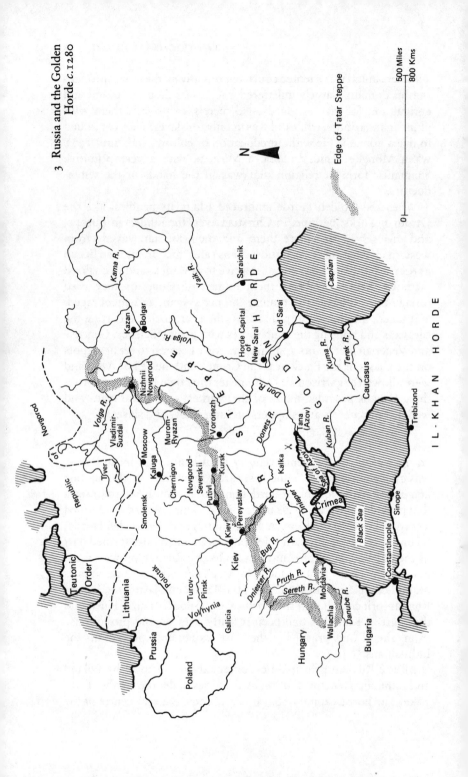

3 Russia and the Golden Horde c.1280

Russian orbit, in that the lives of the princes and the lives and fortunes of the Russian peoples depended entirely on the pleasure of the khan; the Tatar had nothing to fear from Russia but much to expect in the form of tribute, taxes, slaves and levies of troops.[15] Russia became a storehouse to be plundered at will. Although the government was carried out by the princes themselves in the khan's name, and the Tatar allowed remarkable freedom in religious matters, the khan kept his own representative (*daruga*) and tax assessor (*baskak*) stationed in the capitals and main cities of the principalities, these commissioners having power of life and death over the local population.[16] And the princes were elevated, deposed, imprisoned, murdered or executed, sometimes in the most revolting fashion, at the whim of the khan or his representative.[17]

It was Tatar policy to profit from the weaknesses and quarrels of the princes, quarrels that the khans themselves fomented, so that the princes soon became Tatar agents and informers, encouraged to report back to Sarai on each other. Motivated by self-interest and jealousy, the rulers carried their tales and begged the khan for military aid against each other or against the invasions from the west of the Lithuanians, Germans and Danes. But when the Tatar troops did enter the Russian principalities, whether or not in response to requests for such aid, they laid waste the territory of friend and foe alike, murdering, enslaving, plundering and putting to flame what they could not carry.

Since much of the real wealth of the Golden Horde lay in its central position near the mouths of the Volga and Don and astride the water and land caravan routes running east and west and north and south, (routes that extended to Central Asia, India, China, Russia, the Baltic, Constantinople and the Mediterranean), New Sarai soon became a very rich transhipment depot and a centre for international commerce. The main enemies of the Golden Horde, as the khans well knew, were to be found not in Russia but in the other Mongol-Turkic hordes to the east and south that coveted its wealth, and in the Sarai palace revolutions incited by their brother khans. To these threats were to be added others, the expansion of the Ottoman empire that was beginning to menace Constantinople and the Balkans, and the steady encroachment of the Lithuanian and Pole. Yet, in spite of losses of ground in the west, the Tatar fought against the Poles and Lithuanians with undiminished vigour, and, from time to time, inflicted on them bloody defeats and payment of tribute.

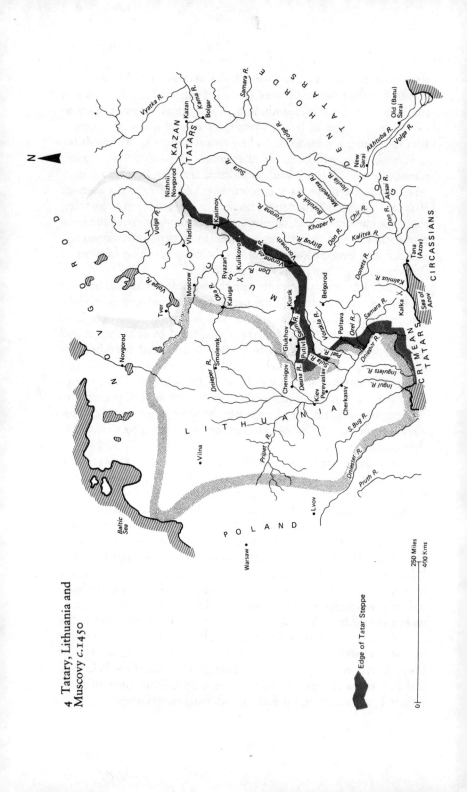

4 Tatary, Lithuania and Muscovy *c.*1450

Edge of Tatar Steppe

0  250 Miles
   400 Kms

NOVGOROD

KAZAN TATARS

GOLDEN HORDE TATARS

CIRCASSIANS

CRIMEAN TATARS

MUSCOVY

LITHUANIA

POLAND

Baltic Sea

Sea of Azov

Warsaw

Lvov

Vilna

Novgorod

Tver

Moscow

Smolensk

Kaluga

Chernigov

Kiev

Pereyaslavl

Cherkassy

Glukhov

Putivl

Kursk

Belgorod

Poltava

Kazan

Bolgar

Nizhnii Novgorod

Vladimir

Kasimov

Ryazan

Kulikovo ✕

New Sarai

Old (Batu) Sarai

Tana (Azov)

Kalka ✕

Vyatka R.
Volga R.
Kama R.
Samara R.
Sura R.
Volga R.
Volga R.
Akhtuba R.
Volga R.
Ilovlia R.
Medveditsa R.
Buzuluk R.
Khoper R.
Vorona R.
Bityug R.
Voronezh R.
Voronezh R.
Don R.
Chir R.
Don R.
Aksai R.
Kalitva R.
Donets R.
Kalmius R.
Ingulets R.
Ingul R.
Dnieper R.
Oka R.
Dnieper R.
Desna R.
Seim R.
Psel R.
Sula R.
Vorskla R.
Orel R.
Samara R.
Dniester R.
Pruth R.
S. Bug R.
Pripet R.
Volga R.
Oka R.

N

Below the surface, however, the decline of the Golden Horde was already well advanced, and this had come about with the weakening of the centralized control of the type originally imposed by Chengis Khan. An outward and exaggerated pretence of discipline, even humility, in the presence of the khan was still there, but when out of his reach many of the nobility acted entirely in their own interests.

The first sign had come towards the end of the thirteenth century when Tatar princes, each with his own powerful horde, began to break away from the khan; some were to attack the khan directly or pass into the service of his enemies.[18] Each new khan had to fight for his own succession, destroying all likely pretenders, brothers, fathers, sons and wives: this had frequently been the case in earlier times, but now the successions gave rise to periods of civil war that were to last for decades, sometimes with two or more rival khans in existence. In 1360 the line of Batu became extinct in the Golden Horde and there followed another protracted period of palace strife and terror purges of the nobility, so that there were twenty-five khans in the twenty-four years between 1357–81. During this time Lithuania defeated the Tatars on the Bug and, by 1370, took the city and principality of Kiev. Mamai, a powerful vizier and khan-maker, usurped the khanate for himself and attempted to restore the fortunes of the Golden Horde; this he might have done, had not the Tatar hordes in the south and east destroyed him first.

One of the principal pretenders to the Golden Horde khanate was Tokhtamysh, a descendant of Chengis Khan through the line of Orda. Tokhtamysh's star at this time was so low that he had been driven out of the White Horde and forced to take refuge with the great warrior Timurlane, a Barlas Tatar who, from his base at Samarkand, was carving out an empire from the lands formerly controlled by the hordes of the Il-Khan and the Chagatai. Timurlane placed Tokhtamysh on the throne of the khanate of the White Horde and prepared to assist him to evict Mamai from the Golden Horde.

Meanwhile, in 1371, the Russian princes, taking heart at the Lithuanian Olgerd's victories and at what appeared to be the imminent disintegration of the Golden Horde, refused to pay homage and tribute, and Mamai's punitive expedition in the upper Don valley was decisively beaten at the battle of Kulikovo field in 1380 by Russian forces under the Moscow leadership of Grand Prince Dmitrii Donskoi.[19] But although many modern Soviet historians have hailed this battle as a main contributory factor in the overthrow of the Tatar, in reality it is very doubtful that this was so. For the Tatar Tokhtamysh appeared with the White Horde on the lower Don and not only routed Mamai's army as it was withdrawing from the Kulikovo field to the Sea of Azov, but, having made himself khan of the Golden Horde as well as of the White Horde, Tokhtamysh rapidly reduced the Russian principalities to their former state of vassalage in a lightning campaign, defeating the Lithuanians at Poltava, taking and burning Moscow and Ryazan, devastating the country and leaving a score of cities in ruins.[20] Dmitrii Donskoi took to flight.

Tokhtamysh, unmindful of his obligation to Timurlane, invaded the lands of his former protector and laid siege to Bokhara. In the fifteen-year war that followed between the two hordes, Tokhtamysh was finally defeated and deposed; the lands of the Golden Horde were ravaged by Timurlane's horsemen and the bordering Russian principalities were once again devastated.[21] New Sarai and Astrakhan were sacked and burned in 1395, the Christian population of the Venetian depot of Tana on the mouth of the Don was massacred or enslaved and the Crimean Genoese trading stations were gutted.[22] Timurlane had finally destroyed the great and prosperous international trading centre between the Far East and Constantinople, and the White Horde was again separated from the Golden Horde.

Edigü, a Nogai vizier and Tatar war-lord and former courtier of Timurlane's, attempted to restore the fortunes of the Golden Horde between 1400 and 1419 by ravaging Central Russia, until he himself was defeated by the advance of the Lithuanians from the west. By 1419, although the Golden Horde still held Russia in thrall and now relied on Russian tribute for its main source of income, the khan no longer had the power to overthrow the Central European Christian kingdoms and he sought instead to use to his advantage the Polish-Lithuanian enmity to Russia.

In 1422 the Golden Horde was struck yet another severe blow from the east when Barak, the khan of the White Horde, drove the khan Mehmet-Ulug out of the Volga delta, forcing him to take refuge firstly with the Lithuanians, and then to move the remnants of his horde to the middle Volga where, in 1438, he set up an independent Tatar khanate at Kazan. Other Tatar princes fled with their tribes from the Volga to the Crimea, where they had the support of some of the Nogai, and here a new khanate was formed by Haggi-Girai who was to be the founder of a dynasty that was to thrive there for three and a half centuries. Other khanates, independent of what was left of the Golden Horde in the Volga delta, were to arise, the Nogai Astrakhan khanate at the mouth of the Caspian, and the Nogai Edisan and Budzhak hordes in the valleys of the Bug and the Dniester. Yet, in spite of these crushing blows, the Golden Horde, thereafter sometimes known as the Great or the Trans-Volga Horde, still continued its existence, always at enmity and sometimes at war with the other khanates, drawing its strength from the nomadic steppe herdsmen, the source that had once made it great.

The splintering of the Golden Horde into separate khanates and hordes had been no relief to Russia—if anything it had actually increased the danger. Under the Golden Horde the tiny principality of Moscow had at first prospered and increased in size and influence by courting the khan and the Tatar. The office and title of grand prince had been bestowed permanently on its ruler and, between 1261 and 1462, Muscovy had absorbed what had been Vladimir-Suzdal and Murom-Ryazan, so that its frontiers stretched against the republic of Novgorod in the north and against Lithuania in the west; in the east and south, Muscovy faced on to the Tatar steppe, the vast borderland of the Kipchak plain. This had always been open and undefended against the incessant attacks of the Golden Horde. But the dispersion of the Golden Horde had resulted in more widespread raiding, not only from the south-east but also from the east (Kazan) and the south (Crimea), and from the many independent Tatar groups living in the basins of the Don, the Donets and the Dnieper; in addition there roamed in the steppe countless bands of robber clansmen who owed allegiance to none. Regular tribute was still being paid by Moscow to the Golden Horde, but that horde was in no condition, even if it had been willing, to protect its vassal against attack from other Tatars. Meanwhile the other khanates and hordes had come to rely on what they could seize in their incursions into Russia and the Ukraine, cattle, goods and, in particular, slaves for sale to Turkey, Persia and the Middle East. In one great raid by the Crimean Tatars in the next century, 130,000 people were taken, so that a Jewish merchant, watching the endless procession passing from the mainland into the Crimea on its way to Kaffa, is said to have asked in astonishment whether there were in fact any more people left in Russia.[23]

In 1462 Ivan III became the last grand prince of Muscovy in that he was thereafter to claim for himself the style, firstly of 'tsar of Russia' and later the 'tsar of all the Russias', even though half of these formed part of the Lithuanian-Polish kingdom. This ambitious monarch finally annexed to Moscow the republic of Novgorod. It has been claimed that Ivan III then finally shook off the Tatar yoke when he refused the payment of the Golden Horde tribute that, so it is said, had been long in arrears.[24] In fact, having incited his boyars and people to defy the Tatar envoys, Ivan fled at the approach of the khan at the head of his horde. Khan Ahmed spent the rest of the year of 1480 encamped at Kaluga on the Lithuanian-Muscovite border immediately to the south of Moscow, laying waste the countryside while he waited for the promised Lithuanian help that did not come. Then, laden with 'gifts' from Moscow as well as such plunder as he could carry, Ahmed withdrew to the south, indiscriminately devastating Russian and Lithuanian lands as he went. The march south was not uneventful, however, for a mixed Nogai-Sheibanide force lay in wait for the Golden Horde in the Donets valley, routed it and killed the khan. Ahmed was succeeded by his infant son Saih-Ahmed, destined to be the last ruler of the Golden Horde.

Neither the Muscovites, the Poles, nor even the battle-experienced Lithuanians could find any satisfactory defence against the lightning forays and fearful devastations of the Tatar Cossack; time and time again events were to prove that Tatars could be soundly defeated only by Tatars. Fortified border towns by themselves gave little defence, for although these sometimes delayed the progress of the invasions, more often than not the fortresses were ringed and bypassed; nor could they save the surrounding country from being pillaged. It soon became apparent that the main defence against the Tatar must depend on mounted men, living in the pattern of hordes, always under arms and military discipline, self-sufficient and relying for their maintenance on their own women and herds, who would ride the northern face of the wild steppe, pushing the Tatar southwards by raids and incursions and seeking early warning of the enemy's intentions by constant patrols, observation towers, spies, smoke signals, by a mounted messenger service, and by the capture of enemy 'tongues'.

This could best be done by Tatars in the pay of the Russian principalities, and it was in this way that the first Russian Cossacks were born.

CHAPTER I NOTES

1  The Hsiung-Nu and the latter-day Mongol-Tatars were people of
   extraordinary arrogance. The Hsiung-Nu envoy to China in 90 B.C., in
   answer to a complaint from the emperor said, 'We are nature's wanton
   boys who do not care to trouble ourselves with petty formalities.'
2  In the year 1200 the Mongol peoples consisted mainly of the Mongols
   proper, together with the Tatars (who were partially destroyed and
   dispersed), the Merkits (who were possibly the modern Buriats) and the
   Keraits (possibly the modern Kalmyks).
3  Chengis Khan's sons were Jochi, Ogedei, Chagatai and Tolui; among
   Jochi's sons were Orda, Batu and Sheiban; Hülegü and Kubilai were
   sons of Tolui.
4  Other than a Mongol aristocracy that provided much of the senior
   military leadership, the Golden Horde, even at the time of Batu, was said
   to have only 4,000 Mongol troops that formed the khan's bodyguard.
5  The Golden Horde eventually minted its own coins, firstly in Bolgar and
   then in Sarai. But, in this primitive society, Tatar or foreign coinage was
   of secondary account, and trade, tribute and taxation were conducted
   mainly in kind. Foreign merchants were expected to pay ten per cent of
   imported goods into the khan's treasury: the overall system of tribute
   and taxes was not so equitable, however, and the khan extorted from his
   princes and vassals what he could; they in their turn collected even
   heavier taxes from their dependent tribes.
6  In recent times in Tatar Crimea an ataman was any form of 'boss', even a
   Tatar shepherd whose labour force consisted of two boys.
7  After the adoption of the Moslem faith a Tatar governor or official might
   be styled a *beg* or *bey*.
8  Camels were also used as mounts by the Tatar hordes in the east, but
   their numbers were insignificant in the Golden Horde. Camels could still
   be found though—even on the Don in 1913—as draught animals,
   usually working mills, rollers or wells and pumps.
9  In later times the Tatar was reluctant to replace his bow with a musket or
   carbine, mainly because of the bow's rapid rate of fire. It was for this
   reason that Alexander I retained Bashkir Cossack mounted archers in his
   1812 field force against the French.
10 Shcherbina, writing of the Nogai and Circassians of the early nineteenth
   century, says the same, 'Hoida' apparently meaning 'surrender' according to some or 'no quarter' according to others. The Tatar arms and
   equipment were, or became, common to all Cossacks, whether Tatar,
   Circassian, Kalmyk, Bashkir or Russian.
11 The migratory pattern of the steppe nomad varied according to the
   availability of water and fresh pasturage. Movement was generally
   unhurried as the cattle had to have sufficient time each day for cropping,
   but even so, great distances (up to 1,200 miles for the Kirghiz in 1913)
   could be covered in the course of a year. Some migration was forced, in
   that tribes were sometimes obliged to flee the incursions of stronger or
   more warlike peoples. The pastoral migratory pattern was, of course,

quite different from the movement of raiding parties that left the herds and set off on their lightning forays that probably covered 600 miles in two weeks.

12   Only in the largest permanent trading centres were the Tatar tented towns replaced by wooden or brick buildings. On the other hand, New Sarai, the winter capital and one of the main trading and administrative centres of the Golden Horde, though founded only in 1253, became large and prosperous and numbered 200,000 inhabitants in 1333; excavations have shown that it had brick and marble buildings, elaborate mosques, mosaic floors, public baths and irrigation systems. New (Berke) Sarai on the Volga tributary of the Akhtuba was forty miles to the east of modern Volgograd (formerly Tsaritsyn and then Stalingrad) near the present settlement of Tsarev, controlling both the Volga and the Don; Old (Batu) Sarai was also on the Akhtuba but downstream about 100 miles from the Caspian standing near the present site of Selitrennoe.

13   Among the wives of the khans were many Moslem and Christian women, and these had both a religious and a cultural influence in the court. The khan Berke (1257–66) had already accepted Islam (though he left it to his successor Möngke-Temür to impose that religion on the horde), and Berke was both scandalized and enraged when Hülegü, the Tatar khan of the Il-Khan, had the Moslem religious leader, the Caliph of Baghdad, sewn up in a carpet and trampled to death. Möngke-Temür considered the relative merits of Islam, Christianity and Judaism before deciding in favour of the Moslem religion. The effect of Islam on the horde was that it reduced the main besetting sin—drunkenness: even so, one of the principal Tatar virtues remained that of forebearance both to foreigners and to other religions. They did not attempt to impose Islam on their vassals (except at a much later date in the Caucasus and then only at the prompting of the Turkish sultan). The Tatar khanates, by and large, remained Moslem throughout their history. The latter-day Russian and Ukrainian Cossack hosts, on the other hand, never were Moslem, notwithstanding that their original leaders and framework may have been Tatar.

14   The principalities that were under Tatar domination at the end of the thirteenth century were Galicia, Podolia, Volhynia, Kiev, Pereyaslav, Novgorod-Severskii, Chernigov, Smolensk, Murom-Ryazan, Vladimir-Suzdal and the republic of Novgorod. Galicia was, in due course, to be overrun by Poland while Lithuania was, by the early fifteenth century, to occupy, in addition to Polotsk and Turov-Pinsk, Podolia, Volhynia, Kiev, the greater part of Pereyaslav, and much of Chernigov and Smolensk. Lithuania joined with Poland under the personal union of 1386 when their rulers married; by the 1569 Union of Lublin the countries merged even closer under a single sovereign, the Lithuanians relinquishing control of the occupied Russian principalities in the south to Poland. This partition of Russia between the Tatars and the Polish-Lithuanians was to give rise to, and perpetuate, the difference between the Great Russian, who remained under the Tatars in the east, and the Little Russian (Ukrainian) and Belorussian in the west.

15  Batu, the first khan, had imposed a levy on all the Russian principalities ordering that *all* unmarried men and *all* unmarried women, together with every third son, should be delivered up to the Tatars for sale as slaves. This was apart from the capricious and incessant slave-raiding that took place most years, sometimes on an enormous scale. In addition, heavy tribute was paid regularly to the Tatars, payments still being made at intervals of every four to six years throughout the fifteenth century and thereafter.

16  There is some difference of opinion as to the function of the *daruga* and *baskak* since both words (one Turkic and the other Mongol) mean 'assessor'. The extent of their powers, however, cannot be disputed: in 1318 for example, one resident *daruga* by name of Kochka had 120 Russians put to death in Kostroma. Each of these Tatar residents had a personal escort of two Tatar mounted squadrons known to the Russian inhabitants as *kazaki* (Cossacks).

17  Among some of the more illustrious of the Russian princes who lost their lives were: Grand Prince Yaroslav Vsevolodovich of Vladimir believed poisoned in Karakorum in 1242; Grand Prince Mikhail Vsevolodovich of Chernigov-Kiev kicked to death in 1246 by Batu's bodyguard for refusing to prostrate himself before the khan or pass between two fires (a Shaman cleansing ritual); a Prince of Ryazan who, while still alive, had all his limbs cut off in 1270; Grand Prince Mikhail Yaroslavich of Tver executed in 1318 by Kavgadyi, a Tatar beg of the khan, after having been led in a yoke at the horse's tail hundreds of miles from Azov to the Terek, trailing behind the khan's hunting party; Grand Prince Dmitrii Mikhailovich of Tver killed in 1324 for having slain Prince Yurii Danilovich of Moscow at the khan Ozbeg's court. In due course Dmitrii's successor Alexander was also executed at the khan's order. As Howorth said, the horde was the cemetery of the Russian princes—'near the khan near to death'. Von Hammer lists nine who fell victim to Ozbeg alone.

18  One very powerful people that was to break away at this time were the Nogai Tatars. Prince Nogai, a grandson of Chengis Khan, had been allotted as his portion what were then the numerous Eastern Tatars or Manguts ('flat-noses'), a different people from the other Tatars of the horde in that they closely resembled the Mongols, being small, copper coloured, with very flat faces; their Tatar language, too, differed somewhat from that of the rest of the horde. Prince Nogai, from whom the Manguts took their name, established for himself an almost independent state running from the Balkans along the north Black Sea coast, and had become so powerful that his friendship was sought by the emperor at Constantinople: Nogai began to nominate the khans to the Golden Horde. In 1299, however, he was killed in battle against his own protégé and nephew, the Golden Horde khan Tohtu. The Nogai then finally broke away. Nogai's horde marked its name on many steppes and continues to exist until this day, although it became dispersed in numerous though still very powerful hordes that eventually included the Edisan, the Budzhak, part of the Crimean and Tauride, the Azov, the

Astrakhan and part of the Siberian Tatars, and the nomadic hordes to the north of the Caspian, all independent of the Golden Horde. Mary Holderness who lived with her English family in great contentment for four years from 1815 among the Crimean Tatars, whom she held in esteem, said of the Nogai: 'Their moral character is of the worst description and there is hardly any kind of mischief that they will not perpetrate. In horse-stealing they have no rivals, the [Russian] Cossacks being much their inferiors in this respect.' The development of all Russian Cossacks owed much to the Nogai, with whom they were continually in contact and from whom, incidentally, they took the Tatar flail-whip (the *nagaika*).

19  Olgerd's conquests had included: Vitebsk (1345), Kiev (from 1362), Podolia (1364), East Volhynia (from Poland 1366), Chernigov (1370) and Galicia (from Poland 1376) and the Black Sea coast: in 1386 came the personal union with Poland: between 1387–96 Moldavia, Wallachia and Bessarabia accepted Lithuanian suzerainty.

20  When Tokhtamysh took the throne of the Golden Horde a large part of the White Horde moved east with him leaving the area north of the lower Syr Darya empty: the Sheibanide (Kirghiz) Horde from the north moved into these former White Horde pastures and eventually (in 1480) subjugated the Siberian khanate at Sibir (Tiumen), holding on to Sibir until they were ousted by the Russian Cossacks in 1598. The Sheibanides also founded (in 1500) the Uzbek empire at Bokhara and Samarkand.

21  Tokhtamysh wanted an ally against Timurlane and had sought the help of the Lithuanians. When he was finally vanquished, remnants of his personal horde, numbering about 8,000, took refuge in Lithuania and fought for the Lithuanians in the victory of Tannenberg in 1410. Their Tatar descendants remained there, providing generations of Cossack cavalry for the Polish-Lithuanians and, in the nineteenth century, forming the basis of a tsarist Lithuanian-Tatar cavalry regiment.

22  New Sarai never recovered and it was not rebuilt, though some of its inhabitants remained. Thereafter coins show the Golden Horde capital as Gülistan (rose-garden) that may have been near Old Sarai.

23  Golobutskii, p. 40. These raids were not just border fights that were common throughout the year along the frontier of the steppe, but were seasonal campaigns that were made deep into Russia from one end to the other. The city of Moscow itself was attacked (and sometimes sacked and devastated) on numerous occasions, principally in 1237, 1293, 1381, 1408, 1439, 1451, 1480, 1521, 1572 and 1591.

24  At about this time the Tatars were threatened by the appearance of the Ottoman Turks who arrived in the estuary of the Don in 1471 and seized the Venetian depot of Tana (Azov). In 1475 the Turks landed in the Crimea seizing all the Genoese forts and trading stations, and put permanent garrisons in Perekop, Gaslav (Evpatoria), Kaffa, Enikale and Arabat, and at the mouth of the Dnieper and Dniester. The Crimean khan Mengli-Girai had been taken prisoner inside Kaffa, where he happened to be on a visit to the Genoese, and was only released two years later on condition that he and his successors should remain vassals

of the sultan, an undertaking faithfully adhered to by the Crimean khans. In the long run, therefore, this invasion from the south rebounded to the disadvantage of both Muscovy and Poland-Lithuania, since henceforth the Crimean Tatars could usually rely on Turkish assistance, and came entirely within the Turkish sphere of influence in foreign affairs and in religious matters; for the sultan himself approved the principal mullah appointments in the Crimea.

# 2 Dnieper and Don

It has been said that the word *kazak* was known on the Russian steppe to the Pechenegs and Kipchaks and other Turkic kinsmen of the Tatars even before the coming of the Mongols. It was certainly used in the tenth century by the Byzantine Emperor Constantine VII (Porphyrogenitus) in describing the Circassians in the Caucasus, a different racial group from the Turkic nomads although somewhat similar in their way of life. For in the Caucasus a Cossack and a Circassian were one and the same, the Circassians being both hillmen and lowland nomads, famous as light cavalry and feared because of their banditry; the very words 'Cossack' and 'Circassian' were interchangeable; and the name of Cossack had been used since the time of the early Arab chroniclers to describe not only Circassians but also the Kabards and a score or so of the other Caucasian peoples; for, although differing in speech, most of the Caucasian tribesmen were indistinguishable in their dress, their arms and their way of life.[1] Both Circassian and Caucasian Cossacks were to have a very strong influence on the development of Russian Cossackdom from the seventeenth century onwards.

In early times, at least from the fourteenth century, the Circassian was called *Cherkes* both by the Russian and by the Ottoman Turk, and his fame as a horseman and warrior was known throughout Turkey, Egypt and the southern regions of Muscovy, Lithuania and Poland. Circassians once occupied the Crimea and the Don estuary and, according to tradition that may be no more than fable, Circassian Cossack horsemen had roamed the banks of the Dnieper so giving their name to the old settlement and fortress of Cherkassy.[2] Both Cherkassy and its twin Dnieper fort of Kanev are believed to have had strong associations with the *Cherkes*, whoever the *Cherkes* might have been, and the towns appear at one time to have attracted Tatar bands who camped nearby and were probably in Lithuanian pay. In Russia as early as the sixteenth century the word *Cherkes* on the southern steppe had come to mean a Cossack, and the two words were synonymous in the official letters between the Tatar, Turkish, Muscovite and Lithuanian rulers. The word *Cherkes* was later used to describe the Ukrainian Cossack (and especially the Zaporozhian Cossack), but it could be applied to a Cossack of any race and was used even of the Cossacks of the Don.[3]

The origin and significance of the word *kazak*, on the other hand, are known more exactly. Among the Tatars themselves its early meaning was close to its Turkic origin in that it meant in essence 'a freeman', that is to say one who was not a bondsman or a slave: but it also had the connotation of 'nomad' and 'adventurer'. It came to be applied in particular to the Tatar herdsman and trooper, the lowest-ranking member and soldier of the horde, since he was both a nomad and a freeman responsible to none but the clan and tribal elders and to the section ataman, in whose election the trooper had probably had a voice. Eventually, and by extension, the word Cossack came to have a yet wider meaning in that it was used by the Tatar to describe any Tatar light horseman or border warrior.[4]

The word Cossack soon gained widespread use in this sense, and from the beginning of the fourteenth century the records of the Genoese merchants and the Greek Synaxarion in Tatar Crimea used 'Cossack' to describe any type of Tatar armed horsemen, whether these were guards, watchmen, escorts or steppe messengers in Genoese employ; it also included Tatar tribesmen who were bringing in cattle or plunder for sale to the merchant depots, or the mounted raiders of the steppe.[5] There was, in any event, little in those troubled times to distinguish between the Tatar raider, the nomad and the guard, for it was not unknown for a Tatar mounted force to convoy a caravan on the outward march across the steppe and then, lacking a suitable hiring for the return journey, plunder its way homewards, attacking other Tatar-escorted merchants whom they met on their way. By association a Cossack was regarded as a plunderer.

In Turkey, Poland, Lithuania and Muscovy the word Cossack came to be used of any steppe horseman since he was, in the early days before 1500, inevitably a Tatar or Circassian. Then, as the pattern of the steppe slowly began to change, it was used to describe a

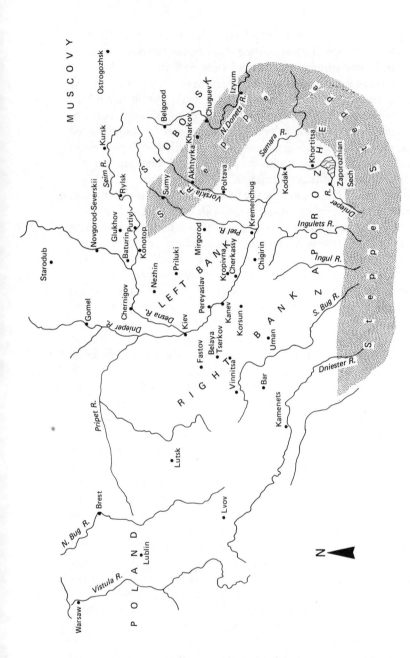

5 The Ukraine and the Dnieper c.1650

variety of peoples of different races that ventured on to the plain or reached its borders, the first of these being, like the Tatars, mounted fighting men and hunters; these were followed by herdsmen, foot-soldiers and boatmen, fishermen and pirates, and eventually by agriculturists and colonists who submitted to no rule except that of their elected leaders. All of them rejoiced in the name of Cossack. Already by the sixteenth century the Russian verb *kazakovat'* was to be found, even in official documents, and could be applied to any people who 'went Cossacking' or lived in the Cossack way.

\*    \*    \*

At the beginning of the fifteenth century, however, the Russias of both Muscovy and Lithuania-Poland were open to the annual invasions of the great Tatar hordes to the east and south, and to the incessant raiding by the Tatar splinter groups and banditry.[6] Pierre Chevalier, a French officer who was with the Polish forces at that time, has told us that since the Tatar brigands roamed the steppe in bands of 3,000 or more, an effective escort had to number at least a thousand men and these always had to be ready for battle. In Muscovy an attempt was made to cobble together some form of border defence along the edge of the steppe, initially by recruiting Tatar Cossack warrior bands to hold key points; in 1444, according to the Nikonovskaia chronicle, a force of 'Ryazan Cossacks', be-lieved to be Tatars, formed part of a Muscovite army that gave battle in the principality of Pereyaslav in the south against a Tatar incursion by the Crimean khan's heir, a Prince Mustapha, who was killed in the encounter.[7] The Lithuanians and Poles also began to bid for the services of Tatar Cossacks to strengthen their own defences, and numbers of Tatars, sometimes whole tribes or clans, deserted both horde and steppe and offered their services to the principalities. Neither side had any religious or racial scruples that might stand in the way of such compacts or alliances. In Moscow, especially, these Tatars were held in great esteem, their leaders receiving grants of borderland and being accepted into the Russian aristocracy as the equivalent of border barons.[8] The Tatar princes, their courtiers and their armed followers, were used not only for border defence but, in time of war, they formed part of their patron's field armies, often holding important military commands and undertaking distant cam-paigns against Tatar, Lithuanian or Russian or the knightly orders in the west.[9]

The migration of Tatars into the Moscow service became particularly common from the middle of the fifteenth century, and Tatar border colonies were set up along Muscovy's and neighbouring Ryazan's eastern frontier on the line of the Oka, with military posts at Kaluga, Tarusa, Serpukhov, Kasira, Kolomna and Tula. The centre of these Oka settlements was at Gorodets, a large fief granted in 1452 by Vasilii II to the prince Kasim, who was the son of Mehmet-Ulug the khan of Kazan, and who had fled to escape murder at his parricide brother's hands; renamed as Kasimov, it was still held by the Tatars in the reign of Peter the Great more than two centuries later. From this time onwards the *émigré* Tatars provided the Russian state with soldiers that came to be known either as Cossacks or, if they had a static role in town defence, as town Tatars. Other Tatar strongholds held for Moscow were Shitov, Rostunovo, Suraz, Berendeev, Izev and Peremysl Lubniya (Peremysh), some of them known to have garrisons of 500 riders or more; for these Tatar fighting communities and marcher barons exploited and recruited many of the local peoples within their fiefs, particularly the Meshcheryaks, Oka-Finns and Mordvins, for the Kasimov Tatars were in fact often known as Meshcheryak Cossacks. When Kazan was finally annexed in 1552 by Ivan the Terrible, the flow of santuary-seeking *émigrés* ceased, but Kazan Tatars continued to be taken into the service of Moscow in increasingly large numbers, and it was on this Tatar-controlled foundation that the border defence first came into being both in Russia and in the Ukraine. The Lithuanians, too, appear to have relied heavily on Tatar bands in their employ, especially in the key areas of Cherkassy-Kanev, as a defence against the hordes and Muscovy. These Tatar border chieftains led semi-independent lives, lording it over the border areas; provided that they were well rewarded, they remained faithful to their paymasters.

Both the Muscovites and the Lithuanians built their early border defences, particularly those in the south and south-east that faced against the Tatar, on very similar lines, relying from about 1468 onwards on what came to be called 'service' Cossacks. Service Cossacks were usually responsible to the local Muscovite or Lithuanian border baron, the *voevod*, and not to a Tatar prince: sometimes they were equipped at state expense and sometimes they provided their own arms and horses: some were foot and some were cavalry: some were full-time soldiers and some were part-time militia: all received payment from the state either in money or provisions or in an allotment of arable or pasture lands. Service Cossacks formed three classes, 'town', 'regimental' or 'outpost' (*storozhevye*), all very different in their composition. Town Cossacks came directly under the town administration and were employed either as horse or foot in its perimeter defence, and these troops led settled lives within the town community. The regimental Cossacks were locally recruited and uniformly organized bodies of cavalry of the size of regiments that had an advantage over those of the central governments in Moscow or Vilna in that they knew the country; these would ride out and engage the Tatars on the steppe.[10] Outpost Cossacks were those who were specially trained for the work of small patrols or outpost lines deep in the steppe. All of these service Cossacks operated from a fortress base under their own atamans, and they were recruited, controlled and paid by the border cities and townships. Originally the outpost and regimental units were largely Tatar, whereas the Great Russian and Little Russian made up the majority in the town units. Although service Cossacks were mainly stationed in the south and south-east as a defence against the Tatar they were to be found also in all border areas, based on towns as far afield as Pskov, Novgorod, Smolensk, Velikie Luki, Vologda, Chernigov, Novgorod-Severskii, Starodub, Rylsk and Putivl. Service Cossacks had little influence on the development of the latter-day Russian 'free' Cossack hosts.

The black-earth region from Ryazan to the Volga, and the steppe to the south of it known as the plain (*pole*), were entirely uninhabited in the fifteenth century, while even as late as 1520 there was not a single dwelling-place on the banks of the Don from Voronezh right down to Azov on the river delta, a distance of more than 600 miles. In the south, where the steppe was usually known as 'the wild plain', there was virtually no permanent habitation south of Cherkassy down the 400 mile stretch of the Dnieper as far as the Turkish forts at the river estuary. Anyone venturing on the steppe ran the risk of being killed, robbed or sold into slavery by Tatar Cossack marauders' or nomads. Yet the whole of the black-earth region and steppe was among the most fruitful in the world since the rivers were teeming with fish, with enormous beluga and sturgeon, with sevruga, sterlet, sheat-fish, carp, perch, pike, bream and roach. The river basins were thickly reeded and heavily wooded and wild fruit trees were plentiful: on the plain itself was a multitude of flowers and luxuriant grasses, some standing as high as a man, that supported herds of wild horses, wild pig, wild honey bees in profusion with honey for the collecting, goose, swan, duck, pelican, bustard, black-cock, partridge, hares, bears, wolves, foxes, otter, beaver, marten and polecat. Salt and saltpetre could be easily dug. Only in spring in the lower reaches of the rivers, following the thaw floods, could the climate be regarded as unhealthy, with its myriads of flies and plagues of locusts.

From about 1450 onwards there had begun a migratory movement of the Little Russian population from the old principalities of Podolia, Volhynia and Kiev, south-eastwards to the edge of the steppe and sometimes beyond, in quest of freedom and of good land, seeking relief from the oppression of debt or of tenant or peasant service, a service soon to be translated into serfdom; these migrants were prepared to brave the dangers of the plain rather than live in penury under a Polish or Lithuanian occupation. The settlers, for many took their families and many moved as complete communities, were mainly cultivators of the soil, but there were also fishermen, huntsmen, saltpetre diggers and artisans among them: understanding the constant threat that the Tatar raider posed to all frontiersmen, they banded themselves together in their own defence as free military colonies with their own appointed leaders, and, since they had heard something of the spirit of Cossackdom, they called themselves Cossacks, although of course these settlers had nothing in common with the brigand, the nomad, or the Tatar Cossack bands. The Lithuanian border area that they began to colonize, on the upper and middle reaches of the Bug, the Dniester and the Dnieper, eventually became known as the Ukraine.[11] These Little Russian farmers and peasants, as well as the artisans and townsmen, because they were jealous of their freedom that under latter-day Polish (and Russian) law could be forfeit if they lost their Cossack status, fiercely defended their Cossack rights even as late as the end of the seventeenth century.

The Little Russians did not in fact venture far beyond the Lithuanian-controlled frontier land, and the Dnieper area of Cherkassy and Kanev was particularly popular with the new settlers, presumably because of the protection given by the forts, for the Lithuanians had refortified them, as a barrier to Tatar invasion, with walls, moats and towers, and set up a *voevod* and small garrisons there. In the latter half of the fifteenth century the *voevod* appears to have enrolled the new colonists, who had by then become numerous, for emergency military service in the event of Tatar attack, and it was for this reason that Cherkassy, already the headquarters of the Lithuanian border hetmanate, was to become the traditional seat of the latter-day military organization of the Ukrainian Cossacks. There is evidence, however, that other peoples, in all probability the Tatar and part-Tatar bands that had formerly occupied the areas near the towns together with numbers of Little Russian adventurers, had meanwhile come to feel constrained by the changing pattern of life on the edge of the steppe that followed the arrival of so many Little Russian colonizers, and possibly by the closer military control of the Lithuanians. The bands therefore had already begun to quit Cherkassy-Kanev and move out to the south along the Dnieper river down below the mighty cataracts.

About 200 miles below Cherkassy, where the Dnieper changes direction to flow due south (near the present site of Dnepropetrovsk) began the first of the twelve cataracts, stretching over sixty miles of the river course, each of the twelve being made up of a series of flat lava beds together with several rows of jagged rocks that towered in sets of dragons' teeth, up to twenty feet high, right across the river. It was dangerous to navigate boats between the cataracts unless the vessels could be controlled by lines from ashore, and this was made particularly difficult since the dry-land approach to the banks was almost impassable. The twelfth and last of the cataracts was the most hazardous since it consisted of a series of seven different sheets of lava table-rock and twelve sets of dragons' teeth, after which the water dropped fourteen feet into a great cauldron. This last cataract was always there, even after the spring thaw when the river, roaring down in spate, covered some of the other cataracts.

Downstream of the cataracts the Dnieper again changed direction and ran quietly south-westwards across the steppe and the Tauride lowlands towards the sea. This lower river was fed by numerous tributaries on both banks and these formed many sluggish channels and backwaters, lakes and marshes, with almost impenetrable high reed beds on both sides of the river. In the area of the rapids and immediately to the south, the banks of the Dnieper were heavily wooded, and the reeds and steppe grasses grew in such profusion and to such a height that they could easily hide a mounted horseman. The river there, that was almost four miles wide, was sown with hundreds of wooded and reed-surrounded islands that were inaccessible without a guide. Of these many islands, five were important in so far as Cossack history is concerned: the greater and smaller Khortitsa, near the last cataract; the Velikii, at the mouth of the river Konskoi; the Tomakovka at the mouth of the river of that name; and finally the Bazavluk against the mouth of the rivers Bazavluk and Chertomlyka.

\* \* \*

At the close of the fifteenth century the bands that had lived near Kanev and Cherkassy for so long began to move southwards to these new island hideaways to the south of the cataracts, that were well beyond the Lithuanian domain. Whether or not they had any families or womenfolk is not known, but it is more likely that they were originally close-knit male military communities and robber bands. Nor is their racial composition clear, but their dress, accoutrements, speech and methods suggest a very strong strain of Tatar superimposed on Little Russian.[12] The immediate origin of this new Cossack host, that came to be called the Zaporozhian, or the people that dwell 'beyond the cataracts', is, however, well documented from Lithuanian and Turkish sources.[13] In 1492, for example, Mengli-Girai, the Crimean khan, wrote to Alexander of Lithuania that steppe Cossacks 'from Cherkassy and Kiev' had plundered a Tatar caravan. In 1527 Sahib-Girai complained to the Lithuanian government that 'Kanev and Cherkassy Cossacks were moving down the valley of the Dnieper and were harassing the Tatar steppe nomads', while the Cherkassy fort records witness that bands had long before established themselves on Tomakovka, Bazavluk and Argachina. They had even got a temporary foothold on Tavan island (near present-day Kakhovka) over 150 miles to the south of the cataracts near the river mouth, not far from where the Tatars and Turks had built the fort of Islam-Kermen (Aslan-Gorodok).

The Zaporozhian host headquarters was set up in a clearing (sech') on one of the islands and this served as a central headquarters, fort and depot, armoury and treasury, where all plunder was cached; this sech was moved, as security demanded, from one island to another. The host was in many respects close to that of the Tatar hordes in that it had an elected koshevoi ataman (known as a hetman in the Ukraine) and elected officials, these being the hetman's deputy (esaul) and the treasurer-secretary (pisar) and (at a later date) a judge; these officials were appointed, usually annually, by a sech

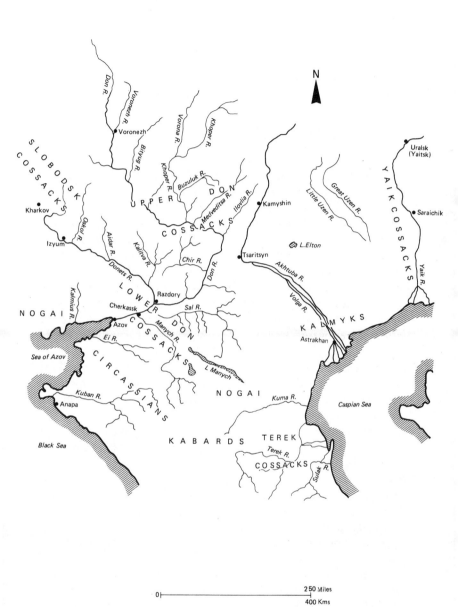

6 The Don and Caspian c. 1690

assembly (*kolo* or *rada*) of all Cossacks within hearing distance of drum and signalling cannon.[14] The sech had a main open assembly square (*maidan*) flanked by the wood-, wattle- and reed-covered huts that served for the host administration, the armouries and stores, the Greek Orthodox church, and the barrack huts (*kuren'*) that housed the sech garrison, the host's immediate fighting force. The garrison consisted of the unmarried or the unattached (the *seroma*), the newly arrived, the homeless and the poor. These were maintained at the host expense until permanent work and quarters could be found for them in the surrounding countryside, the very great area that came to be controlled by the sech.[15]

Women were not permitted inside the sech on pain of death and from this it has sometimes been assumed that the Zaporozhian Cossack host was a celibate, almost monastic, order. But there are grounds for thinking that the rule applied only to the sech itself, for the host eventually came to own or control an area of about 150,000 square miles, with great fishery industries, boat-building yards, farmsteads and settlements, and this host area was peopled by families: men were continually leaving the sech for employment in outlying districts and might not see the sech again unless called in for military service, particularly if they were too far away to attend the rada meetings. But the Cossack, together with his horse or his boat, remained at the call of the host, even though he might be summoned only at times of emergency.

Fishing was the main summer industry that occupied a large part of the host in netting, drying, smoking and salting and transporting the fish, together with fur, honey and high-grade salt, by boat or cart to markets as far afield as Cherkassy, Kanev and Kiev; the winter was spent hunting and trapping. In addition there was some cattle-raising in spite of the danger of Tatar raids, and even as early as the beginning of the sixteenth century large stock farms (*zimovniki*) began to appear near the northernmost cataract in the area of the Orel river.

There was no lack of new recruits for the Zaporozhian host, and these were principally Little Russians that had either been service Cossacks or Ukrainian Cossacks or were migrants or fugitives from the old principalities further to the west and north. Tatars and Great Russians were also represented, together with Turks, Poles, Lithuanians and Germans. The language commonly spoken was Little Russian with a strong Tatar admixture. Most would-be recruits were accepted after a trial period; and the accepted recruit was usually given a name that was not his own, and he was allotted to one of the kuren, the name of the kuren being permanently coupled with his new name as a clan identity.[16] All faiths were admitted, although the Cossack was expected to join the Greek church that was in effect a community church in which the host appointed its own clergy from among its own ranks, and which was independent of the church of Constantinople, Kiev or Moscow. Once accepted, no man would be given up, whatever his crime and no matter who demanded his return, a practice common to all other early Cossack hosts and to the North Caucasian and Iranian people of the steppe. This was an important factor in cementing trust in the little community.

Although the Zaporozhians said that they could put a force of 12,000 men into the field, there rarely appear to have been more than 6,000 men in the sech. And because of the lack of nearby pasture land in the wooded and marshy Dnieper valley there were insufficient horses to hand to mount this force. Necessity and environment changed the way of life of these Zaporozhian Cossacks so that they became fishermen, mariners and foot-soldiers, in addition to being horsemen. They were excellent boat-builders and, according to the French officer Chevalier, they could build up to 100 boats in three weeks. These open keel-less boats, known as sea-gulls (*chaiki*), were sixty feet long, twelve feet wide, with a freeboard of only thirty inches that could be increased by slotted planks or the use of water-tight dried reed bundles: they carried a single sail but they usually moved by oars, up to fifteen to each side, with two steering oars for better manoeuvrability, and they were much faster than a Turkish galley. Each boat was armed with six falconet guns and two arquebuses and carried a crew of about sixty men. Their boat provisions were biscuit and boiled millet, together with a paste and water, that, said the Frenchman, 'they think delicious: for, heavy drinkers though they are, they never take intoxicating drink with them when going on expedition.' Flotillas of these boats, sometimes fifty- or a hundred-strong, would row rapidly down the Dnieper, moving usually by night into the open sea, and they would sack settlements and forts as far away as the north coast of Turkey, even the suburbs of Constantinople. Turkish war vessels were not safe from them for they could be boarded by night, plundered and sunk.

As foot-soldiers, too, these Cossacks were redoubtable, particularly in forest fighting where they could quickly fashion great barriers by felling trees, barriers that sometimes extended for a mile or more. No troops were better at storming fortifications. Nor did they fear to move far out on to the steppe, the pikemen, bowmen and musketeers plodding alongside the columns of covered carts, while the light cavalry ranged far and wide observing and reconnoitring the distant horizon. In the event of Tatar attack the carts were quickly closed up in nomad fashion into a tight circle, known as a *tabor*: teams were unharnessed or unyoked and taken into the circle while the carts were chained or lashed together to prevent them being dragged away. All Cossacks then set to, for the spade and axe were never far from their grasp, digging out the earth and throwing up a rampart of soil among the wagons. From behind these mobile ramparts, said our French officer, a thousand Zaporozhians could easily hold at bay six times their number of Tatars, particularly as they usually carried light cannon with them, whereas the Tatars rarely had any form of artillery. But even when powder and arrows were used up, their pikemen, sheltering from Tatar fire behind the earthern fortifications and below the carts, could not be approached too closely, for their long pikes, often provided with the Tatar hook, were murderous to rider and horse alike. On occasions, thought Chevalier, the Tatar would have been better advised to have fought dismounted, but nothing could ever prevail upon him to do so. But where the Zaporozhian was essentially a practical man, the Tatar was already becoming an anachronism, out of harmony with the times.

The Zaporozhians were capable of sending out cavalry expeditions, perhaps 3,000 riders strong, as far afield as Moldavia, but 3,000 horse was not a force of great significance in the steppe where the Crimean khan could put out ten times that number without burden to his resources. The Zaporozhians' ability to wage this type of war was severely restricted by their lack of horses and men, and so they remained principally footmen and mariners.

The reputation of the Zaporozhian Cossacks grew rapidly during the sixteenth century so that Chevalier said of them, that 'there was no warrior better fitted to outfight a Tatar than a Zaporozhian.' The sultan sent frequent complaints to the Lithuanians, and later to the Poles, who replied, with truth, that 'these people were not their concern since they were outlaws outside their domain;' Turkish galleys were lost below the cataracts coming up the Dnieper in pursuit of Zaporozhian flotillas, and the Turks tried in vain to close the mouth of the river by drawing a chain across its estuary at the island of Tavan. The Turk and Tatar did of course inflict defeats on the Zaporozhians, at one time burning their flotilla and capturing 2,000 horses when the host was away on a land expedition; and in 1593, again when the main host was absent, burning the Tomakovka sech. But the Zaporozhians were adaptable and resilient with remarkable powers of recovery: casualties in men, that were occasionally heavy, could be made good, since the supply of recruits was never lacking; a fleet of new boats could be built in a month; only the loss in horses could not easily be replaced. The Zaporozhians attacked, as they thought fit, Turk, Tatar, Russian, Lithuanian and Pole, thinking nothing of penetrating deeply into the Lithuanian-Polish area and laying siege to Kiev. And although their relationship with the Little Russian of the Ukraine was generally good, they did not hesitate, if occasion demanded, to include among their enemies the Ukrainian Cossacks in the Polish-Lithuanian service. The renown of the Zaporozhian became such that Pope Clement VIII and the Hapsburg emperor, and at times even the Poles, sought their friendship as an ally against the Turk. Their fame was well known, too, in Moscow where Fedor Ivanovich, the Russian tsar, had described the Zaporozhians to a visiting Austrian delegation as being 'good fighters, but cruel and treacherous'. These foreign powers frequently sent envoys to the Zaporozhians, and it is from the envoys' reports that the descriptions of the sech are drawn.

The approaches of the Zaporozhian sech were covered by high look-out towers giving observation down the river and across the steppe, these being provided with warning beacons of straw and tar, so that the alarm could be sent from beacon to beacon; horses were kept standing by all watch towers. The sech at Bazavluk, that replaced Tomakovka after 1593, had ditches and a wooden palisade with corner towers, and inside the sech were the usual maidan square, the church, the official huts and the kuren barracks. The day-to-day government was entirely in the hands of the hetman and his elected staff, as advised by the committee of elders (the *skhodka*); on the other hand the annual re-election of the hetman and his officials, and any great matters of policy, had to be discussed, and voted, by the assembled rada, at which the meanest Cossack entered on the host roll was entitled to speak and vote.

When a rada was summoned, the traditional procedures were strictly adhered to; these procedures were also common to the other great free host, the Don Cossacks. Some of the origins were Mongol-

Tatar; the others are lost in antiquity. The assembled Zaporozhians, dressed more like Tatars or Turks than Little Russians, with their heads shaved in the fashion of the steppe nomads, sat in a circle on the ground or on the shed roofs, awaiting the arrival of the hetman bearing the mace of office (*bulava*), together with the esaul carrying the *bunchuk*, the Cossack horse-tail standard surmounted by a brass ball that had its origin in the Mongol yak-tailed standard.[17] The judge and secretary followed bearing their badges of office.[18] The hetman then took off his hat and bowed ceremoniously to the assembly in all four directions, addressing the members Tatar fashion as *tovarishchi*, and then he proceeded to business. If an election was involved, the departing officials laid down their regalia and thanked the assembly for the honour of their trust. A newly elected hetman had, as a matter of course, to refuse the office, accepting it only on the third proposal. He was then showered with mud to remind him that he was only the servant of the host.

Often, however, the meetings of the rada went on for days, sometimes ending in violence. In 1581 the Pole Zborovskii visited Tomakovka with an invitation to the Zaporozhians to join Warsaw in an attack on the Muscovite region of Putivl. But either the reward to be paid was insufficient or the proposal was little to the liking of the assembly. The talking dragged on, and the proceedings became disorderly to a background of the firing of weapons in the air, to singing and the playing on the *kobza* (an old Ukrainian stringed instrument): eventually the only matter being debated was not whether the Zaporozhians should attack Putivl but whether the rada should hang Zborovskii and his delegation. During the night the Poles slipped off, thankful to have got away with their lives.

In 1594 the Austrian Lassota von Steblau, the envoy of the Hapsburg Holy Roman Emperor, visited the sech at Bazavluk with a proposal from the emperor that the Zaporozhians should enter Moldavia to the rear of a Turkish army that was threatening Hungary, and so prevent the Tatars from joining the Turks. Von Steblau remained in the sech during the three-week discussions and recorded a description of events in his diary. The hetman Mikoshinskii had just returned with fifty boats and 1,300 men from an expedition to the mouth of the Dnieper where he had been attacking forts and settlements. A rada was called which von Steblau was invited to attend and there put his case, and this went on for a number of days. The Cossacks gladly accepted the emperor's money as an advance on payments yet to be made, but wanted more precise information as to what further sums were to follow. They also doubted the wisdom of moving on foot so far afield as Moldavia, particularly as they were short of horses anyway and did not trust the Moldavians. But von Steblau had to take some sort of answer back as to whether the Zaporozhians would co-operate in the emperor's plan in the event of the other objections being met; and so the rada broke up into two separate circles, one for the elders and the other for the rank and file (the *chern'*), to take a vote on the matter. The *chern'* quickly decided in the emperor's favour, announcing their decision by a great shout and the throwing of caps in the air. They then rushed over to the elders' circle threatening them with 'throwing in the river', that is to say death, if they did not agree likewise. And so the matter was settled.

The next morning, however, the situation had changed entirely and the *chern'* was no longer in favour of a new expedition—such was the volatile nature of these Cossacks. It was then the turn of the hetman Mikoshinskii to become angry. There was, he said, no dignity in serving a host that was without honour or good name, and, laying down his regalia, he resigned. The rada dispersed in confusion. After dinner, however, the esaul called another assembly, sending out his henchmen with whips to urge in the reluctant. Mikoshinskii was begged, in front of the entire gathering, to take up his office again, and this he eventually agreed to do. The emperor's envoy returned to Austria satisfied that he had achieved what was possible in the circumstances.

\* \* \*

That the Zaporozhian host was never destroyed by Turk or Tatar was due, in the main, to the difficult river channels and marshland that surrounded the sech; that it was never suppressed by Lithuania-Poland was due partly to the cataracts but, more particularly, to the troubled conditions, often bordering on anarchy, that existed in the settled Ukraine.

The Ukrainian Cossacks there did not develop into a free and independent Cossack community, in the fashion of the Zaporozhian or the Don hosts, because the area that they had chosen to settle was already under the control, firstly of Lithuania and then, after 1569, of Poland, and these powers reached out and absorbed them. Ukrainian Cossackdom, even in the early free days, appears to have been no more than scattered communities each of a few settlements of perhaps a hundred souls banded together in little military colonies under their own elected chiefs. These were soon made subject to a Lithuanian *voevod*, and some were enrolled into a Lithuanian militia administered by a Lithuanian soldier or a Lithuanian-appointed Little Russian official; and so these tiny Cossack communities lost their identity and a large measure of their freedom at a very early stage. Not only were they obliged to be ready for military service in emergency but they were conscripted for regular labour to rebuild the forts. The Cherkassy *voevod* from 1514–35, Evstafii Dashkevich, appears to have enjoyed an extraordinary independence even from his grand duke, for he sent out forays on his own account against both Muscovy and the Crimean khan, and he and the *starosty* of Cherkassy and Kanev began to assume feudal rights over the local population. In consequence, there was a rebellion in 1536 and Cherkassy was seized by Cossacks, the revolt being put down by a Lithuanian force sent from Kiev. This was the first of a long series of revolts, mutinies and wars of Ukrainian against Lithuanian, Ukrainian against Pole and eventually Ukrainian against Ukrainian. Each revolt, as it was crushed and followed by repressions, caused the flight of more colonists to the Zaporozhians or to the Don.

Lithuanian military leaders and, more frequently, Little Russian officers and officials in the Lithuanian service, were given grants of land in the border areas that were already occupied in part by Ukrainian Cossack settlers; once again this new gentry assumed feudal rights and used their own strong-arm men, private retainers whom they also called Cossacks, to oust the colonists from their holdings, to levy taxes or demand a share of produce and labour. Yet, however much the settlers might have been angered by the confiscations and brutality of the newly arrived nobility, those Cossacks that remained in the Ukraine were willing, even anxious, to serve the Lithuanian grand duke either as a militia or as campaign soldiery. In their view the worst that could happen to them was to be denied their right to bear arms, for this could bring with it a reduction to serfdom. In times of war the Ukrainian Cossacks were a welcome addition to the Polish-Lithuanian armies; but in peace they were regarded as a numerous, unreliable and potentially explosive element in the borderlands: and wherever there was trouble with the Ukrainian Cossack, the Pole was of the firm belief that the Zaporozhian had incited it.

DNIEPER AND DON 43

It was to the advantage of both Lithuanian and Pole to bring the Zaporozhian Cossacks under their influence and this they repeatedly tried to do. To disperse the Zaporozhians was not necessarily in the Polish-Lithuanian interest since the sech formed a bulwark against Turkish-Tatar aggression, provided of course that the Zaporozhians did not ally themselves with the Tatar. To force the Zaporozhians out of the sech might drive them into the arms of the Crimean khan or those of the Muscovite tsar; this would not have been to Vilna's or Warsaw's liking. But in any case it proved militarily impossible to track the Zaporozhians down and assail them. So the Lithuanian and Polish governments alternated their policies and tactics from blandishments and promises to threats and raids, all with little success. From 1541 the governorship of the twin fortresses of Cherkassy-Kanev had passed into the hands of the Vishnevitskii family, the office passing from father to son or brother to brother. Dmitrii Vishnevitskii, a powerful and rich magnate with properties in Lithuania and Podolia, a man of great personal as well as political ambition, in 1556 attempted to neutralize the Zaporozhians by putting a Ukrainian Cossack garrison on the island of Khortitsa just below the last cataract—but still forty miles to the north of the Tomakovka sech. Sigismund II, who was both king of Poland and grand duke of Lithuania, had ordered Vishnevitskii to control the Zaporozhians and also to bar the Muscovites from entering into the middle Dnieper valley: but Vishnevitskii was in secret correspondence with the sultan Suleiman and the tsar Ivan IV, in some design that was presumably based on personal aggrandizement. In 1557 Vishnevitskii raided Islam-Kermen, but the Tatars in return attacked and destroyed Khortitsa. Vishnevitskii and the remnant of his force fled back to Cherkassy, from whence Vishnevitskii, already suspected in Warsaw of treason, went on to Moscow: the Cossack rank and file were arrested by the Lithuanians.[19]

In 1569, after the Union of Lublin, Lithuania, at the insistence of the last of its Jagellon monarchs, had unwillingly ceded the Ukraine to Polish administration, and this had deepened the discord between the border government and the Little Russian Cossack. One of the first Polish measures, that same year, was to subordinate all Ukrainian Cossacks to a Polish state official, directly under the crown, who was to be known as 'the *starshina* of the Cossacks'. In 1575, following an interregnum of three years after the death of Sigismund Augustus, Stefan Batory, who had married Anne, the last of the Lithuanian Jagellons, was elected Polish king; thereafter the crown, that had formerly been elective in theory, now became so in fact, the new king being very much subject to the control of the Polish nobility. This nobility began to move into the Ukraine in numbers and required the crown to control, disarm and disperse the Ukrainian Cossacks.

Stefan Batory's first measure was to order the licensing of Ukrainian Cossacks by the recording of their names in a central register (initially at Cherkassy), the numbers admitted to the register being severely restricted according to a Polish approved quota, at first only 300, a figure that was soon afterwards increased to 6,000 men. These registered Cossacks were not liable for taxes or subject to the control of *voevod* or Polish government except through their regiment, and they were permitted to retain land under privileged conditions; their pay, however, was so small that the cost to the Polish crown was not 1/20th of the upkeep of a Polish soldier. The registered Cossack was in fact a militiaman, his position being roughly equivalent to that of a Muscovy service or town Cossack. In 1590 Stefan Batory decreed that the overall Cossack command should be held by a crown-designated hetman, who was usually a Polish or Lithuanian army officer stationed in Warsaw or Vilna: as a special mark of grace the registered Cossacks were permitted to elect the commander (*starshina*) for each regiment but the appointment had to be confirmed by the Polish crown. The electing of commanders, like the privileged ownership of land, was a favour that could be, and often was, rescinded, whereupon Polish and Ukrainian officers would be appointed to the regiments from the nobility or gentry. It was Stefan Batory's intention that all former self-styled Ukrainian Cossacks, of whom there were a very great number, possibly nearly 100,000, if not admitted to the register should revert to the status of peasants or townsmen; it was an intention that, for a number of reasons, the Poles were never able to fulfil.

Due to the constant warfare between Poland and its neighbours and the perpetual civil disorders within the Ukraine, disorders that bordered on anarchy, the crown was unable to insist on any set limit to the register. In the few peaceful years, Warsaw made determined efforts to reduce even the earlier agreed figure of 6,000: in times of war against external enemies every armed Ukrainian Cossack was needed and, in the next century, the limit on registered Cossacks was increased, at one time to 40,000 and at another to 60,000 men. In actual fact, such was the frequency of the emergencies and such was the sudden need that it is doubtful whether there was time for the registering formalities to be completed on each occasion that the Ukrainians flocked to join the king of Poland's forces.

After the Union of Lublin the Polish restraints increased in the Ukraine against both town dweller and countryman, and these repressions took several forms: arbitrary and illegal taxation, confiscations of property and land, the introduction of the semi-feudal socage system, the threat or reality of serfdom, racial discrimination and preference, and lastly the religious intolerance against the Orthodox church motivated by the Jesuit order that had become particularly powerful in the Eastern Ukraine. In 1587 there were widespread peasant disorders throughout Podolia and a serious uprising of Cossacks north of the Dnieper; in consequence Polish officers were drafted into the Cossacks, and the *Seim* appointed commissars whose duty it was to report on the reliability of the registered Cossacks. A restriction was placed on the movement of all Ukrainian Cossacks (in case they escaped to the sech) and it was ordered that all Zaporozhians found in the Ukraine were to be executed.

The Zaporozhians were a source of acute embarrassment to Poland in its relationship with Turkey and the Crimea, since Poland was unable to control the sech or prevent Zaporozhian attacks in the area of the Black Sea; yet Poland persisted in claiming the Zaporozhian area as its own. The Poles also regarded Zaporozhian incitement as the main cause of their internal security problems in the Ukraine. In 1590 they built a Polish river-fort below Cherkassy at Kremenchug to serve as a base of operations against the sech; they also made a number of ineffectual expeditions below the cataracts, using registered Ukrainian Cossacks as part of the raiding forces. The conduct of the Ukrainian Cossacks in such a role was unpredictable; sometimes they deserted to the Zaporozhians in large numbers; on other occasions they fought with great determination, suffering and inflicting numerous losses. Meanwhile the Zaporozhians were not idle, for they advanced boldly into Polish Ukraine, attacking Kiev, Belaya Tserkov and Cherkassy, this last fortress being the scene of much fierce fighting in September 1598 between the Zaporozhians and the Ukrainian Cossacks; Warsaw may have hoped that the Zaporozhians and the registered Cossacks would weaken each other in the struggle. Meanwhile the Poles sought to assert their claim on the sech and confuse both the local population and foreign envoys by calling *their* registered Cossacks 'Zaporozhians', and even went so far as to include the words 'and hetman of the Zaporozhians' in the official title of the Polish-appointed crown hetman, thereby, as Golobutskii has said, confusing historians for many centuries. When in correspondence with the sultan or the khan, however, the Poles and Lithuanians denied any responsibility for the Zaporozhian sech.

\* \* \*

The situation in the wild borderlands to the east and south-east of Muscovy developed somewhat differently from that in the Zaporozhian steppe. In the very early days, before 1430, the Nogai and the powerful Golden Horde were closer to Ryazan and Muscovy than they were to the Lithuanian-held frontier, and the princes of Moscow were neither as bold nor as militarily capable as the grand dukes of Lithuania. After 1430, however, the position changed with the break-away from the Golden Horde and the move westwards of the Crimean khanate, for thereafter the authority of the Golden Horde and the Nogai over the black-earth region and the steppe to the south-east and south of Muscovy that had previously been virtually absolute, was challenged by the khans of Kazan and of the Crimea and by the Tatar and Circassian banditry: to these were added many foreign riders who began to appear on the open steppe. The wild plain had become an even wilder place, for dangers were to come from all sides.

The Moscow archives give a reliable, even graphic, picture of the perils attending any venture out beyond the borderlands, however great the escort. No one could live permanently on the steppe and it was soon to become dangerous even for the Tatar nomads and their herds, for the pasture lands had become the territory of warring factions. In 1489 the tsar complained to the Crimean khan that an escorted caravan of official envoys returning to Moscow from the Crimea had been attacked near the junction of the Oskol and Donets (near present-day Izyum) with much plundering and killing; in 1493 it was the turn of the khan to complain to Moscow that Meshcheryak (Kasimov) Tatars were hanging about on the outskirts of Azov 'looking for tongues [prisoners]'.[20] In 1496 the Moscow ambassadors to Moldavia and the Crimea, travelling together for safety across the steppe with a joint escort, were, nevertheless, attacked and robbed: four years later the Crimean Tatar ambassador to Moscow and the Moscow ambassador to the Crimea were moving in a single convoy across the steppe with a large mounted escort, when they were attacked by an even larger force of 'Azov Cossacks' and only the Russian ambassador, Prince Kubinskii, and fifty of the escort escaped. The next year, in 1501, the Russian ambassador was captured by Azov Cossacks.

The Azov Cossacks were said by some to have been Nogai; by others they were described as Circassians, for in those days the Circassian territory stretched as far as the estuary of the Don; whatever their origin they soon disregarded both khan and sultan, for Ottoman rule did not extend beyond the Azov fortress walls and the river banks. Under pressure from the sultan, the khan stationed a body of Tatar horse in Azov to protect convoys in and out of the town, and this led to frequent fighting between the escorts and the Azov Cossacks, a situation that was only resolved, and that temporarily, by the Turks having to come to terms with the Azov Cossacks and employ them as guards and escorts.

The turn of the century saw the final destruction of the Golden Horde. In 1501 the tsar Ivan III had promised its khan Saih-Ahmed that he would resume the payment of tribute that was again in arrears; but, in the following June, the Crimean Tatars routed Saih-Ahmed's forces, so forcing the khan to flee for refuge, firstly to the Belgorod-Akkerman Nogai Tatars, then to the Astrakhan khanate, and finally to the protection of Alexander of Lithuania-Poland who, from time to time, had been his ally. But an ally without troops is no ally indeed, and in 1505 Alexander had the last khan of the Golden Horde murdered in order to better his standing with the Crimean khan Mengli-Girai I. Mengli-Girai in his turn demanded and received from Moscow the tribute that had been outstanding to the Golden Horde, tribute that continued to be paid intermittently until the reign of Peter the Great. It was the disappearance of the Golden Horde that was to transform the steppe to the south-east of Muscovy and bring into being one of the most powerful of the Russian Cossack hosts on the Don.

The period from 1501 to 1530 was one of intense border fighting and steppe raiding so that it was impossible for caravans or government officials to move without a great escort; this devil's cauldron was so inviting that the Belgorod-Akkerman Nogai Cossacks began to feel that they were in an unprofitable backwater and could only improve their fortunes by 'moving to the area of Putivl [on the Muscovite border] and selling their services to the highest bidder'. The Lithuanian, Ryazan and Moscow borders were under constant attack from Crimean, Azov and Nogai Tatars; on the other hand the Kasimov Meshcheryak were very active on Moscow's behalf raiding Azov and the Black Sea coast. In 1523 the tsar Vasilii complained yet again about the Azov Cossacks and asked the sultan to strengthen his garrison there to quieten them; thereafter, however, the pattern of the correspondence began to change in that there was a very marked increase in Tatar and Turkish accusations about the Moscow-controlled Tatar Cossack raiders and the presence of Russian horsemen on the open steppe.

In 1520 the Don valley was completely uninhabited from the Russian border town of Voronezh right down to the Turkish fortress of Azov on the river delta, a river distance of over 500 miles. At one time the tsar had proposed to the khan, though nothing came of it, that fortified staging posts should be set up over the steppe to give some security to travellers and merchants. From 1530 onwards there began a series of complaints from the Turks, the Crimean Tatars and the Nogai, about the number of *new* marauders on the steppe, for Muscovite Russians were venturing out on to the plain in ever increasing numbers. Many of the new arrivals sought adventure; many were would-be brigands; many of them, like the migrant Little Russians on the Dnieper, were in search of a new life away from poverty and servitude.[21] Some were fugitives from the law and readily reinforced the steppe robber bands; others became fishermen, boatmen, hunters and herdsmen, although there was rarely any clear distinction between the robbers and the others, for these new-found Cossacks turned their hands to whatever was profitable. The early attraction was in the freedom, the way of life; the acquisition of land at first meant very little, for these first migrants, like the nomads, were not rooted to the soil but used it and moved where it could best serve them. Because of the great dangers on the steppe these people soon became trained to arms and learned that the way of safety was the way of the Tatar, for the bands were in no way homogeneous but were made up of Little Russians, Lithuanians, Finns, Turks, Mordvins and others, with the largest element being Tatar and Great Russian. But as Stökl has said, 'the original Tatar bands were not so much Russianized, it was rather that the Slavs joined the Tatar framework in increasing numbers, for the Tatar was the unchallenged authority in steppe warfare,' the Slav content, according to

Zasedateleva, thus 'growing over two centuries into a preponder-ance'. There were no Russian Cossacks while the Tatar controlled the steppe—they arose only when the mastery was being disputed —and these Russians took on the ways of the Tatar Cossacks.

In 1538 Mirza Kelm-Ahmed wrote to the tsar about the ravages caused 'by *your* town Cossacks', by which the prince may have meant the border 'town' Cossacks or, more likely, the Kasimov (Gorodets) horde: but Ivan Vasilevich shrugged off the complaint saying: 'On the steppe there are many Cossacks, Kazan, Azov, Crimean and other trouble-makers (*balovni*) and you are mistaking them for our Ukraine [Great Russian border] Cossacks.' Yet it is not impossible, as was noted by the nineteenth-century historians of the Don host, that the border towns could indeed have added to the confusion in that many of the service regiments had already begun to patrol as far as the Volga and the middle Don; some elements may indeed have reinforced the free Cossack bands, for there was always a place there for the soldier.[22]

In 1549 the tsar Ivan Vasilevich sent his envoy Ivan Borshevich to Prince Iusuf of the Nogai in an attempt to incite the Nogai to attack the Crimean Tatars, saying that if the Nogai should choose to do so, then he, the tsar, would be pleased to help them with *his* Putivl and Don Cossacks; in all probability, however, the tsar was offering only the service Cossacks from the towns in the upper reaches of the Don, since the free Don bands out on the steppe were entirely independent of Moscow. In June of that same year Iusuf wrote to the tsar reporting that a party of *Sevriuki* Cossacks 'living on the Don' had plundered a Nogai caravan returning from Moscow and killed a number of people; he wanted the handing over of the criminals and vengeance. To which Ivan replied that 'these plunderers live on the Don outside our realm and are in fact fugitives from us.' Mirza Iusuf was not convinced, for four months later he told the tsar that 'a certain subject of yours, Sari-Asman, with three or four of his settlements already sited on the Don, has been shadowing the movement of our ambassadors and envoys and indeed attacking them.'[23] From this archival material it is now generally accepted that the free Don Cossacks were certainly in existence much before 1549 and that one of their principal leaders, to judge from his name, was probably a Tatar.

The flight of Muscovite citizens to the Don began before the reign of Ivan the Terrible, but the numbers increased considerably during

his time and during that of his two successors, that is to say in the
period between 1547 and 1605. Those with families tended to settle
at first on the Medveditsa, the Buzuluk (a tributary of the Khoper)
about 100 miles or so from the Volga, and on the upper Donets;
relatively few, as yet, made their way to the lower Don. The
unmarried and the unattached, however, who intended to live by the
horse and the gun, having few women and no settled habitation,
wandered from the Russian to the Tatar border, from the Crimea to
the Don and the Don to the Volga, in search of plunder. Their
hide-outs were in the woods, in the steppe ravines or on inaccessible
and hidden islands in the rivers. Inevitably they were drawn to the
land-bridge between the Don and the Volga, the junction of the
thriving water and caravan routes where Batu had once reigned
supreme. To the strong they offered their services for payment: the
weak they would destroy.

By the mid-sixteenth century there was already a collection of both
winter and summer settlements on the Don and its tributaries,
usually in the marsh or on the islands, but the boldness of these free
Cossacks can only be wondered at in view of the hideous fates that
awaited them in the event of capture. In 1551 Don Cossacks actually
attacked Azov and a few years later they began to settle on the banks
of the lower Don only a few leagues upstream of the Turkish fortress.
The sultan described them as 'a creeping disaster and grave threat not
only to Azov and the lower Don but to the Volga, to Astrakhan and
Kazan and even to the Moslem faith'; in 1551 he urged Prince Ismail
of the Nogai to destroy the Don Cossack settlements 'that were
nothing more than pawns of Moscow'. Whether these free Cossacks
were in the service of Moscow at this particular time is doubtful,
thought a mid-nineteenth-century Don Cossack historian, 'but
among what would now be regarded as the diplomatic corps, the
envoys and the ambassadors, it was widely believed at the time that it
was so.' Precariously exposed as they were in this dangerous area, the
presence of the Don Cossacks in that vital region was highly convenient to the tsar. He, meanwhile, continued to maintain that the
Cossacks were no concern of his.

In 1570, however, Ivan the Terrible wrote to the Don Cossacks
requiring their services, for which they would be paid; and among
the tsar's requests were the provision of boat and mounted escorts to
conduct the Muscovite and Turkish ambassadors in safety across the
steppe and the furnishing of military detachments for the tsar's wars

against the Tatars in Kazan and Astrakhan and against the Livonians. In 1571 an agreement was settled between Moscow and the Don that 'gunpowder, lead and money' (to which were later added other provisions not obtainable on the Don) should be sent regularly from Moscow in return 'for the freeing of prisoners'. These prisoners were the unfortunate population dragged off from Russia during the many Tatar invasions and raids. The Don Cossack bands, made up in part of, and often led by, Tatars, rarely had the strength to beat back the incursions, but, in time-honoured nomad fashion, they marched on the flanks of the invaders keeping them under observation, harrying them and cutting off stragglers. But their main effort would be kept in reserve to waylay the Tatars on their return march when, tired and loaded down with plunder, split up and very disorganized in guarding columns of thousands of prisoners, they would be much easier prey for the Don lancers. The Don Cossacks were paid a bounty by Muscovy for all Russian prisoners released, together with 'expenses incurred for looking after them'. This 1571 agreement was renewed again in 1584 and 1592. One of the Don Cossacks' main tasks, however, was to roam the Don and Volga steppe and provide Muscovy with early warning of Azov, Crimea or Nogai Tatar Cossack intentions.

The sultan's gloomy prognostications sent to the Nogai in 1550 were partially realized when Ivan IV finally took Kazan the next year and moved down the Volga on Astrakhan. The Don Cossacks took a part in the fighting round Astrakhan and then, in 1556, at Moscow's invitation, raided Islam-Kermen, Ochakov and part of the Crimea in company with the Nogai, some of whom had a grievance against the Crimean khan. In 1569 the Cossacks on the lower Don were obliged to abandon part of their home settlements when a 70,000 strong Turkish and Tatar force moved up the Don to the Don-Volga land-bridge. The Don Cossacks returned, however, as soon as the enemy had left.

In 1571 the Crimean khan Divlet-Girai again attacked Moscow, and although the Don Cossacks sent timely warning to the tsar they were helpless to influence events. The chastened tsar that same year sent a Don ataman, Nikita Mamina, on a mission of friendship to the Turks in Azov; yet, at the same time, the tsar encouraged the Don Cossacks 'not just to observe' but to make constant attacks into the Tauride and on Azov. There appears little doubt that, from 1571 onwards, the tsar was playing a double game when he pretended that he had no dealings with the Cossacks.[24] And when Divlet-Girai's son Mehmet-Girai sent Araslam-Mirza as an envoy to Moscow in 1578 to present the khan's demands that all foreign Cossacks be removed from the Dnieper, the Don and the Volga, the tsar replied that 'the Dnieper Cossacks were Batory's [Poland's] affair, while the Don Cossacks were fugitives from Lithuania and Russia for whom he [the tsar] was not accountable.'

The situation with Muscovy's temporary ally, the Yaik Nogai, was otherwise, however, for the Don Cossack boatmen had moved over to the Volga where the Nogai Prince Iusuf complained that their piracies were threatening his people. In 1553 Ivan the Terrible had several men whom he declared to be Volga pirates hanged in the presence of the Nogai ambassador, and he sent an expedition under the boyar Grigorii Zholobov to police the river, after which he assured the Nogai ruler that only 'good' Cossacks remained on the Volga. But after two or three years these good Cossacks started pillaging and killing Russian travellers from Astrakhan. In 1557 Ivan sent more expeditions under Stepan Kobolev and Lianup Filimonov from Kazan to the mouth of the Samara river and to Perevolok.[25] But this did not satisfy the Nogai, for by 1570 there were so many Russian boats on the Samara, the lower Volga and the Yaik that they did not know friend from foe. The final blow came when the Volga Cossacks destroyed the Nogai capital of Saraichik on the Yaik and set upon and robbed the Moscow and the Nogai ambassadors when they were crossing the ferry near the island of Sosnov. The tsar then ordered their extermination; in 1579 the robber bands under Ivan Koltso, Bogdan Borbosha and Nikita Pan, fled, moving up the Volga and the Oka on their way to the Urals.

The new tsar Fedor Ivanovich attempted to patch up a peace with the sultan and the Crimean khan, for the sultan had said he wanted the foreign Cossacks removed from the Don and the Terek, in return for which he would restrain the Tatars from their warlike incursions against Muscovy. In 1584 the tsar sent his envoy Boris Blagii to the lower Don Cossacks on his way to Azov and Constantinople for talks with the sultan: Blagii advised the Don ataman Kishkin to leave Azov severely alone, at least as long as the talks were going on. He then journeyed on via Azov and Kaffa to Turkey. His return was not without incident for, when he arrived in Kaffa in company with the Turkish ambassador to Moscow, a Circassian prince was awaiting him to protest against Don Cossack piracy on the Crimean and

Kuban shores, and the prince's retinue became so violent that Boris Blagii feared for his life. And when Blagii arrived back in Azov it was to hear that a certain petty ataman Iushko Nesvitaev of the upper Don Cossacks, after having plundered English and Armenian travellers on the Volga, had moved back to the Don to lie in wait for a tsar's convoy coming down the river to escort Blagii back to Moscow; Nesvitaev had done this most successfully, seizing boats and stores. Blagii also found that Azov itself was ringed by lower Don Cossacks whose attitude to his companion, the Turkish envoy, was so threatening that the sultan's ambassador refused to continue his journey. Eventually, at the express request of the tsar, the Don Cossacks found an escort to accompany Blagii back to Moscow, where he arrived at the end of 1585.[26]

In 1588 a band of Zaporozhian Cossacks under a campaign hetman Matvii Fedorov arrived in the upper Donets valley near Livensk to prey on the traffic moving between the Crimea and Moscow, and eventually put a stop to all movement. The next year Moscow had to send an envoy Petr Zinovev to the Crimea, accompanied by a returning Crimean ambassador, and although Zinovev was provided with a mounted town Cossack escort together with 150 foot-soldiers, Moscow still feared that its convoy would be routed. Zinovev was therefore armed with letters from the tsar addressed personally to Matvii Fedorov, asking for safe passage in the tsar's name. In the event, the convoy arrived at its destination unscathed, for the Zaporozhian band had already moved southwards to join the lower Don Cossacks in an attack on Azov, pillaging a great part of that Turkish settlement and taking 300 prisoners.

In 1591 the Crimean khan Kazy-Girai mounted an expedition with 150,000 men that included Azov and Belgorod-Akkerman Cossacks and the Kazyev and Kramtsev *ulus* of the Nogai, and this reached Moscow. The following year the frightened tsar sent an ambassador Grigorii Afonasevich Nashchokin to beg the sultan to restrain the Tatars from raiding Moscow, blaming 'the Lithuanian Cossacks and Don fugitives' for stirring up all the trouble. Nashchokin had been instructed by the tsar to call on the lower Don Cossacks and urge them to keep the peace, if only for the period during which these delicate negotiations were being conducted: the tsar was prepared to pay the Don Cossacks for their co-operation, but to this he added a threat that he would send an expedition against them if they failed him. But even before Nashchokin arrived at Razdory, the lower Don capital, the Azov Cossacks had attacked some Don settlements and, in return, the Don Cossacks had attacked Azov, several hundred lives having been lost on both sides; the lower Don Cossack field ataman had thereupon taken a fleet of boats out pirating in the Azov Sea and was still absent when the tsar's envoy arrived. The tsar's ambassador had brought with him Vishata Vasilev, the field ataman of the upper Don Cossacks, to help him state his case to a general assembly (krug) meeting that began at the end of May and went on for several days.[27] The lower Don Cossacks would not agree, however, to peace with Azov or to the return of prisoners 'that had been bought with their blood'. Tempers flared and they set on and killed the ataman Vishata Vasilev, and afterwards seized by force the tsar's ambassador's 'presents' and goods.

The angry mob then quietened down and came to its senses and, somewhat subdued by what it had done, tried to win the envoy's favour by telling him that it *would* agree to peace with Azov. Nashchokin went on to confer with the Turks and Tatars in the fortress and speedily concluded an agreement. But, when he returned up river to Razdory to announce the settlement before leaving for Constantinople, Nashchokin found that the Cossack krug had changed its mind again and wanted an enormous ransom in gold for one Turkish official and six Caucasian princes held prisoner by them. And as earnest of their intention they cut off the hand of one of the princes and sent it to Azov.

When Nashchokin sailed from Azov on his way to Kaffa and Constantinople the Turks imprisoned and misused his 130 strong Muscovite escort that had remained in Azov awaiting the ambassador's return; the Don Cossacks then attacked and overran the fortress and released the surviving Muscovites. They gained further credit with Moscow when, in 1594, they intercepted returning raiders of the Crimean horde, together with a Nogai Kazyev *ulus*, laden with plunder and convoying Russian slaves; in routing this convoy the Don Cossacks released a further 600 prisoners. And the meek tsar Fedor Ivanovich soon restored them to favour, sending presents to them regularly together with an annual subsidy.

\*　\*　\*

Although the Don Cossacks, speaking the Great Russian tongue with an admixture of Tatar, eventually became a tightly knit and unified host, in the earlier days they were split into the upper and the lower, the dividing line between the two being at Tsimlyansk. The lower Don was to become well populated in the next two centuries so that it was to form the powerful centre of the host, but at the end of the sixteenth century the Cossacks there numbered only seven atamans and about 1,800 fighting men. In the early days, there were few families on the lower Don and the lower Don Cossacks were obliged to take their women from Tatar, Caucasian and Turkish Moslem captives, and this accounted for the distinctive racial traits that were still common among the lower host even in the twentieth century, for the Cossack there was often smaller, slighter and much darker in complexion than his fellow in the north. The women on the lower Don tended, too, at least until the eighteenth century, to favour Oriental clothes and to be more retiring than those on the upper Don. The dress of the men in the south was little different from that in the north in that they wore what was to hand, looted garments, furs and sheepskin, that might be as much Russian in pattern as Tatar, and they did not necessarily share the Zaporozhian taste for Tatar-Turkish styled clothing. The lower Don Cossacks looked towards Azov and the Azov and Black Seas while the upper Cossacks roamed more or less due east to the Volga, that was not much more than 100 miles away, and to the Nogai territory beyond, between the Volga and the Yaik.

The upper Cossacks were no less adventurous nor more law-abiding than the lower Cossacks in the south, for they were river pirates as well as fishermen on the Donets, the Don and the Volga, and their robber bands preyed also on the Volga, Don and the north Donets land routes. Nor did they hesitate to attack the properties of the Russian boyars in the borderland of Muscovy. But, in the main, a higher proportion of their number led a more settled existence than the Don Cossack in the south, in that many had families; and since large numbers of refugees from Muscovy were continually arriving at the upper host, the Cossacks in the north, both men and women, were by race mainly Great Russian with an inherent love of the soil. Some began to farm cattle and other livestock; then, by the end of the next century, necessity forced them to take the plough into use, notwithstanding the draconian Don laws that forbade it.

On the lower Don the cultivation of the soil was entirely impracticable due to the closer proximity of the Tatar; but, in any case, the Cossacks there, like the Tatar, thought labour was for slaves and agriculture was for serfs. In the south every man was a warrior, a horseman and a boatman, and, like the early Tatar hordes, the lower Don Cossack lived for war, loot and plunder, protection money, ransom and subsidies. Like the Zaporozhian he was a river pirate and sea mariner, venturing far into the Black Sea in open *chaika* row-boats, similar to those on the Dnieper; and although all early Don Cossacks were not necessarily mounted men, horses were much more easily acquired than in the sech since they were usually stolen from the Tatar herds. Their tactics, too, were those of the steppe nomad, for surprise and mobility were the secrets of success, and they liked to move by night, each man with two horses. If they were themselves surprised when mounted they would usually scatter; if dismounted and flight was impossible they would form a square.

At the end of the sixteenth century the banks of the Don from the mouth of the Khoper to the river Aksai, a distance of about 500 miles, were already covered with settlements, although the inland area between these two rivers (away from the river basins) was empty. The main centres were at Razdory, Manotsk, Cherkassk (formerly Akhas) and Medveditsk (now Serifamovich). Settlements were of two types, *gorodki* made up of huts or semi-basement dug-outs surrounded by a double wattle-fence or double moat, these settlements being occupied the whole year round, or *zimovishchi* that were huts or dug-outs that gave winter quarters to the homeless unattached or unmarried, those who, in the summer months, were always with the herds or campaigning. Generally, most of the settlement population changed house or went afield as soon as the spring arrived, partly because they became easily bored if they remained in the same winter surroundings and partly because this was the pattern of steppe life, the nomad heritage common to all Tatars from the khan to the shepherd. For the Don Cossack retained many of the Tatar usages and some of his early and dark Shamanistic superstitions and beliefs, even into the nineteenth and twentieth centuries.[28]

The Don Cossacks, like the Zaporozhians, were religious in their primitive and superstitious fashion; like the Tatars, they were usually honest amongst themselves.[29] They considered the worst crimes to be treachery, cowardice and theft from each other. Like the Tatar they could be tolerant of other faiths and in the next century they accepted without question the large numbers of Old Believers that fled from Muscovite persecution, together with Moslems, lamaists and heathens.[30] In common with the Zaporozhians, they prided themselves on never returning a fugitive to his place of origin; and it was partly for this reason that they refused to give Moscow precise information as to their rolls, membership or strength, threatening to put to death any Muscovite who tried to inquire too closely. For the people on the Don regarded themselves as Cossacks and not Russians, being subject to no laws except their own. This, too, was recognized in Moscow, at least in the early years, for all business with the Don was conducted through the main military department of the government, and then, from 1614, through the foreign office, it being confirmed that the Don Cossacks had the right to conduct their own foreign relations with other powers as they thought fit, as though they were an independent sovereign state. For although the Don Cossacks were often a diplomatic embarrassment to Moscow since they stirred up trouble with Turk and Tatar, they were also the first line of defence against the Crimea, the Nogai and the Turk, and for this reason they merited special care and consideration. Muscovy was surrounded by enemies and it would have been ill-considered, as Boris Godunov was yet to learn, to have added the Don Cossacks to their number.

The Don Cossack community was a very strange one in that it was a disorderly collection of brave, wild and freedom-loving people, impatient of restraint, yet accepting, by and large, a common code; and the result, in the view of the Soviet writer Popov, was 'a thoroughly muddled *muzhik* form of democracy'. The form of government was generally similar to that of the Zaporozhians, with the authority of government resting in the Cossack general assembly (the krug) that appointed the ataman and his two esaul deputies, the judge and the secretary, (*d'iak* on the Don), forming what came to be known as the council and later the chancellery: these appointments were usually made in November each year at the time that the Cossack ambassador to Moscow was selected and sent off as part of a retinue known as the light stanitsa. The council's legal and judicial authority was all-powerful, and laws were made and cases judged according to its will, the sentence of death apparently being fairly common even for theft within the host; its assembly decided all matters of war and peace, the appointment of the field or campaign ataman should an expedition be under way, the admission of recruits to the Cossack roll, and the siting of new settlements—for without proper sanction a settlement was likely to be destroyed. Settlements eventually became known as stanitsas.[31]

Although all matters of policy had to be put to the assembly, the responsibility for the day-to-day and week-by-week control of the host rested on the ataman, his chancellery and the committee of elders on whose advice he might rely. It was theoretically possible for the youngest and meanest of the Cossacks to be proposed and elected ataman, but in practice it could never be so. For the post demanded experience, judgement, courage, military ability and intellect, if not education. As the new stanitsa settlements came into being they also formed local assemblies and elected their own ataman, and, although their individual responsibilities were not great, jointly they took much of the load from the central council. Each of these stanitsa settlements provided a body of troops for the host, usually in squadrons (hundreds) or half squadrons, the commanders of these sub-units being elected, Tatar fashion, by the Cossack troopers themselves.

CHAPTER 2 NOTES

1 The Circassian or Adighé (literally 'the gentlemen') and the Kabard are two branches of the same racial group, the one in the west around the Kuban river and the other further east in the upper Terek basin. To this day the Circassian is still known by the Ossets and Georgians as *kazak*.

2 The settlement of Cherkassy is said to have been founded by these *Cherkes* before 1300 and the Lithuanian fortress there to have dated from about 1380. It is also said that a Tatar *baskak* in the frontier settlement of Kursk had a *kazak* escort of Circassians that he had brought with him from Beshtau and Piatigorsk (in the foothills of the Caucasus). These are reputed to have settled in Kanev and terrorized the surrounding steppe for a quarter of a century. In 1386, after the Lithuanians had driven the Golden Horde out of the middle Dnieper, Cherkassy became the capital of the Lithuanian border command (the hetmanate).

3 Early maps show the Don Cossack area as *Cosacci Circassi*, while Circassia proper (in the Caucasus) is shown as *Circassi Tartari*. The popularity of the word *Cherkes* among the Don Cossacks is illustrated by the naming of their capitals Cherkassk and Novocherkassk. By its early association with the Ukrainian Cossack, the word *Cherkes* was sometimes used by the Great Russian to describe Ukrainians in general!

4 Among the Kirghiz the word *kazak* is still used to describe themselves.

5 Tatar couriers, known at the time everywhere as Cossacks, were recruited not only by the Genoese but by Moscow, Warsaw and Vilna, for duties in which they excelled, the messenger service between the capitals and the Golden Horde, the Crimea and the Nogai. Their Tatar names are

recorded in the Moscow archives and it is a proof of their trustworthiness that some carried out their courier duties for one paymaster for periods as long as twenty years: not before 1521 did Russian names appear on the record. One of the main advantages in the use of a Tatar Cossack was that he knew the language and ways of the steppe: he usually formed one of an armed party, each man leading a spare horse, such a group being known as a *stanitsa* or mounted troop, a word that was to become commonplace with the latter-day Russian Cossacks. The messenger was instructed to hand the message or present personally to the intended recipient, even though that be the khan himself, and he was schooled in the answers that he was to give should he be cross-examined.

6  Lithuania continued, for a short time, to extend its territories along the Black Sea and into Rumania, but after the personal union with Poland in 1386 and its defeat by the Golden Horde on the Vorskla in 1399 its expansion was virtually halted.

7  The Ermolin chronicle records that the Tatar khan of Kazan (Mehmet-Ulug) in 1445 was also trying to attract into his service a splinter group of 2,000 Cossacks, presumably Tatars or Circassians, from 'Cherkassy': it is uncertain, however, whether this meant Cherkassy on the Dnieper or Circassia.

8  Boris Godunov was one such boyar (and eventually tsar) of Tatar origin.

9  In 1491 when Ivan III took the field against Lithuania in the west he took with him his own allied Tatars, described in the chronicle as 'Mirzas [princes], uhlans [captains] and Cossacks [riders]'. In 1551 the Kasimov Tatar Cossacks found 5,500 cavalry for Ivan the Terrible's war against Kazan.

10  The activity of the steppe patrols, the dates they rode out and returned (they were usually out for 14–16 days at a time), the names of the atamans that led them, of the enemies taken or killed, were reported by the 1586 *voevod* of Putivl directly to the tsar Fedor Ivanovich in a series of regular reports.

11  'Ukraine' in Russian means 'the borderland' and the word was used widely in the sixteenth and seventeenth centuries by both Great and Little Russian to describe *any* borderland including that of south-east Muscovy.

12  It is assumed by some historians that these bands were originally Ukrainian fishermen and hunters who spent the summer months in the steppe as seasonal workers and returned each autumn to Cherkassy, Kanev and Kiev for the winter. Golobutskii challenges this, basing his argument on the great distance they would have to travel and the time lost in travelling each year; these bands must, he reasons, have lived all the year round below the cataracts right from the start. Another cogent reason, not advanced by Golobutskii, is that these were established military (and outlaw) communities unlikely to want to winter in Cherkassy or elsewhere, even as private individuals; nor would the *voevod* have welcomed them; moreover their social and military pattern of life was a close reflection of the Tatar and suggests an unbroken linkage with

the bands that infested the steppe around Cherkassy a century or more before.

13 Although, admittedly, the Zaporozhians were, or came to be, predominantly Little Russian (Ukrainian), they were free and independent Cossacks and entirely separate from the Ukrainian Cossacks to the north. A Ukrainian Cossack was not a Zaporozhian; a Zaporozhian might be Ukrainian but he was not a Ukrainian Cossack.

14 *Koshevoi* is from the Tatar *kosh* meaning a 'field' or 'campaign': here it signified the sech hetman. It is possible that the chief of the host was originally an 'ataman' and that the word 'hetman' was a later substitution after the Cherkassy bands had come into contact with the Lithuanians, where the word 'hetman' was in use as a military rank; 'hetman' may be derived from the German *Hauptmann. Kolo* and *rada* mean a circle or assembly.

15 There were in all eight recorded *sechi*: Khortitsa, Bazavluk, Tomakovka, Mikitin, Chertomlyka (1652–1708), Kamensk (1710–11), Aleshkovsk (1711–34) and Podpilensk (1734–75).

16 The kuren names were geographical and were towns or regions in Little Russia and Belorussia; it has been said that they signified the place of origin of the members, though this could hardly have always been the case. In all probability the names were those of convenience. Each kuren (there were eventually thirty-eight) had its own elected hetman, who controlled his own long hut inside the sech.

17 The *chub-oseledets*, the long forelock on the shaven head, common to the Zaporozhians, was also to be found on the Don in the eighteenth century.

18 According to Rigelman, the latter-day judges bore the seal while the secretary carried an ornamental silver inkpot.

19 Some Ukrainian writers have credited Vishnevitskii with being a nationalist patriot and the founder of the original sech. This latter does not seem to be the case. Having lost the trust of the Poles, Russians and Turks, Vishnevitskii became a wanderer. He was eventually seized in Moldavia and executed in Constantinople.

20 Kasimov is 600 miles from Azov as the crow flies—this gives an idea of the range of action of these early Cossacks.

21 The *voevod* of Putivl, Prince Mikhail Troekurov, wrote to the tsar in 1546 reporting that there were 'now many Cossacks on the steppe, both of the khan and of Muscovy—they come from all the border areas.'

22 Any of the following border towns could have put out 'Don' Cossacks: Pronsk, Ryazsk, Kozlov, Lebedyan, Epifan, Sapozhok, Mikhailov, Voronezh, Elets, Livny, Chernyavsk, Donkov, Chern and Novosil.

23 The Nogai despatch continued: 'And if you wish to retain our brotherly love, then remove them!' To which Ivan Vasilevich replied with some asperity: 'Then kill them yourself, or, if you so wish, deliver them to us and we will kill them for you!'

24 In 1576 the tsar replied to the sultan's and Crimean khan's complaints through his ambassador Elizar Rzhevskii that 'these Cossacks lived on the Don and were independent of him, and this applied, too, to those on

the Volga and near Azov, and he had already given orders that if any came near the Muscovite border towns they were to be killed.'

25 In 1558 Ivan IV, hoping for Nogai aid against the Crimea, sent his envoy Elizar Maltsov to the prince saying that all guilty Cossacks had been punished or 'dispersed to the Crimea or Azov.' He went on, in what was presumably a fiction though it sounded impressive enough: 'Our Kadomtsy and Temnikovskii [both town Cossacks], Don, Volga and Astrakhan Cossacks beg us humbly for our permission to attack you, but we, in view of our friendship for you and for your father before you, will not permit it.'

26 Blagii reported to the tsar his amazement at the many settlements that had recently sprung up on the lower Don 'inhabited by Cossacks—a fugitive people'. The first lower Don capital was at Razdory (Razdorov) on an island at the junction of the Don and Donets not 100 miles above Azov.

27 The *krug* (circle) was the Don equivalent of the Ukrainian and Zaporozhian rada.

28 Among these were strange funeral practices including the burial of weapons and saddlery; the curing of the sick, particularly animals, by the Shamanist ritual of passing between two fires 'or earthen gateways'; a fear of the evil eye, a profound trust in sorcerers and witches, and a belief in the prophetic powers of whirlwinds.

29 Whereas the Orthodox church of the Ukrainian Cossacks was subject to the control of Kiev, the so-called Greek Orthodox church of the early Don Cossacks (like that of the early Zaporozhians) had no connection with Moscow or Kiev. The Don churches were built by the host settlements, and the clergy, usually semi-literate preachers, were appointed from among their own ranks.

30 Old Believers were members of the Greek church who refused to accept the 1667 reforms of the Patriarch Nikon.

31 The use of the word 'stanitsa' to describe a mounted cavalcade was in accordance with Tatar precedent where it usually meant an envoy's or messenger's troop. The light or winter stanitsa was housed, incidentally, at Moscow cost and received a daily allowance in money and goods. The word 'stanitsa' to describe a settlement was not in general use among the Zaporozhians who favoured 'kuren'. With the Don Cossacks, however, a 'kuren' meant a section, usually about ten men.

# 3 Siberia and Caspian

The Don Cossacks had, from very early times, moved overland to the Volga and had begun to settle along the banks of that river, according to some accounts joining up with other settlers, the descendants of the Ryazan service Cossacks who had already moved out across the steppe to the Volga basin; there they became known as Volga Cossacks. In the main, however, this new Volga community owed its parentage to the Don, although it did, from time to time, take in further migrants from elsewhere, particularly from the Kazan Tatars further up river. From the Volga, numbers of these boatmen made their way to more distant lands, to the Caspian and to the Yaik river where they were to form the Yaik (later known as the Ural) host.

The Cossacks of the Don and the Volga were a very lawless body and many of them lived by plundering the rich convoys that came north, both overland and by boat, from Persia and Bokhara on their way to Muscovy or to the Siberian khanate. One of the tsar's embassies had been attacked when carrying presents to the shah, and envoys travelling between Moscow and the Nogai and Moscow and Persia were frequently plundered or killed, so that the lower Volga, in particular, was entirely unsafe for merchant caravans or shipping. Eventually, in 1577, Ivan the Terrible despatched an expedition under Ivan Murashkin against this banditry, an expedition that, with the help of the Don Cossacks who furnished a military detachment to aid the tsar's troops, killed those that fell into their hands and dispersed the remnants of what came to be known as the first Volga Cossack host. Those that scattered either returned to the Don, moved into the Caspian to the Yaik or the Terek, or made their way northwards up the Volga and Kama towards the Ural mountains.

The Urals, standing at the edge of what is now Siberia, was an area that was quite foreign to early Muscovy, for the only contact had been through the republic of Novgorod in the far north, and the Russians there knew only the indigenous Samoyeds, the Ugri and the Voguls, all very poor and primitive peoples. The Tatar khanate of Sibir was little known to Moscow because of the barrier made by the peoples to the east of the Volga river, particularly the Bolgars and the latter-day Kazan Tatars.[1] Yet the khanate of Sibir, that was in fact a pagan feudal and military Tatar aristocracy that had imposed itself on the scattered groups of conquered native peoples and in particular on the Ostiaks and Voguls, had a history nearly as old as that of the Golden Horde. The khanate had long been disputed by the Nogai and by the Sheibanide Tatars, but by the middle of the sixteenth century the throne was held by Kuchum, a grandson of Ibak and son of Murtaza, who came of Sheiban-Bokhara lineage and who had recently introduced Islam to the Siberian horde.

By the sixteenth century, however, there was some intercourse between the khanate and Moscow and it is said that the Tatars had paid a tribute to the tsars in pelts from the time of Vasilii Ivanovich. His son, Ivan the Terrible, who had recently annexed Kazan and thereby advanced Russia's eastern frontiers to Perm in the foothills of the Ural mountains, had concluded a treaty with Kuchum in 1569 by which Ivan 'took Kuchum under his protection' in return for an annual tribute of 1,000 sable and 1,000 squirrel skins. Sometimes this tribute was paid; at other times Kuchum returned truculent demands and occasionally attacked the Russian border areas.

In 1558 the tsar had already permitted the two brothers Stroganov, living in the borderland settlement of Perm, to develop the resources, govern the indigenous population, build and maintain forts and raise a local body of troops in the area between the Kama, the mouth of the Sylva, Chusovaya and Puskorsk-Kura. In 1564 and 1568 the tsar gave the Stroganovs two further licences and these were extended to a third Stroganov brother and two nephews of the same name. The Stroganovs built the town of Kankov, at the mouth of the Chusovaya, and the fort of Kerghedan together with other border settlements, until they became threatened in 1573 by Tatar attacks made by Mehmet-Kul, the nephew of the khan. The Stroganovs appealed to the tsar for assistance but received nothing except orders to subjugate the Tatar khanate to the Russian crown and protect those peoples that were already tributaries of Moscow;

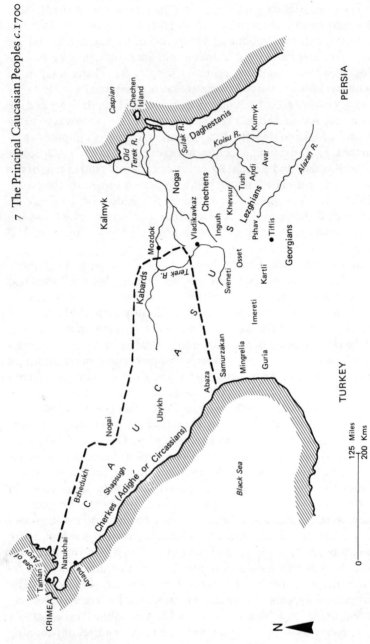

7 The Principal Caucasian Peoples *c*.1700

1. Steppe Tatar Cossack scouts in the 14th century, armed with bow, sabre and lance fitted with a hook for unseating an enemy rider (from an artist's impression). 2. *above right* A Zaporozhian Cossack of the Dnieper in the early 17th century wearing the usual Tatar dress (from an artist's impression).

3. Repin's famous painting of the Zaporozhian Cossacks writing the insulting letter to the sultan. The letter was in fact dictated by Ivan Serko, the hetman, presumably the standing figure on the right, in December 1678, after an unsuccessful attack on the *Sech* by Tatars and janissaries. Weapons and dress were mainly Tatar, and the heads were shaven nomad-fashion.

4. Ermak's Cossacks (from the Don and Volga) disembarking from river boats and firing on Tatar forces during the war with the Siberian khan c. 1580. The destruction of the Ural khanate quickly led to the Muscovite occupation of Siberia as far as the Pacific (detail from a painting by Vasilii Surikov, himself a Siberian Cossack).

5. An early 18th-century Don Cossack armed with pistol and the traditional sabre without a hilt-guard (from an early print).

6. An early 18th-century Don Cossack fisherwoman (from an early print).

7. *above left* Stepan Danilovich
Efremov holding the *bulava*; Efremov
was ataman of the Don Cossack host
1753–72, the son and immediate
successor of a former ataman Danilo
Efremov 1738–53, for, from the 18th
century, the office was in the gift of
Russia. Efremov, on the tsarina's
orders, was kidnapped and spent the
rest of his life in exile and in chains.
8. *above right* His wife, Melanie
Karpovna. The regalia, robes, and
the headdress in particular, are of a
distinctly Caucasian pattern. Melanie,
a woman of great character and of the
people, kept a market-stall in
Cherkassk before her marriage: her
daughter was the wife of ataman
Count Platov. 9. *left* A Zaporozhian
of the second *Sech* about 1750 (from
an early sketch).

10. Black Sea Cossacks c. 1800, clearly showing the influence of their Zaporozhian origin (from an early sketch).

11. Platov, the ataman of the Don Cossacks who commanded Cossacks from all the hosts in the 1812 campaign, together with Kalmyk, Bashkir, Kirghiz and Tatar Cossacks. In the centre will be noted the Mongol features of a Kalmyk Cossack (from a contemporary painting).

12. From a painting by Doré depicting Cossack lancers destroying stragglers during Napoleon's 1812 retreat from Russia.

in return they were to be allowed additional mineral rights and trading privileges.

The Stroganovs had attracted wild vagabond adventurers, and to these were to be added the bands of Volga Cossacks that had been dispersed by the tsar's forces in 1577. Many of the Cossack leaders, including Ermak (Yermak) Timofeev, Ivan Koltso, Ivan Grosa, Iakov Mikhailov, Nikita Pan, Matvia Meshcheryak and Bogdan Briaga, were outlaws who had a price on their heads, wanted by Moscow to answer charges of attacking the tsar's and other diplomatic envoys. Necessity, however, knew no law, and, as the Stroganovs had too few men to overcome the khanate in accordance with the tsar's decree, the new arrivals were welcomed, being provisioned and equipped at the Stroganovs' expense. This banditry, together with three priests and a monk, set up a fort at Ermakogo Gorodichi and began to loot and plunder Moscow's Vogul allies.

It took until mid 1579 to equip Ermak's expeditionary force with boats, armament and stores before setting out for Sibir. According to legend its strength was only 800, though some historians have subsequently reckoned it to have been much stronger, probably several thousand men. Ermak moved off up the Chusovaya river to the mouth of the Serebrenka, then to the Zhuravlin, so crossing the Ural watershed, and then down the Rahil to the Tura, an expedition that lasted several years and cost the greater part of its strength in disease and casualties caused by the fighting. Its purpose was to conquer and plunder, and the loot that it could not carry it buried; but its robberies and extortions were indiscriminate, rather in the fashion of the Tatar hordes, and this made enemies of many peoples who would otherwise have assisted the Cossacks against the Tatar khan. As it was, a prince of Pelim, together with an army of Ostiaks, Voguls and Bashkirs, arrived on the Muscovite frontier area near Perm and burned the Russian settlements on the Kama in the area of Cherdin, Usol, Kankov, Kerghedan and Chusovsk, murdering or enslaving the Christian population.

The Muscovite border *voevod* at Cherdin, Vasilii Pelepelitsin, who was no friend of the Stroganovs, wrote to Ivan IV criticizing them for their folly in using untrustworthy Cossacks for an expedition that had incited the tribal peoples and led to such grievous losses to the border population. The tsar sent an angry letter to the Stroganovs accusing them of treason and recounting all the former crimes of these same Volga pirates, including the robbing of state funds and the killing of the tsar's ambassador. But by the time that this letter, that augured little good for the Stroganovs, had arrived, the Stroganovs had already sent a messenger to inform Ivan the Terrible that Ermak had overthrown the Siberian khanate. Since the new territories were believed to be very rich, the tsar immediately saw the situation in a different light and sent his pardon.

Ermak's progress had been strongly contested by the Tatars, but the bulk of the khan's forces had been made up of vassal native tribesmen, cavalry and foot, without fire-arms or artillery. Several battles had been fought on the Tura and the Tobol before the deserted Isker (Sibir) capital of the khan was finally occupied in 1581. Mehmet-Kul, the khan's nephew, said to be an experienced leader of large armies of cavalry, had been captured. The fighting continued, however, and the Tatars frequently assailed the Cossacks, causing many losses by ambushes and skirmishes: the plunderers and so-called tax-gatherers who were obliged to move detachments away from the main body were often killed, and Ermak himself met his death in such a trap. The tsar had no intention of leaving the occupation of the khanate in the hands of privateers, and he sent a *voevod* Simeon Dimitrovich Bolkhovskii with a small reinforcement to take possession of Sibir in the tsar's name; but death and disease soon whittled away the little force and Isker was abandoned by the Russians in 1584 and reoccupied by Tatars under a prince Seidiak, an enemy of Kuchum's. The tsar's troops and the Cossack remnants withdrew from Sibir to Russia. Ermak had left no lasting colonies but he had shown what could be achieved by small boldly led forces.

Ivan IV died in 1584 but his son Fedor Ivanovich determined to reoccupy the Siberian khanate; another new expedition set off in 1587, this time entirely under Muscovite military control, for the force had a small regular infantry (*streltsy*) nucleus, together with Asiatic and non-Russian Cossacks. This little army entered Siberia by way of the Yugorian mountains and, making its way up the Ob, arrived at the Tatar fortress of Chingi on the river Tura, where a new town was built and given the old Tatar name of Tiumenda. Other towns and forts were laid out at Tara and at Tobolsk (near the old Isker capital of Sibir). It did not prove difficult to subdue Seidiak, but a force had to take the field to track down and finally defeat Kuchum who was still active in harrying settlements. The patchwork composition of the military under the command of the Russian Prince Andrei Vasilivich Eletskoi is revealing in that it shows the extent to which Moscow could make use of what was to hand, often its former enemies. For, in addition to the *streltsy*, the troops consisted of fifty Polish soldiers and 100 Polish and Lithuanian Cossacks, presumably former prisoners or deserters, about 1,000 Tatar Cossacks from Kazan, from the Tauride (Crimea), Sibir, and elsewhere, and 300 Bashkir Cossacks.

When the war was finished and the khanate pacified, many of the Tatar nobility, including Mehmet-Kul, were given commands in the Russian Army and were shortly to see battle against the Crimean khan's forces; Kuchum's family and some of his cavalry joined the Tatar colony at Kasimov. Kuchum himself, old, blind and friendless, refused all surrender terms and fled to the Nogai by whom he was murdered.

This provided the pattern by which, in the seventeenth century, that part of northern Asia now known as Siberia was to be overrun as far as the Pacific; for the Russians were in what is now Omsk at the head of the Ob in 1604, and on the Yenisei and the Lena twenty years later. And the troops used consisted of a Moscow-led but largely Asiatic force made up of Tatars, Mongol Kalmyks, Turkic Bashkirs, Mongol Buriats and others, mainly boatmen and cavalry, that in the next century came to be known as Siberian Cossacks.

In 1639 a Cossack force was detached in the country of the Buriats beyond Lake Baikal, and by 1650 the Russians had reached the Bering Strait and Okhotsk on the Pacific Ocean. Northern Asia thereafter formed part of Russia.

*    *    *

There is no precise information as to the origin of the Yaik (later the Ural) Cossacks, but it is generally assumed that they came from the Don Cossacks during the sixteenth century, since their pattern of life, their Great Russian dialect, their manners and, as was noted at the end of the seventeenth century, their political and military structure, closely followed that of the Cossacks on the Don.[2] The Yaik Cossacks were much influenced by what went on in the Don territories and, although decisions made on the Don were not binding on the Yaik, the Yaik Cossacks usually followed suit. If the Don Cossack was stirring up trouble, the Yaik would be sure to lend a hand. The Yaik Cossacks were entirely independent of Moscow.

The main pursuits of the Yaik Cossack were fishing, hunting and cattle-raising, and in the early days there was little agriculture because of the danger of attack by nomads. The Yaik Cossack herdsmen often moved, together with their families, in the two-wheeled *kibitka* that carried tents and all their possessions. Although they were frequently at war with the Tatar, the Kirghiz and the Bashkir, they also traded with their neighbours, particularly with the distant Uzbeg province of Khiva near Lake Aral.

Across the other side of the Caspian Sea another Cossack people had begun to settle in the basin of the river Terek, to the north of the Caucasus range, in lands, like those of the Yaik, that were once controlled by the Golden Horde. The first European Cossacks arrived before the middle of the sixteenth century and it is generally accepted that these colonists either came from the Don Cossacks or migrated through the Don territories. Some accounts have surmised that the Terek settlers may have owed their origin to Novgorod free companies and pirates; others believed that they were Ryazan or Volga Cossacks, reinforced by refugees from Kazan and Astrakhan, who came to the estuary of the Terek by boat across the Caspian Sea; yet another view is that the settlers were Don Cossacks who came to the foothills of the Caucasus either by sea from the Volga or direct from the Don territories overland on the old caravan route to Persia from Tsaritsyn through the Derbent pass, or possibly by the more direct route of the Manych river, the Kuma and the upper Terek.

The true origin of the Terek Cossacks has been impossible to determine because of the confusion of early place names and the lack of contemporary documentation and of good archeological evidence —there is indeed little agreement even as to where the early settlements were. The names of the atamans, the settlements and the rivers on which they stood have, admittedly, sometimes been recorded, but the settlements have long since disappeared and, due to the many tongues spoken in the Caucasus and the many different names used for the same geographical feature, some river tributaries can no longer be identified. It has been said that the rivers Sulak, Aktash, lower Terek, Sunzha and Argun may have been the areas originally settled. But the traditional view, and the one that is most widely accepted, is that these colonists eventually concentrated near the junction of the Argun and Sunzha rivers about 100 miles from the coast, midway between present-day Groznyi and Gudermes, and that this people spread over the *greben'* (ridge) from which they took their latter name of the Grebensk Cossacks, this ridge being either the Terek ridge or the Sunzha ridge to its south, two ridges that in reality form part of the same feature standing about 2,300 feet above sea level. The Grebensk were probably the original Cossacks on the Terek and were in place by the middle of the sixteenth century. Racially they were already mixed, being mainly Great Russian and Tatar, and shortly became even more so as they began to marry with the local Caucasian peoples, the Little and Great Kabards from the area of the Terek, the Circassians from further west towards Piatigorsk, the Kumyk and the Okok and the Chechens from the country to the east between the Terek and the Sulak; these were mostly feudal societies, partly pastoral and partly nomadic, some even being partly agricultural. All of these tribal hill peoples, like the Nogai in the open steppe between the Terek and the estuary of the Volga, were warlike communities.

With the destruction of the Golden Horde in 1502, the area of the North Caucasus fell to the khan of the Crimea and his overlord the sultan: but it was Ivan the Terrible who exploited the new situation by his movement down the Volga from Kazan to Astrakhan and thence to the Caspian, so that by 1550 Russia had easy access to the Caucasus. Whereas the tsar and the Crimean khan had once had a joint interest in their common enmity to the Golden Horde, when that horde had disappeared there was no longer any cause for an understanding between Russia and the Crimea, particularly after Ivan IV had angered the khan by annexing Kazan and Astrakhan. And the fears of an earlier sultan came to be realized when Moscow began to undermine the khan's influence in the Caucasus, encouraging the Tatar's vassals to break with the Crimea. Even as early as 1552 the Nogai prince Ismail was asking for Moscow's protection, and that same year the Circassian and Daghestan princes were also seeking the tsar's aid against the khan; so it was that Ivan determined to put a permanent Russian military garrison on the Terek, since this would serve as a stepping stone into the Caucasus and also protect the caravan way and coastal Caspian sea-route between the Volga and Persia, at that time the enemy of Turkey.

The first fort was built near the junction of the Sunzha and the Terek in the country of the Grebensk Cossacks near the ferry point on the Osmanovsky road (the exact site is no longer known), and this had a garrison of 2,000 men with artillery under the command of Prince Babichev and Petr Protasev. Many of the Cossacks there were taken into the Russian service as couriers, guards, picquets and for general mounted duties. And when, following the sultan's protests and threats, the *streltsy* garrison was temporarily withdrawn, the Cossacks remained in occupation of the fort. The relationship between the Grebensk Cossacks and the local hillmen was good, since they were much intermarried, and both moved about freely in each other's areas and joined in a common defence against outside raiders and invaders. Large numbers of the Cossack wives were women from the hill tribes.[3] So the Grebensk Cossacks grew steadily until they numbered more than 1,000 riders, a half of whom were permanently under arms in paid government service or campaigning under Russian orders, while the remainder were at home defending and farming their own settlements, where they and their wives fished and grew millet, maize, mulberries and grapes, and made wine, cloth and lace.

In 1588 a second town was built to house a Russian *streltsy* garrison, this time close to the sea at the mouth of the Terek delta on the Tiumenk river, this being known as the Terek or Tiumensk new town; it stood on a reed-covered estuary about three miles from the sea, had a fort, a monastery and a wooden bridge across the river. A new community began to gather there since the fort provided both employment and a market for their wares, and these became known as the Terek Cossacks. These Terek Cossacks were made up of some Grebensk Cossacks that moved down the river, and of new arrivals from across the Caspian, Volga Cossacks dispersed by Ivan the Terrible, some of the remnants of Ermak's Siberian expedition and migrants from the Yaik; part of the host consisted of Kabard and Kumyk groups that lived scattered by *yurts* in the marshy Terek estuary. All of these Cossacks, whatever their origin, at first considered themselves well off and secure both from Moscow and outside interference because the land was both rich and remote.

The Cossacks recently arrived from Russia were, however, little interested in agriculture, since they were hunters, fishermen, sailors and merchant-shippers, the owners of boats who bought and sold cargoes; but they also had amongst their number pirates who occupied the Caspian island of Chechen from which they controlled the Terek estuary. This new element of the population mirrored the old Volga host and was difficult to control, and it is doubtful whether it acknowledged the host or any other authority, for these new immigrants were at the centre of the troubles at the beginning of the seventeenth century; nor was the strength of this very unstable element constant, for, from time to time, some of these bands would take it into their heads to sail away and resettle in the Yaik or elsewhere. More reliable, both in numbers and in allegiance to the host, were the Cossack families living in the settlements on the banks of the river, and these often received payment from the host in the form of a regular bounty, since the ataman could count on them as a military asset. Generally, however, it was the more settled element that began to suffer from the heavy duties imposed by the Russian *voevod*, duties for which they were not paid by the Russian crown, and this led to a rapid decline in their strength, a decline that could not be stemmed even by the large scale recruiting of the 'new Christians', mainly hillmen who formed their own units within the host.

The location of settlements depended largely on the type of settlers and their means of livelihood. Those that were mariners, fishermen or hunters were usually to be found in the estuaries and marshes; the agriculturists were in the fertile valley and the herdsmen in the lowland plain. Those that were in direct government service would be found near the forts, while those that were in military settlements were scattered far out on the plain or in the hills to give early warning of enemy attack. All settlements, wherever they might be, were sited where they could be best defended, on a hill, on river banks or cliffs, on an island or in a marsh, and were stockaded and ditched. In the early days, numbers of settlements were grouped, for ease of control, into kurens, but later all larger settlements that numbered more than thirty families were known, as on the Don, as stanitsas.

The seventeenth century saw the beginning of the massive migrations from Russia to the Cossack hosts, mostly to escape serfdom but also as fugitives, firstly from the troubles and civil war and then later from religious persecution, for many of the peasants were Old Believers. Many of these refugees chose to settle on the Terek since it was distant from Moscow and the climate and soil were believed to be fruitful; but, as against these benefits, the Terek was in no way a free and independent Cossack host in the fashion of the Don or Zaporozhian, since Moscow controlled it directly, though loosely, through its garrison there. But in spite of this the refugees still came, the Grebensk being the usual goal of the Old Believers since it was more distant from the Russian *voevod* headquarters on the Terek estuary; for the loosely scattered communities still contrived to retain some independence, and, although they sent military detachments to assist the tsar in the Chigirinsk and Crimean campaigns of

1677–9 and that against Khiva of 1716–17, they also sent rebels to support the uprisings of Bolotnikov and Razin.

## CHAPTER 3   NOTES

1  The Tatar khanate of Sibir stretched from the Urals to the middle Irtysh and then eastwards roughly as far as the Ob, forming only a small western part of what is known today as Siberia.

2  When in 1721 a Yaik delegation visited Moscow it told questioners that the host owed its origin to the Don Cossacks: some of the members maintained that 'there had always been Cossacks on the Volga and Don even when Timurlane was there [1395].' This is probably true, but it is the racial origin of these very early Cossacks that is to be questioned.

3  Islam, that eventually proved a barrier between the Cossacks and the tribesmen, was not introduced to the North Caucasian peoples until relatively late, towards the end of the eighteenth century.

# 4 The Ukraine

At the beginning of the seventeenth century the inhabited northern Ukraine on both sides of the Dnieper was controlled by Poland, for Muscovy was still no closer to the river than the frontier garrison of Putivl about 160 miles away. But the Polish commonwealth also laid claim to a vast area where no Polish soldier ever set foot, virtually the whole of Zaporozhe as far south as the second Dnieper bend and the uninhabited Tatar steppe to the east of the Ukraine, steppe that stretched as far north as the semi-circular line that ran from the valley of the Vorskla through Putivl to Kursk and Voronezh. Poland's first line of defence in this area, against the khan and against the tsar, depended on a line of Ukrainian Cossack garrison regiments in Chernigov, Nezhin, Priluki, Mirgorod and Poltava, a cordon of fortress towns about eighty miles away to the north-east that ran parallel to the river.

The whole of the south of the Ukraine that came under the Zaporozhians was entirely independent of Poland, for the Zaporozhian owed no allegiance to Warsaw or to Moscow and of course none to the Tatar or Turk. When the occasion demanded, the Zaporozhians sought the alliances that suited them, pacts that were broken again as soon as they had served their purpose; so, too, did the Pole and Russian seek to use the fighting strength of the Zaporozhians each against the other and against the Tatar. The Pole, however, seems to have come off worst in attempts to negotiate with the sech so that Warsaw found itself, from time to time, more likely to be at an understanding with the khan than with the Zaporozhian host, such understandings being directed against the sech or against Moscow.

The situation with regard to the Little Russian population inside the Polish-occupied Ukraine was complicated; the Little Russian gentry and landowner, no less than the Polish magnate and *pan*, were generally in favour of Warsaw rule, at least for the time being, for there was much to be gained in the Polish service. This was true, too, of the majority of the officers of the Ukrainian Cossacks held on the Polish register, for the commanders and officers were elected or appointed, often for life. The simple registered Cossacks, that is to say the rank and file, also enjoyed certain advantages bestowed by the Poles and could be relied upon to fight Tatar and Russian, and sometimes even the Zaporozhians who were their near kinsmen; but they were volatile and their dislike of the Pole was often deep-rooted so that they would, on occasions, mutiny and kill their Polish-appointed or Cossack-elected commanders and either take the field against the Poles or desert to the Zaporozhians. Since the unregistered Cossacks and the peasants were much poorer than the registered Cossacks, they were less kindly disposed towards the Polish *voevod* in the Ukraine because status and land were being denied them; there was intolerance of their religion and they were in constant fear of serfdom. For these reasons many migrated from the Polish Ukraine to the Zaporozhian or to the Don Cossack hosts, particularly between the years 1630–50. Others went to the Muscovite borderland to the area between the Psel and the upper Donets that came to be called the *Slobodskaia Ukraina*; there they were taken into the Russian service and became known as Slobodsk Cossacks.

The unregistered Cossacks and peasants that remained in the Polish Ukraine often formed an explosive and lawless population: with each uprising, landlords were murdered and estates were looted and burned, so that many of the Polish gentry were forced to employ squadrons of mercenary German troopers as bodyguards.[1] Yet, notwithstanding their enmity to the Polish landowners, the unregistered Ukrainian Cossacks and peasantry would willingly flock to join the king of Poland's forces when the registered quota was increased or when their aid was demanded, for many hoped that the register would be permanently enlarged to include all who claimed Cossack status. In this, however, they were disappointed since, as soon as the danger was passed, the Polish government reduced the register to its former size, and the Cossacks who were eliminated reverted to the status of petty townsmen, peasants or serfs.

The Polish magnates and aristocracy, and this applied also in part to the Little Russian gentry and landowners, regarded the Ukrainian Cossacks as rival claimants for land; they also viewed the armed Ukrainian masses as a danger to Polish law and order and they urged the Polish king to abolish all Cossacks. The elected Polish monarch, who was responsible for the safety of the realm, was dependent on a self-seeking aristocracy and *Seim* that were often a hindrance to him in managing the country's affairs. It was not necessarily in the Polish king's or Poland's interest to disband all Ukrainian Cossack units since these gave some protection against the raiding Tatar and, if need be, against the Muscovite and the Zaporozhian; in time of war they were a valuable source of recruits that had cost the Polish state very little in time of peace. It was for this reason that the king was forced to play a double game, outwardly agreeing with the views of his Polish nobility but being slow to take action on their demands, while at the same time having clandestine talks with Cossack representatives and giving secret encouragement to some of their aspirations and lending a sympathetic ear to some of their complaints, even though, here too, the king took no action to remedy them.

The crown hetman of the Ukrainian Cossacks was a Pole or Lithuanian appointed by the king and usually living in Warsaw, most of his day-to-day duties being carried out at Cherkassy by the principal commander (starshina) of all registered Cossacks together with a council of a deputy (esaul) and secretary (pisar), these appointments being filled by crown nomination.[2] The registered regimental commanders were either directly appointed by the crown or were elected by the Cossacks subject to the approval of the Polish king.

In the early part of the sixteenth century there were frequent Polish wars both with Russia and with the Tatars and Turkey, particularly in Moldavia, and during this time there were incessant peasant and Cossack uprisings everywhere in the Ukraine that, in 1617, caused the king to station 10,000 Polish troops in Dnieper garrisons from Kiev to Cherkassy. The registered Cossacks had also mutinied from time to time, killing or driving away their officers and appointing their own; meanwhile the Zaporozhians were making frequent raids into the Ukraine and had been organizing a collection of money throughout Polish Little Russia for the purchase of guns. The Poles countered by threatening with death and confiscation of property any Little Russian who had dealings with the Zaporozhians, and they tried to control all registered Cossacks by severely restricting their movement. Yet, because Poland was at war and needed every soldier that it could muster, it was still obliged to seek Cossack recruits and had to bargain even with its own successive starshinas, and in particular with Samuel Kishka and Petr Sagaidachnyi, for their support in finding the men to increase the register from 6,000 to 20,000 in return for a restoration of some of the Cossack rights and privileges that had been rescinded in 1594.

The history of the Ukraine in the seventeenth and eighteenth centuries is in effect a story of Cossackdom, admittedly a very different Cossackdom from that of the Don, but Cossackdom nevertheless. To the south was the free Cossack host of the Zaporozhians, while to the north there developed a Ukrainian state that was sometimes partly and sometimes wholly in the hands of a Cossack military and civil administration, sometimes independently Ukrainian but more often the satellite of the Pole, the Russian or the Turk. The Ukrainian Cossack himself was a small farmer or peasant, organized in militia companies of horse or foot. The story of that unhappy country is one of war, reprisals, terrorism, bloodshed and ruin: many of its leaders appear to have been the puppets of foreign powers; many of them were opportunists primarily concerned with the improving of their own fortunes, with their own aggrandizement and the killing of their rivals; even the patriots had to temper valour with discretion in trying to achieve or retain some national independence in the threatening presence of the foreigner. For the remedy of a protective alliance was often worse than the Polish ill: to call for Tatar or Turkish aid against the Pole usually resulted in Ukrainian land being devastated by murder and plunder from end to end; to invite the Muscovite as an ally was to bring in an equally brutal invader that too rarely had any intention of leaving.

At the end of the sixteenth century there had been Cossack uprisings under Kosynskii and Nalivaiko against the Poles, together with a Zaporozhian invasion under Loboda and Shaula. But in the early part of the next century there was comparative quiet since the Zaporozhians' attention was engaged in a series of strong expeditions against the Tatars and the Turks.[3] And while the Zaporozhians had been engaged in the south the energies of the Ukrainian Cossacks had been fully used in the Russo-Polish war and the expedition to occupy Moscow, a campaign in which 30,000 Ukrainian Cossacks fought in the Polish service.

By 1618, however, the Polish intervention in Russia at the time of the troubles had ended, and there followed a new period of civil war and anarchy in the Ukraine. Sagaidachnyi, the principal starshina of the Ukrainian registered Cossacks who was a good friend of the king of Poland, determined to interfere with his neighbour in the south. So, in 1620, Sagaidachnyi attacked the sech with a force of registered Cossacks and burned a number of boats there, but was then faced with a revolt among his men and the emergence of Borodavka, a rival Ukrainian starshina, whom Sagaidachnyi countered by proposing that they should merge their forces (at that time each had about 20,000 men); at a subsequent parley Sagaidachnyi had Borodavka arrested and killed. Zhmailo, a Zaporozhian, raised a new rebellion against Sagaidachnyi in the Ukraine; this was suppressed. It was then the turn of Mikhail Doroshenko, the new principal starshina of the registered Cossacks, to invade the area of the cataracts in 1626 and leave a garrison of 1,000 men at Khortitsa. Two years later Doroshenko was succeeded as starshina by Chernyi; but Chernyi did not hold his office for long, since the Zaporozhians under Triasilo entered the Ukraine and, laying siege to the Cherkassy base of the registered Cossacks, they captured Chernyi and killed him. The Poles appointed Petrazhitskii as the new commander of the registered Cossacks, and he, on their orders, invaded the sech in 1632, took Triasilo prisoner and, leaving a further 1,500 registered Cossacks at Khortitsa to replace the earlier garrison that had been driven out, returned to Kanev where his own Cossacks killed him. His successor was another Doroshenko who was also murdered by his own men. Then followed widespread disorders among the registered Cossacks, the main leaders of the uprisings being Pavliuk (a registered Cossack who had escaped to the Zaporozhians), and the Zaporozhians Ostrianin and Gunia.

In 1634 the Poles built a fortress at Kodak at the site of the first northern cataract, employing a Frenchman Guillaume Le Vasseur de Beauplan to construct it, using Tatar prisoners and serf labour. It took a year to build and, when finished, was regarded as a feat of military engineering; it housed two squadrons of Polish dragoons and some registered Cossacks under the command of a French officer Jean Marion. But it fell in a single night to a Zaporozhian force under a hetman with the Tatar name of Sulim. After a long siege it was retaken by registered Cossacks—it is said by a breach of parole. For there was no faith amongst these people in their dealings with each other, any more than in their negotiations with Turk or Tatar; the conditions of parleys, truces, safe-conducts or agreements were rarely observed, and hangings, mutilations, impalings and quarterings were the more common order of the day.

The Polish crown hetman Konetspolskii and, in particular, his field hetman Pototskii took the most energetic action to suppress the uprisings and mutinies, slaying and burning in a reign of terror that forced much of the population to flee to the Zaporozhians, to the Don or to the Muscovite Slobod. But, although Pototskii was successful in defeating the Zaporozhian-led insurgents, he could never overcome the sech base. In 1638 Pototskii was appointed principal starshina of the registered Cossacks, by then reduced again to six regiments, with a council consisting of Karaimovich as his deputy and Bogdan Khmelnitskii as secretary; all were Polish appointments and in Polish pay. That same year the Zaporozhians once more invaded the Ukraine and rebellion flared up everywhere.

Bogdan Khmelnitskii would appear to have been a politician well versed in intrigue as well as being a soldier. He was a landowner and member of the Ukrainian gentry, and probably no friend to the peasant or to the unregistered Cossack. In due course he became an officer of the registered Cossacks, was in Polish pay and was personally known to the king of Poland. It is said that Khmelnitskii eventually fell foul of his Polish masters and was victimized by them, and this may have been the case; but the real cause of Khmelnitskii's unpopularity appears to have been that he was not trusted, either by the Poles or by the registered Cossack leadership. However this may be, the Poles put him in arrest from which he escaped to the Zaporozhian Cossacks. There in the old Chertomlyka sech he made an excellent impression by planning an operation that led to the elimination of the registered Cossack garrison at Khortitsa, and by visiting the Crimean khan to bring the Tatars over to the side of the Zaporozhians. The delighted Zaporozhians thereupon elected Khmelnitskii as their hetman and, in 1648, together with Tatar forces, invaded the Ukraine, and this time with signal success. Pototskii was captured, his son killed and their forces routed; and, while the Tatars devastated far and wide, Khmelnitskii's men, in a civil war that became known as the national war of liberation, slaughtered foreigner and countryman, those of their own and other faiths, Poles, Jews and Little Russians, Catholic and Greek, regardless of sex or age, sometimes whole communities being put to the sword.

The Poles recovered from their earlier losses, and since the Tatars, laden with spoil, had withdrawn from the war, Khmelnitskii was obliged to come to terms with Warsaw.[4] By the 1649 Zborov agreement the registered Cossack ceiling was set at 40,000 (this was later increased to 50,000 with a further supplementary list of 20,000) and the Poles, having removed their *voevod* fortress commanders from the eastern part of the country, lost real control over the left-bank Ukraine to Khmelnitskii.[5] The peace was an uneasy one and operations against the Poles continued sporadically over the next few years with particularly fierce fighting in Moldavia and Wallachia.

The Ukrainian (as opposed to the earlier Polish) hetmanate really dated from the 1649 Treaty of Zborov, since it was at that time that the hetmanate state was allowed by the Polish *Seim* to become an autonomous unit of the Polish-Lithuanian commonwealth; this was the recognition of the emergence of the Ukrainian people as a nation. But the hetmanate was, in essence, a military and Cossack dictatorship since the principal starshina, henceforth known as the Ukrainian hetman, took over the civil government of the former palatinates of Kiev, Bratslav and Chernigov. Seventeen registered Cossack regiments (made up in all of 272 companies) were used to form the territorial framework of the executive of government from its new hetmanate headquarters at Chigirin.[6] So it came about that the regimental colonels controlled regions while the company commanders ruled counties, the officers functioning simultaneously as military commanders, civil executives, and controllers of the judiciary and the legislature. These soldiers had to command and administer their own troops in peace ready to take to the field in war, police the area allotted to them, administer the law, assess and collect taxes, and maintain highways and public services; all these duties had to be supervised by Cossacks who were usually ill-fitted for the task by education and by temperament.[7] The Cossack administrations did not control the Kiev Orthodox or Roman Catholic clergy, or the large towns, since these had internal autonomy based on the Magdeburg charters; in consequence the clergy, the city councils and the hetmanate were often at loggerheads. The hetmanate and the military government representatives had little understanding of, and often little interest in, the welfare and the problems of the serf, the peasant and the poor Cossack. Peasant uprisings soon broke out anew.

In 1651 the Ukraine was again at war with Poland and the hetmanate was forced out of most of western (right-bank) Ukraine so that Khmelnitskii turned to Moscow for an ally, and, by the terms of the 1654 Pereyaslav Rada, the hetmanate and left-bank Ukraine became a Russian protectorate and this in effect brought Muscovy to the Dnieper and close up to the Ottoman empire.[8] It also heralded the annexation of the Ukraine, for the tsar soon introduced his own *voevod* fortress commanders to the major cities in the eastern Ukraine and, in due course, these were to be followed by Russian garrisons; meanwhile Moscow bought over the Ukrainian Cossack officers (including Khmelnitskii) by condoning their seizure of lands and their use of serfs, and by granting them Russian military ranks and by ennobling them. And since Khmelnitskii and some of his successors began to style themselves hetman of the Ukraine 'and of the Zaporozhians' it might be supposed that the sech was part of this Moscow protectorate. This, however, was not really the case since Poland still laid some claim to the area and the Zaporozhians themselves remained, as before, independent of Poland, of the hetmanate and of Russia. Indeed, inside the sech it was even considered that the hetmanate was a dependancy of the Zaporozhian host, and the host demanded not only that it should have a vote in the appointment of the Ukrainian hetman but also that the candidates should be Zaporozhians and nominated by the sech.

When Khmelnitskii died in 1657 he was succeeded by the council secretary Vygovskii, a bitter enemy of the Zaporozhians. This appointment did not have general approval and some of the registered Cossack regiments disassociated themselves from the hetmanate; Vygovskii thereupon had their commanders shot. The Zaporozhians supported two candidates, their own man Barabash and the colonel of the Poltava regiment, against Vygovskii; in return Vygovskii had the Poltava regiment and its families and dependants sold into Tatar slavery. Vygovskii, pressed on all sides, turned to the Poles for support, but, by 1659, Serko, the hetman of the Zaporozhians, finally unseated him and Vygovskii fled to Poland. Iurii Khmelnitskii, a son of Bogdan, became hetman until 1663, but he steered a very unsteady course, under such heavy pressure from Moscow to accept Russian garrisons that he was finally forced into the Polish camp and resignation. In 1663, at what became known as the Nezhin

'Black Rada', the Zaporozhians put forward a candidate from their own host by name of Briukhovetskii, who disposed of his rivals by having them killed on the spot and was therefore elected. But this election must have had the blessing of Moscow since the tsar sent his own observer to the rada, Prince Velikogagin, with the support of 8,000 troops to give proper significance to his presence. For, from 1654 onwards, the Zaporozhians, in consequence of the Pereyaslav Rada agreement, for a time at least, leant more towards Moscow than to the hetmanate, and, so it is said, began to receive the Moscow subsidies doled out to the Cossack hosts.

The original hetmanate of the Ukraine, that had included most of the eastern and western regions, was thereupon split into two separate hetmanates—right and left bank with the Dnieper in between—so that from this time onwards the Ukraine, as it is known today, was divided into five parts: the right and left banks, the Slobod, the Zaporozhian sech and the Tatar Tauride. Briukhovetskii held sway only in the left bank with Muscovite and, in the early days, Zaporozhian support. The Poles and their Tatar allies had their own placeman hetman in the west Ukraine, Teteria from 1663 and Petr Doroshenko from 1666, the right bank having at its disposal the ten right-bank Cossack regiments. The right- and left-bank hetmanates were continually at war with each other. The Zaporozhians under Serko invaded the Polish-controlled right-bank Ukraine; then, when it became apparent that Briukhovetskii of the left bank was the pawn of Moscow and that, at the tsar's bidding, he had put a garrison into Kodak, the Zaporozhians began to withdraw their support from their former candidate. Nor was Serko's suspicion of Moscow allayed when a Russian garrison of 500 men under Kosagov arrived in the sech, ostensibly to support the Zaporozhians against the Tatars but in reality to spy. Serko determined to remove Moscow's ally Briukhovetskii, and the left-bank hetman was eventually lynched by his own Cossacks.

Just as left-bank politics were controlled from Moscow, so were the Tatars and Turks taking an increasingly active role in right-bank Ukraine, and the intervention of the Zaporozhians in the hetmanates was resented both in Moscow and in the Crimean capital of Bakhchisarai.[9] In December 1678 the sultan tried to destroy the sech when he sent 15,000 janissaries and Tatars to attack it by night, an attack that foundered with very heavy losses to the attackers. And it was on the morrow of this attack that Serko dictated his famous letter, the writing of which has been immortalized in Repin's painting *The Cossacks' letter to the Sultan.*

The left- and right-bank hetmanates were used by the Russians on the one side, and by the Turk, Tatar or the Pole on the other, to further their own national interests, provoking and protracting incessant and bloody civil war; and the Ukrainian hetman who failed them was deposed, exiled or murdered. In the left bank, Mnogogreshnyi was deposed in 1672 by a Moscow inspired *coup* and replaced by Samoilovich who, with Russian forces, invaded the west bank and besieged Doroshenko in Chigirin; many right-bank Cossack regiments went over to Samoilovich. But then the Turks arrived in the west Ukraine and, bent on vengeance, rapidly emptied an already devastated country. The Turks eventually rid themselves of Doroshenko, who fled and later died as a guest of Moscow, replacing him by Iurii Khmelnitskii who had been resurrected from retirement. Iurii Khmelnitskii did not meet the Turks' needs and they later killed him. When the Poles returned to the west Ukraine and Podolia in 1699, following their victory over the Turks, the country was a ruin from which much of the population had fled, and it took a generation to repopulate it with new Little Russian settlers from Galicia and Volhynia. What was left of the old right-bank Cossack regiments was in course of time disbanded and reformed as a component of the Polish Army. The hetmanate, as far as the west bank was concerned, had ceased to exist.

Meanwhile, in 1686, the Zaporozhians had expelled the Russian garrison, as the relationship between the sech and Moscow had much deteriorated; but, little daunted, the regent Sophia decided the next year to attack the Crimea directly, relying instead on Samoilovich's left-bank Ukrainian Cossack forces, together with a Russian army under Prince Golitsyn. The Tatars set the steppe on fire and the expedition failed. Samoilovich paid the price of failure, for he was arrested in another Moscow-directed *coup* and exiled to Siberia: his replacement, his colleague and deputy Mazeppa, is said to have paid Golitsyn 10,000 rubles to ensure his election and confirmation as hetman.

The brief period of Ukrainian independence, such as it was, was now over. According to Golubutskii, Mazeppa had great estates that numbered tens of thousands of serfs and was Moscow's faithful servant.[10] In the period 1686–9 he put down numerous mutinies and uprisings with the greatest of cruelty. Russia had the left bank and

Poland again held the right bank. Meanwhile the Ukraine was being impoverished by migration and by providing large numbers of troops to serve its foreign masters.

Under Mazeppa's hetmanate the remaining vestige of independence was extinguished in the left-bank Ukraine. It was due to Mazeppa, too, that the first Zaporozhian sech met its untimely end at the hands of Russia, untimely in that there was still a real need there for a protective frontier force. Mazeppa, like so many of his hetman predecessors, was an ambitious intriguer who dreamed of uniting the Polish west bank and Zaporozhe with his own hetmanate. He was in league with Palii, a Cossack colonel of the Fastov regiment on the right bank, against the Poles; he sent peremptory demands (usually at Moscow's prompting) to the sech, and, when these were ignored, counselled Moscow to destroy the Zaporozhians. But finding that Moscow's pressure on his own hetmanate was increasing and that it was the tsar Peter's apparent aim to turn the Ukraine into a Russian province, Mazeppa looked about for other allies. Russia, allied with Poland, had invaded Swedish Livonia in 1700, so starting the Great Northern War that was fought mainly on Polish soil; and it was Charles XII of Sweden to whom Mazeppa turned, making him secret assurances that the Ukrainian Cossacks would rise against Moscow as soon as Swedish troops should appear on Russian soil.

Mazeppa then went to great pains to conciliate the Zaporozhians and make the hetman Gordienko privy to his plot. The Zaporozhians, no less than the hetmanate, felt threatened by Moscow's expansionist policies and resented the Russian detachments and observers that were appearing on Zaporozhian territories; and so a secret accord was struck between the two hetmans. The relationship between the sech and Moscow had further deteriorated since large numbers of Zaporozhians, defying Gordienko's orders, had left the sech and gone campaigning in support of the Don Cossack rebel Bulavin against the Moscow government.

Charles XII is said to have paid out hundreds of thousands of *zloty* to ensure Mazeppa's and Gordienko's support; and when tsar Peter heard that the Zaporozhian loyalty was in doubt he wrote to the sech hetman trying to detach him from Mazeppa, and made a subsidy payment of more than 12,000 rubles. But he was unsuccessful, for on 28 March 1709 Gordienko and 8,000 men declared for Charles XII. Instead of marching on Moscow Charles XII turned south into the Ukraine; there the aid promised by Mazeppa did not materialize. The

Russians captured the Swedish supply and reinforcement train, and Menshikov, the tsarist field commander in the Ukraine, acting with despatch and great brutality, effectively paralysed all opposition and destroyed Mazeppa's capital at Baturin. Menshikov detached two Russian regiments under a Colonel Iakovlev and these entered and occupied the sech on 14 May, a few weeks before the Swedish army of Charles XII, and those Ukrainian and Zaporozhian Cossacks that had rallied to him, were destroyed at Poltava.

The Russians occupied the sech, almost without resistance, taking fifty guns, the treasure, the regalia and stores. Most of the Zaporozhians, under their last hetman Sorochinskii, slipped away in boats downstream, and the old Bazavluk or Chertomlyka sech had ceased to exist.

*   *   *

The Ukrainian Slobodsk Cossack regiments had come into being as a result of the migration, early in the seventeenth century, of Ukrainian Cossacks and peasants from the Dnieper into the southern border regions of Muscovy on the edge of the empty steppe near Belgorod. Sometimes these came as individuals or families, sometimes they arrived as small communities or military detachments. One such Cossack force was that of Iakov Ostrianin, 800 men strong, that, having recently been defeated in the Ukraine, sought refuge in 1638 at Chuguev.[11] Like many other hosts they consisted of the electorate (male Cossacks) and the auxiliaries (dependants and peasants), and, retaining this social distinction in their new home, they were allocated land and became self-ruling communities answerable to the local Russian *voevod*; in return they were expected to provide the tsar with a reserve of troops. Their liability for military service was not, however, restricted to the frontier locality and they eventually served as part of the Russian Army as far afield as Persia.

In 1651 the unrest and fighting in the Ukraine caused a new wave of immigrants that founded Ostrogozhsk in 1652, followed by Sumy, Kharkov, Akhtyrka and Izyum. The Slobodsk political organization was in no way a replica of the hetmanate, for the new arrivals there formed what were, in effect, five town or service Cossack regiments each with its elected colonel, captains and officials, commanding and administering itself. In 1670 there was yet another great influx of colonists, mainly from the right-bank Ukraine.

The starshina and the colonels of the five Slobodsk regiments, although Ukrainian, served Russia well, notwithstanding that tsar Peter had, in 1700, restricted their strength to 3,500 men, for they and their men were much removed from the mentality of the free Cossack hosts in the south. The Slobodsk Cossacks were well placed to catch Russian or Ukrainian fugitives and migrants on their way to reinforce the Don Cossacks, and as, from the beginning of the eighteenth century, the Don Cossacks were in a foment of rebellion against Moscow interference and oppression, the Slobodsk regiments volunteered to catch the runaways, an offer that was accepted in St Petersburg.[12] One tenth of those caught were to be committed on the spot to penal servitude and the remainder sent under guard to Moscow. In return and by way of payment, the regimental colonels were trying to get their hands on the northern Don Cossack territories. The Slobodsk regiments also served the *voevod* Bakhmetev with distinction, assisting in the defeat of Bulavin's Don Cossacks on the river Kurlak and in the repulse of 1,500 Zaporozhians who were on their way to the Don. In recognition of these services, the Don Cossack area of Aidar was distributed to the elders of the Ostrogozhsk regiment in 1708.

No Cossacks were, however, completely trusted in Russia. In 1722, as if to emphasize that they were Russian auxiliary troops and not Ukrainian Cossacks, the command was removed from the Ukrainian *divizia*, and all border and legal matters had to be referred to Kursk; in 1726 their leadership was put under the St Petersburg military collegium (the war office). From 1730 onwards the Cossacks of the Slobodsk regiments were employed on field works and the digging of canals, together with the local peasantry, often far from home and working under the most harsh conditions. Then between 1733–7 the government reformed the Slobodsk Cossacks in order to reduce their number, all former Cossacks who were not actually serving, together with their Cossack dependants, being reverted to peasant status. These changes were admittedly cancelled by the empress Elisabeth in 1743, but the old order of life had by then been so shattered that it was impossible to restore it, and for this the host starshinas had been largely to blame in that they had apparently seized on common lands and, aiming at providing these lands with serfs, they had used every measure in their power to turn the Cossacks into peasants.

By 1763 the Slobodsk Cossacks no longer existed. They had never had any political significance nor, after the steppe frontier began to recede southwards, even a static military role; being Ukrainian and Cossack they tended to be the object of tsarist suspicion. The five regiments had been cut, then expanded to go to war for Russia; then disarmed and used as a labour corps, then rearmed and Russianized, and finally, taking their names from their depot towns and losing their Cossack designation, they became regular hussar regiments of the Russian Army, remaining in the service until 1917. The administration of the area once occupied by the Slobodsk Cossacks reverted to the civil government as part of an ordinary province of the Russian empire.

*　*　*

The subsequent course of events in the Ukrainian hetmanate on the left bank of the Dnieper was in many respects similar to that in the Slobodsk. Long before Poltava, even as far back as the 1654 Treaty of Pereyaslav, Moscow had begun its policy of encroachment, firstly to turn the Dnieper territory into a dependency and then to annex it, the tsarist ambitions being tempered only by circumspection in its dealings with its rivals in that area, Poland and Turkey. The tsar had sought to influence and then to control the eastern Ukraine by appointing Russian *voevod* commanders in the principal cities; and the lack of experience and political acumen of the Ukrainian Cossack officers of the hetmanate made them unfit to counter the intrigues of the *voevod* who often became the secret centre of subversion against the Ukrainian government.

Under the Briukhovetskii régime, the Russian representatives had actually succeeded in taking over the government and the taxation of the non-Cossack Ukrainian population of the east bank, all taxes collected being payable to Russia; and although this was revoked after the lynching of the hetman, the Russian *voevod* fortress commanders remained. Russian garrisons were stationed in the country and the tsar's representative took to attending the national rada assemblies accompanied by a large armed escort. Meanwhile the high-ranking Ukrainian officers of the hetmanate were bribed by the bestowal of Russian nobility, ranks and honours and the grant of estates on Ukrainian soil.

After the defeat of Charles XII and the failure of Mazeppa's bid for independence, Peter the Great treated the hetmanate and the Ukraine with scant respect. Skoropadskii, the next hetman, was selected from the Starodub regiment by Peter and instructed to move his capital from Baturin to Glukhov near the Russian border: from that time onwards the tsar alone appointed the commanders of regiments while the selection of the captains was made by the hetman, subject to the approval of a Russian resident-general. The Russian resident-general, as the tsar's representative, advised and controlled the hetman, while the Ukrainian government and economy was subordinated to that of St Petersburg. Russians were appointed to many of the key appointments and granted great landed estates in the Ukraine, and a number of Russian cavalry regiments were brought into the country and maintained there at hetmanate cost. The Ukrainian Cossack regiments were put to work building canals and fortifications.

When Polubotok became hetman in 1722 after the death of Skoropadskii, Peter the Great had already decided that the real government of the Ukraine should be exercised by the ministry known as the Little Russian college made up largely of Great Russian representatives; Polubotok and his council were imprisoned in St Petersburg. In 1723 the emperor confirmed a law allowing the change from Cossack to peasant status, since this was favoured by both the crown and the landowners, but making it very difficult to reverse the process. In 1727 the hetmanate was temporarily resurrected under Apostil, but then the government passed into the hands of a council under Prince Shakhovskoi until 1750, when the empress Elisabeth nominated Razumovskii, a court favourite, as hetman. Razumovskii, who transferred his capital from Glukhov back to Baturin, made some efforts to restore the earlier functions of the hetmanate, but his achievements were more apparent than real. Catherine the Great, on coming to the throne, required Razumovskii in 1764 to resign his office; she then appointed Rumiantsev with a new Little Russian college to prepare the abolition of the hetmanate and the conversion of the ten regimental regions into the three vice-regency provinces of Kiev, Chernigov and Novgorod-Severskii that were put under a governor-general of Little Russia and incorporated into the Russian empire. This was done in 1783, and that same year the ten Ukrainian Cossack regiments were reformed as regular carabineer regiments of the Russian Army.

Ukrainian Cossacks were, however, to be resurrected in the next century, when there would be a need for them and when it would be convenient for the tsar to have them at his service. But in reality the Ukrainian Cossack had, in the tsarist view, ceased to fulfil any purpose, since the frontier had long since moved and the Ukraine was no longer an independent national state.

In the right-bank Polish Ukraine the old Ukrainian registered Cossack regiments virtually disappeared at the beginning of the eighteenth century, and they were replaced by two different bodies of troops known as Polish Cossacks. Firstly there was a small regular cadre inside the Polish Army, recruited from Ukrainians but officered by Poles; and secondly there was the irregular militia, drawn mainly from Little Russian peasants and serfs in the private service of the Polish landowners. These were in addition to the Lithuanian Tatar Cossacks whose long history predated that of the Ukrainian or the Russian Cossacks; these Tatar Cossacks were to remain within the Polish commonwealth until its partition towards the end of the century when they passed into the Russian service.

*    *    *

After the Zaporozhians had stolen away down the Dnieper at the time of Poltava, they set up, in 1710, a new encampment at the junction of the Kamenka and the Dnieper, from which, the next year, they were driven out on the tsar's orders by Buturlin's Russian forces and Skoropadskii's Ukrainian Cossacks. They then camped further down the river at Aleshki (Aleshkovsk) near the junction of the Ingul and the Dnieper, in Tatar territory, where they were permitted to remain by the khan Kaplan-Girai on condition that they served the Crimea. There they led a troubled and stormy existence at the mercy of the Tatar and Nogai, and soon wished to return to Russia.

Their supplication to return, addressed to tsar Peter in 1716 and 1717, fell on deaf ears, but the empress Anna Ivanovna and Graf von Veisbakh (Weissbach) had different ideas. The southern border of the Ukraine had been open and vulnerable since the removal of the Zaporozhians in 1709, and von Veisbakh needed them back to build a defensive line there. A secret agreement was made with the field hetman Ivan Milashevich that the host could return to the Ukraine on condition that it would join in any future war against Turkey. In 1733, when the expected war broke out over the Polish succession, the Zaporozhians were ordered by the Crimean khan to move north towards Poland to fight for the sultan; this served to bring the host to the river Podpolna, only five miles from the old sech of Chertomlyka, and there the Zaporozhians left the khan's service and, changing sides, went over to the Russians and built the new Podpilenskaia sech.

The Russian government allocated to the Zaporozhians a great area to control and defend that later became the Ekaterinoslav and Kherson provinces (with the exception of the Odessa, Tiraspol and Ananevsk districts). The area was divided into five (and from 1735 six) regions, each region being known as a *palanka*[13] The sech itself was divided as before into thirty-eight kurens and in 1755 numbered 13,000 Cossacks. An initial bounty of 20,000 rubles was paid by Russia to the host.

The main strength of the host was still found by the *seroma*, the unmarried or unattached, and these lived, as before, either in a kuren in the sech or as part of the working force in one of the 400 great estates (*zimovniki*) in the surrounding countryside. The kurens in the sech also controlled areas of surrounding land held in common by the members, and every year this land was redistributed by lot.

Only the unattached Cossacks had a vote in the rada, and by their vote the host hetman and his council, consisting of the deputy, secretary and judge, were chosen, usually on the first day of each year. The sech still had its square, its houses, school, church (the Pokrov Bogoroditskii) and kuren long huts. Recruits continued to be accepted by a kuren vote before being presented for enrolment, usually under an assumed name; the accepted recruit could then stay in the kuren or go out to a *palanka*, provided that he could find work there. Each of the outside *zimovniki* estates employed between fifteen and sixty men, and the number of the estates increased rapidly from the original 400 in 1736 to over 4,000 thirty years later.

Each of the outlying *palanka* regions had an administrative centre, the *sloboda*, together with a small garrison, with a hetman and council elected at a rada by the Cossacks within the area. The *palanka* hetman was responsible for implementing the orders issued from the host, for administration, finances and taxes, for mobilization and keeping law and order within his area. In addition to the unattached Cossacks in the garrisons, in the *zimovniki*, and in the host and kuren working parties, there were numerous married Cossacks and free peasants in the regions: married Cossacks were part of the host and had Cossack responsibilities and military duties, but could not vote at the rada: the peasants elected their own starshina whose duty it was to attend rada or council meetings when peasant affairs were under discussion and to represent the peasants' case when asked to do so. All members of the host, whether Cossack or peasant, paid taxes. Although the sech garrison in 1755 numbered only 13,000 Cossacks, by 1760 the total Zaporozhian population exceeded 100,000 people, and Zaporozhe eventually became a great trading area exporting salt, wine, vodka, tobacco, pelts, fish and cattle to the Crimea, Moldavia, the northern Ukraine and Poland, transport being by boat or by the *chumak*, the Ukrainian ox-cart: imports included grain, cloth, gunpowder, lead and finished goods. Except in the last years of the life of the new sech, agriculture was still not fully developed, but the Zaporozhians became the middlemen providing intermediary markets between the Black Sea and the interior.

The new Zaporozhe was unlike the old in that it was entirely dependent on Russia; it received an annual subsidy (4,600 rubles in 1742, later increased to 6,600) together with material grants that were mainly powder and lead. In 1736, as soon as the sech was established, a Russian fort had been built there with a permanent Russian garrison; and the sech was tied into the central government in that the host was originally made subordinate to the governor-general of the Ukraine and then, from 1750, to hetman Razumovskii; at the end of the hetmanate, in 1764, the sech came under Rumiantsev. The Zaporozhians had been used by Russia in the 1736 war against Turkey and they had mounted expeditions by land and water against Perekop, Evpatoria, Bakhchisarai and Kinburn. A grateful Russian monarch had, admittedly, honoured them by the presentation of a banner bearing the Russian coat of arms; and the Zaporozhian regalia, seized in 1709, had been returned; besides which the host was permitted, as a special concession, to keep its own plunder. But, as time went on, the Zaporozhians came to be held in less regard by the Russian emperors.

The new sech suffered from social ills that had not beset the old. The annual election of the host hetman became somewhat fictional in that the election began to be looked upon as an accepted extension of office of the rich and influential council, so that a hetman and his colleagues might serve continuously for ten years or more. The hetman, the council and the starshina elders who acted as the hetman's advisers usually lacked nothing: but the situation with the rank and file was otherwise. The sech continued to accept fugitives in numbers above the capacity that it could accommodate: the kuren housing for the *seroma* was poor, uncomfortable, cold and over-

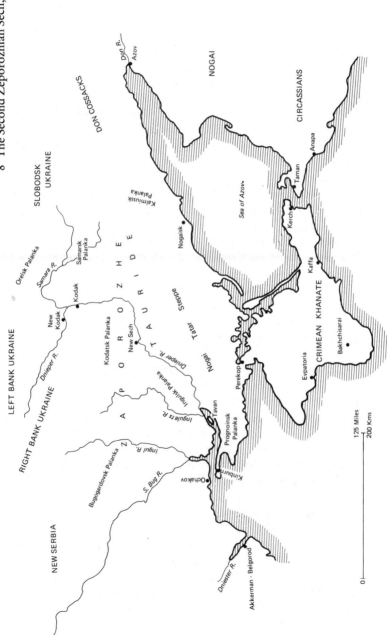

8 The Second Zeporozhian Sech, 1734–1775

N

LEFT BANK UKRAINE

RIGHT BANK UKRAINE

NEW SERBIA

SLOBODSK UKRAINE

DON COSSACKS

Don R.

Azov

Oreisk Palanka

Samara R.

New Kodak

Kodak

Samarsk Palanka

Kodatsk Palanka

New Sech

Ingulsk Palanka

Bugogardoevsk Palanka

Ingul R.

Ingulets R.

Dnieper R.

Kalmiussk Palanka

Nogaisk

Z  A  P  O  R  O  Z  H  E

T  A  U  R  I  D  E

Tatar Steppe

Nogai

Nogai

Tavan

Prognoinsk Palanka

Kinburn

Ochakov

S. Bug R.

Perekop

Sea of Azov

NOGAI

Kerch

Taman

Anapa

CIRCASSIANS

Kaffa

Eupatoria

CRIMEAN KHANATE

Bakhchisarai

Dniester R.

Akkerman - Belgorod

0      125 Miles
       200 Kms

crowded and the food was meagre, and there was always a pressing need to find work in the *palanki* for the kuren dwellers so that they could be moved out to make room for new arrivals and so keep down costs. Since those Cossacks that had acquired wealth were living in luxury and were even paying for substitutes to perform their military service, a great gulf, hitherto unknown among the Zaporozhians, had arisen between rich and poor, between those in authority and those in the kuren huts. This was good neither for the welfare nor for the discipline of the community.

In the old sech the frequent change of hetman had tended to keep the leadership in touch with the rank and file; this leadership was in itself adventurous and bold and was generally well able to deal with the wild and unruly elements within the host. The leadership of the new Zaporozhe was of a milder kind and was far less able to cope with the subversive and mutinous movements, sometimes in the form of secret societies, that existed among the poor Cossacks. For many of the recruits accepted into the second host were formed bands of outlaws, murderers, arsonists and robbers who, under the name of *haidamaki*, had been terrorizing the west bank for a number of years, their usual prey being the Polish or Ukrainian landowners.[14] These regarded their new homes in the sech as being a safe haven or base from which they could continue the plundering of the Polish right bank and, defying the hetman, many soon broke away from the kuren and set up their own marshland island fortresses within the Zaporozhian area, often numbering several hundred men, with their own boats and cannon; in addition to making forays on the right bank these began to attack the *zimovniki* and other properties of the sech. The *haidamak* attacks on the Polish-controlled west bank and the failure of the hetman to maintain order in his own territory were regarded with much disquiet in St Petersburg, for Russia, after the 1738 ratification of the Treaty of Vienna, had a powerful voice in the affairs of Poland, and was prepared to use Russian troops in restoring order in the Polish Ukraine, partly because it had come to regard itself as the protector of the Poniatowsky kingdom and partly because it did not want the disorders to spread across the Dnieper into Russian-held Ukraine.

There were many other causes of discord between the Zaporozhians and the Russians. Zaporozhe continued to accept Russian fugitives, serfs and outlaws, even soldier deserters with horses and full equipment, under the very eyes of the Russian troop commander in the sech. And there was frequent wrangling, even armed conflict, between the host and its neighbours, Poles, Ukrainians, Don Cossacks and Tatars who had encroached upon the old Zaporozhian territories during the absence of the host after 1709. Zaporozhe expected Russia to support its border claims; St Petersburg had neither the patience nor the inclination to listen to these Zaporozhian complaints.

*Haidamak* uprisings and other Cossack mutinies and lawlessness became commonplace within the sech from as early as 1749, and these extended to the Zaporozhian free peasants. Muscovite troops had to be brought in to quell them. In 1768 the Polish Ukraine was aflame throughout Podolia, Volyhnia and Galicia, in uprisings led by Zalizniak, a poor worker from the Zaporozhians who had turned *haidamak*; the general revolt, once again, had to be put down by Russian forces. That same year there was another mutiny inside the sech itself and the hetman Kalnishevskii fled, disguised as a monk, taking refuge in the Russian garrison-held 'retranchment', while other starshinas fled to Kodak; in consequence Rumiantsev, the governor-general of the Ukraine, ordered two Russian cavalry and two infantry regiments to the sech. Many of the Zaporozhian Cossacks had been called away in 1768 to serve in the new war against the Turks and this had caused great hardship, particularly to those with families; but in 1773 there were still enough men at home to provide numerous volunteers to join the Pugachev uprising against the empress. Then, when Pugachev was captured, many of his former supporters swarmed back to Zaporozhe for refuge. In 1773, possibly as a result of this home-coming, the *haidamak* robberies started all over again.

Meanwhile fortune had favoured Russia in its war against Turkey, that was weakening and was without allies, and from 1764 Catherine the Great was already planning the founding of great southern provinces carved out of the steppe that would bring the empire on to the Black Sea; these provinces were to be called New Russia.[15] Slavian Serbia and New Serbia, forming part of the Russian new territories, already encroached on the Zaporozhe borders, but the empress coveted the lands even beyond the sech. When, by the 1774 Treaty of Kuchuk-Kainarji that ended the Turkish war, Russia acquired Kinburn, Enikale and Kerch with free navigation for commercial ships in Turkish waters (the Tatars of the Crimea being recognized as independent of the sultan, that is to say dependent on the tsar), Russia had arrived at the Black Sea and the way was open for the 1783 annexing of the Crimea. And, by the first partition of Poland, in 1772, that unhappy country, having lost one third of its territory and about one half of its inhabitants, was virtually a Russian protectorate.

Russia no longer had any need of the very troublesome Cossack host in Zaporozhe that it regarded as a nest of robbers and haven of sedition, and Potemkin, the newly appointed governor-general of New Russia, believing that its continued existence could only be in conflict with the provinces of New Russia, advised Catherine to suppress the sech. Zaporozhe was, in any event, in an advanced state of demoralization and threatened to break up of its own accord.

On 5 June 1775 General Tekelii, with a force of Russian cavalry, infantry and Don Cossacks, occupied the sech by surprise, without meeting any resistance, and by a Russian manifest of 5 August the Zaporozhian host was dissolved. The lands were distributed to the Russian military commanders, nobility and officials (Potemkin, Prozorovskii and Viazemskii all received great estates of 100,000 *desiatin*—about 275,000 acres), and some of the land was made over to the Zaporozhian dignitaries; the remainder was retained by the state. The administration of the Zaporozhian territory was divided and transferred to the Azov and New Russia provinces and to the Ekaterinoslav region.

Kalnishevskii and his council were exiled to Siberia or the north. Once again, many Zaporozhians fled, firstly to the Dobrudja at the mouth of the Danube that still formed part of the Turkish empire. From there some went on to the Austrian Banat, returning to Dobrudja in 1812 where a new sech was formed at the junction of the Danube and Little Danube, and there they lived by fishing and agriculture as Turkish subjects, taking part in military expeditions when ordered to do so by the Turkish ruler.

Of the large Zaporozhian Cossack population that remained on the Dnieper, most were reduced to peasantry and many of them to serfdom. But Russia soon found itself in difficulty when it extended the boundaries of New Russia into the Kuban and the Caucasus, for this gave rise to a new war against Turkey in 1787 and the first Russian experience of fighting the very warlike peoples of the north-west Caucasus, mainly the Circassian Cossacks. Sweden, too, had come into the war against Russia.

So it came about that there was a need once more for Cossack colonists, preferably those of the Terek Cossack type, in order that Russia should gain a permanent foothold in the Kuban. The most readily available people for this task were the dispersed Zaporozhians. So they were brought together again, by Potemkin, only eight years after the sech had been dissolved, and were transported into this new land as Black Sea Cossacks.

CHAPTER 4 NOTES

1 They also kept numerous Little Russian armed retainers, and they demanded from the Polish government that these be allowed against the quota of registered Cossacks; the purpose of this demand was to reduce the numbers of registered Cossacks not under their control and at the same time have their own retainers maintained partly at government expense in that they would qualify for bounties and land grants.

2 The principal starshina of the registered Cossacks at this time was also called a hetman; he will, however, be referred to here as a starshina in order to distinguish him from the crown hetman and the hetman of the Zaporozhians.

3 In 1604 the Zaporozhians took Varna and in 1608 Perekop in the Crimea; in 1609 they stormed Ismail and Kiliiu on the Danube and Akkerman-Belgorod on the Dniester; in 1615 they attacked Kaffa and the mainland of Turkey at Trebizond, Sinope and Constantinople. Then, together with the Don Cossacks, in 1622 the Zaporozhians again stormed Trebizond, and in 1624 and 1630 Constantinople. In 1637 4,000 Zaporozhians joined the Don Cossacks to take Azov, this being held against Turkish counter-attack until 1642.

4 The Tatars mistrusted Khmelnitskii and before withdrawing took him prisoner; determined to profit by the event, they charged a heavy ransom before releasing him.

5 The Ukraine is divided by the Dnieper that runs diagonally across it from north-west to south-east, so that the northern and eastern part (eventually controlled by Russia) became known as left bank, while the southern and western part became the right bank.

6 The six permanent registered Cossack regiments were (in 1625) at Kiev, Belaya Tserkov, Korsun, Kanev, Cherkassy and Pereyaslav. By 1638 the Kiev regiment had moved to Chigirin. In 1649 the seventeen regiments covered both east and west Ukraine and were at Bratslav, Uman, Kalnyk, Belaya Tserkov, Pavolich, Korsun, Chigirin, Cherkassy, Kanev, Pereyaslav, Kropivna, Poltava, Mirgorod, Priluki, Nezhin, Chernigov and Starodub.

7 The hetman's staff had been increased, but it still followed the traditional pattern: a general quartermaster (his esaul and chief of staff), a general-judge, a general-chancellor, a general-treasurer, together with general-ADCs, flag and standard bearers; the regiments had a similar

staff of commander, quartermaster, two judges, ADCs and standard bearers.

8   From 1654–1663 hetmanate affairs were dealt with in Moscow by the *posol'skii prikaz* (the foreign office); then from 1663–1717 by the Little Russian office and thereafter by the college of foreign affairs and senate.

9   In 1668 Doroshenko, seeking Turkish aid against his Polish masters, acknowledged the right-bank hetmanate as a *Turkish* protectorate, and in 1672 Turks and Tatars attacked Poland: the right-bank hetmanate was the loser, however, for the Turks removed Podolia from the western Ukraine and took it under their control.

10   Theoretically and in law there was at this time no serfdom in east-bank Ukraine; in reality it was already widespread.

11   Ostrianin, originally a Zaporozhian, was killed by his own men in 1641; most of the men then returned to the Dnieper.

12   The Russian capital was moved from Moscow to St Petersburg (now Leningrad) in 1703; in 1721 tsar Peter (it is said at the proposal of the senate) assumed the titles of 'emperor' and 'the Great'.

13   The *palanki* were: Bugochardov, Ingulsk (or Perevezsk), Kodatsk, Samarsk, Kalmiusk and Prognoinsk. In 1766 Orelsk was added and Samarsk was split into two, the southern half being called Prorovchansk.

14   *Haidamak* (or *Gaidamak*) from the Turkish word for robber.

15   New Russia was to cover the northern littoral of the Black Sea, stretching from part of Moldavia and Bessarabia across the Tauride and, eventually, into the Kuban.

# 5 The Cossacks of the Don

Boris Godunov, who in 1598 succeeded Fedor Ivanovich, the good friend of the Don Cossacks, took a very different view of that distant community, and he tried to control it by orders and threats and the building of a fort on the upper Donets at Tsarev-Borisov. As this availed him nothing, he stopped all subsidies, forbade the border towns to trade or treat with the Don, and ordered that all Cossacks taken should be imprisoned or killed. This only served to add Muscovy to the list of the Don Cossacks' enemies, and they began once more to raid the boyar estates in the border areas.

When the first false Dmitrii, the rival claimant for Godunov's throne, appeared in Poland, he sent to the Zaporozhe and to the Don for support. The Zaporozhians refused help, presumably because Dmitrii was a protégé of the Poles: the Don Cossacks sent a deputation under ataman Andrei Korella to Cracow to try to learn the truth concerning Dmitrii, and this came back convinced of the justice of the pretender's claim, partly because king Sigismund and the Polish nobility professed to be sure, and partly because Boris Godunov was hated on the Don. And when the Don Cossacks came across a boyar, Semen Godunov, sent by Boris to Astrakhan to gain support for the tsar's cause, they killed him and sent a message to the tsar saying that they would soon be in Moscow. Boris Godunov had learned too late that even the tsar might need Cossack support; so, at this eleventh hour, he tried to win the Cossacks over by sending an envoy Petr Khrushchev to the Don to denounce Dmitrii as an impostor. When the ataman Korella set off with 6,000 Cossacks to join Dmitrii at the Moscow border, he took the reluctant Khrushchev with him; Khrushchev, on seeing Dmitrii and being in fear for his life, declared the pretender to be no impostor but the true heir to the throne, and this confirmed the Don Cossacks in their determination to be rid of Godunov.

The Don Cossacks, together with the Poles, helped the first false Dmitrii win his throne. When, the next year, this Dmitrii was murdered by the boyars and Vasilii Shuiskii became tsar, new pretenders arose. The second Dmitrii was a Terek Cossack named Sleik who received some Don Cossack support when he marched to his defeat at Tula; the third false Dmitrii (the Tushino felon) was also joined by part of the Don Cossacks simply because the rank and file were credulous; but even they finally tired of the pretenders and of the Poles, and in 1613 they took part in the Moscow *zemskii sobor* and the election of Mikhail Fedorovich Romanov as tsar. In 1614 the tsar restored the Don Cossacks to the royal favour, and confirmed their autonomous rights as an independent state free to conduct its own foreign relations, with no extradition liability to return fugitives to Muscovy; Don Cossack affairs, that had previously been handled by the main military department in Moscow, were transferred to the foreign office. Henceforth the Don was to receive an annual subsidy in return for escorts for the tsar's envoys to Azov, the Crimea and the Nogai, and the Don host was to continue to be responsible and to be paid for the freeing of Russian prisoners and slaves in Tatar, Turk or Circassian hands.

Some of the rebels against the Romanov tsar still held out, however, and in particular the Cossack Zarutskii, who had a great following among the Cossacks of the upper Don, the Volga, the Terek and the Yaik, and who had set up a camp in Astrakhan together with a new pretender, the young felon of Tushino, and the pretender's mother Marina Mnishek. The tsar Mikhail, because he wanted to keep the loyalty of the Don Cossacks, sent his emissary to address the krug on the lower Don; the krug voted in favour of the tsar and sent off their own men to detach Zarutskii's mutineer supporters on the upper Don and on the Volga, and the influence of the lower Don Cossacks was already so powerful that Zarutskii was also abandoned by the Terek and Yaik hosts. The grateful tsar bestowed on the Don Cossacks a banner and the title of 'the great host' (*velikoe voisko*).

This good relationship between Mikhail Romanov and the Don host was not to last, however. The tsar felt threatened by Poland, Sweden, the Tatars and Turkey, and he badly needed Cossack help in the many wars of his long reign that lasted until 1645. Russia could not hope to fight all these nations and so needed peace in the south in order to muster its strength against its northern enemies. For this reason it was both dangerous and galling to Moscow when the Don Cossacks, who were regarded in Constantinople as being Russian and therefore part of Muscovy, started fighting again with Tatars, Nogai, Circassians and Turks, partly because the Don host was provoked by its warlike neighbours and partly because it willingly allowed itself to be led astray by its very good friends the Zaporozhians to take part in joint raiding expeditions in the Black Sea.[1] There was a renewal of the running warfare between the Cossacks and Tatars and the Turkish garrison of Azov, with the sultan ordering the stopping up of the estuary of the Don delta by the building of artillery towers and chain barriers across the Katancha and the Mertvyi Donets.

In 1617 the tsar told the sultan that the Don Cossacks were thieves and rogues and he promised to destroy them without trace as soon as the war against Poland had come to an end. This was, in effect, Moscow's attitude to the Cossacks over the centuries; for all the tsars' fair words and promises, there was never any intention of allowing the hosts either autonomy or freedom. But Mikhail Romanov took pains to hide his anger and at first remained on apparently friendly terms with the Don: he tried to deflect the sultan's wrath on to the Poles and the Zaporozhians, and not without reason did the tsar suspect the Polish king Sigismund of fishing in the troubled waters there. Yet Mikhail Fedorovich suffered, as his predecessors had done, from the unreliability, even wantonness, of the Cossacks, for no sooner had he sent envoys to the host to explain the necessity for keeping the peace, and had received in exchange the Cossacks' fervent assurances of their obedience and loyalty to his person, than the next messenger brought in a despatch that the men on the Don were pleased to announce the capture of an important Turkish pasha and were demanding 30,000 *zloty* as ransom for his return.

The Don Cossack leadership was not guileless in the intricate maze of foreign relations, however. It knew its worth to Moscow. For although the tsar's subsidy and provisions were being sent regularly, so, too, were the requests for troops, both horse and foot, for use against the Poles.[2] At this time the Zaporozhian hetman Borodavka was trying to enlist Don Cossack support for a joint Cossack war, together with Poland, against the Turks, since the king of Poland was offering a bounty of thirty rubles a man. But the Don krug said that it could not commit itself to Borodavka; for although the Don Cossacks were normally willing to join in most escapades with the Zaporozhians, they were suspicious of the politics of outside nations: at that time they estimated their fighting strength at between seven and eight thousand men, a large number of whom were away on campaign; 'not before these returned would they be in a position to consider the matter.' Russia was fully occupied in its struggle with Poland, and Turkey was at war with Persia, and it was in the Don Cossack interest that these wars should be prolonged; peace could bring a determined effort by the tsar or sultan to clear the Cossacks from the Don.

The Don Cossacks continued, however, to mount great expeditions together with the Zaporozhians against Tatar and Turk throughout the Black Sea, expeditions in search of plunder; much of the loot went to decorate the hosts' churches and monasteries. The losses in men were sometimes heavy, although this apparently did not deter them. The skirmishing and raiding by land were at times also costly; Azov and Kerch were stormed with little success.[3] On the other hand, as the Turkish envoy Uma Kontakuzin observed and reported, few could equal the Cossacks of the Don as horsemen, particularly in the nomad tactics of the steppe, as they shadowed, ambushed and trapped Azov and Nogai raiding parties and relieved them of their plunder and slaves. By 1625 the Don Cossacks had joined up in a temporary alliance with the Astrakhan Nogai in great horse-raiding forays against the Tatars in Perekop.

The Don Cossacks' standing with the sultan and the tsar had worsened by this time so that it was little different from what it had been during the reign of Fedor Ivanovich fifty years before. Mikhail Fedorovich Romanov's two envoys, Kondurev and Bormasov, on their way to the sultan, were detained by the Don Cossacks and the tsar's subsidy was forcibly removed from them; the Cossacks would give no undertaking to the tsar to observe the peace, and they were subsequently denounced by the envoys, both to the sultan and to the tsar, as 'thieves responsible to none'. In 1625 the tsar replied by having the Don Cossack envoy to Moscow, ataman Aleksei Staryi, and his companions imprisoned; and Mikhail sent a warning to the Don threatening fearful punishments should there be any further Black Sea raiding. This, presumably, had little effect since, in 1626, the Cossacks were raiding Kozlov and besieging Azov, while the Don Cossacks of the upper river, together with those on the Volga, were robbing Russian and Persian ships on the Volga and the Caspian. In subsequent years, in 1628–9, there were numerous attacks on Balaclava, Karas-Bazar and other Crimean townships and on the Rumelia coast.

During the years following the 1625 imprisonment of ataman Staryi there were few official dealings between Moscow and the Don, but the Don Cossacks continued to provide escorts if required, and presumably, if paid for.[4] Mikhail Fedorovich, however, was no longer referred to as the tsar by the Cossacks, but had become merely 'the grand prince'. Romanov was already following the same painful path trodden by his predecessor Godunov; for by 1630 he was forced to try and enlist Cossack help, but he did this by 'demanding that the Cossacks should aid the Turkish pasha' defending Ochakov against the Poles, to which the Cossacks replied that they were 'no servants of the sultan'.

The tsar that same year sent his *sanovnik* Ivan Karamyshev to the Don as his ambassador extraordinary, together with other Russian and Turkish envoys on their way to Azov. Karamyshev read to the Cossacks a letter conveying the tsar's displeasure together with the patriarch's warning of excommunication, and, since this left them unmoved, he changed his ground and began to threaten them with hanging and the knout. So the Cossacks killed him. Then, regretting their action, they penned a letter of apology to the tsar and sent it to Moscow by the hand of two of their more prominent members, Denis Parfenov and Kirei Stepanov; and, while they awaited the return of the deputation with a reply, they thought it advisable to cease all raiding. The messengers did not reappear, however, for the tsar had ordered the cutting of all communications with the Don. But the strain of living without raiding or fighting made the Cossacks restless, and so they moved to the Volga, the Caspian and the Yaik to prey on Russian and Persian shipping, setting the Russian *voevod* of Astrakhan at defiance. By 1632 the Don host was back plundering in the Black Sea once more.

In 1633 Mikhail Fedorovich was finally forced to come to terms with the Don since he had to have help not only in his war against Poland, particularly in the area around Smolensk where his boyars were fighting the Lithuanians, but also against the Crimean khan and part of the Nogai who had resumed their pillaging of south-east

Muscovy. The tsar released all imprisoned Cossacks and offered a renewal of the subsidy, provided that the Don Cossacks would go to war against the Tatars. This was the sort of proposal that the Don host liked to hear, and that year Don Cossacks penetrated south-eastwards from the Don towards Caucasia, the home of the Little Nogai. The tsar ordered that a large force be assembled in the south, made up of about 20,000 men, a mixed collection of Russian troops, some hired Edisan and Nogai Tatars, Circassian and Daghestan Cossack mercenaries of various types, and Grebensk, Terek and Don Cossacks under the princes Vasilii Turenin and Petr Volkonskii; its task was to advance to the south-east and isolate the Crimean khan from his newly found ally, the Kazyev *ulus* of the Nogai that he had succeeded in detaching from an alliance with Muscovy.

The Don Cossacks carried out their part in this new war by deep raiding that took them to the foothills of the Caucasus and to the Caspian. In 1633 they fell on part of the Kazyev Nogai that had just arrived in a fresh pasture land between the Don and Kalanch, and they then sent a mounted party of 500 men (of which 200 were Tatars in the Don host) to assist the Russian *voevod* at Mazharsk on the river Kuma. Other Don Cossacks then moved south-eastwards towards the Terek. There they met and defeated part of the Great Nogai horde returning towards Astrakhan; the Don men took some Nogai prisoners, together with many head of cattle, and released 1,500 Russian captives. As the tsar wished to keep the friendship of the Great Nogai he ordered the release of the Tatar prisoners; but the Great Nogai (as well as the Little Nogai) had secretly committed themselves to the Crimean khan, and the next year, in 1634, they began to move from their old pasture lands to the north of the Caspian westwards to the lower Don in order to join up with the Crimean Tatars in the Tauride. To do this, however, they, their families and their herds, had to run the gauntlet of the Don Cossacks in the open country above Azov and the Don estuary.

The tsar had instructed the Don host to meet the Great Nogai as the horde approached the lower Don and try to persuade them to return to their old grazing grounds; only if all else failed were the Don Cossacks to attack these Tatars. What actually happened is not known, except that the Cossacks transported men and horses across the Don and fell on the Great Nogai by night, killing about 1,500 and taking 1,300 prisoners. Then, two months later, the Don Cossacks moved out again southwards on to the Nogai steppe where they came upon the *ulus* of the Great and Little Nogai near Chubur, made up of about 2,000 families: there the Cossacks took another 150 prisoners and released a further 800 Russian captives. In February 1635 they dispersed more of the Great and Little Nogai on the Ochakovsk peninsula (in the Caspian) taking another 900 Tatar prisoners. They then returned to the Don by way of the river Kagalnik. So it was that the Don Cossacks had succeeded in doing far more than the task allotted, for not only had they prevented the Tatars from joining the Crimean khan and moving into the Tauride pasturages so much closer to Muscovy, but they had, by 1636, finally broken the power of the eastern coalition of the Great and Little Nogai. The host then contrived to detach the Little Nogai by bribes and promises, and with these new allies attacked the Great Nogai once more, forcing this latter horde to accept Moscow suzerainty and return to the Astrakhan grazing lands. At the end of this lightning campaign the Don territories had been extended well south of the Don estuary to the river Ei.

In 1637 the Don Cossacks, with some Zaporozhian help, took Azov by storm and held it against Turkish counter-attack and siege for nearly five years; the Don host capital was moved there. At times the Don Cossacks were so hard pressed that they were forced to ask for Russian aid, aid that was not given because the tsar Mikhail Fedorovich was again trying to patch up his quarrel with the sultan Murad IV, denouncing the Cossacks once more as thieves in his letters to the Porte. In 1642 the Don host was eventually forced out of Azov and returned its capital to Razdory.

The Cossacks on the lower Don had from early times formed a solid central wedge between the Kazan, Astrakhan, Nogai, Circassian-Kabard and the Crimean Cossack hordes, and they had ringed the toe-hold of the Turk in the key area of Azov; they were thus an obstacle to the movement between the hordes and to the advance of the Turk inland. By their very presence on the Don the Cossacks were the protectors of the south-east boundary of Muscovy and offered to the tsar a ready pretext and an aid to a Russian advance to the Black Sea and the Caucasus. Moscow, at the time of the timid Mikhail Fedorovich, was not yet ready to begin the march to the south, and so it reverted once more to the Godunov role of acting as the bad stepmother to the Don Cossacks, blaming them for all its ills. The Cossacks, however, were little daunted by the tsar's change of heart and did not remain long in the service of him whom they regarded as their Russian oppressor, but, taking to arms, they once more made bold raids on the Muscovite boyars' ancestral border homes, freeing the dependent and serf population that often made off with them. Many of the nobles' petitions to the tsar in the sixteenth and seventeenth centuries were requests for assistance against the Cossacks who robbed the estates and emptied the houses and the stables for, said one complainant, 'they know good horses to a T'.

Between 1642 and 1647 the Don Cossacks were under heavy attack from the Turks that forced them, whether they liked it or not, to appeal to the tsar for help, for the Turks had advanced inland and burned to the ground the settlements of Manych, Yar, Cherkassk and Razdory. Meanwhile the Turkish artillery towers and chain barriers on the Don delta prevented the Cossacks from reaching the sea and taking the war into the Turkish homeland.[5] Then, in 1647, a mixed force of Tatar and Circassian Cossacks laid siege to the rebuilt Cherkassk (that had since 1644 become the Don capital).[6] This put the tsar in a quandary, but since he had no wish to see the Don fall into Turkish hands he was forced to send the Don Cossacks secret military supplies, together with *streltsy* and other 'volunteers'. In spite of all these difficulties and misfortunes, the Cossacks still believed themselves to be the envy of the world and strove to be independent of Moscow. They had already refused to swear allegiance to the tsar in 1645 and, two years later, when the tsar was hoping to make the aid and subsidy conditional upon binding the Cossacks closer to Moscow, the Cossacks refused even to meet his envoy. Yet, in reality, the Don host could not afford to keep up a prolonged struggle on two fronts against both tsar and sultan, particularly since the Cossacks relied upon Muscovy for trade and assistance, often for the very necessities of life.

\* \* \*

In the middle of the seventeenth century the Don Cossacks lived in thirty townships or villages, known as stanitsas or *gorodki*, on the Don and on its tributaries the Medveditsa, the Khoper, the Donets and the Zherebtsa, the number increasing by the end of the century to about 125 settlements. The main pursuits in both the upper and the lower Don were war, raiding and looting, together with cattle- and stock-raising, trapping, hunting, fishing and some salt-farming. There was no agriculture at all on the lower Don because it was associated with serfdom and regarded as incompatible with the hazardous nomadic frontier life and readiness for war; in the conditions that existed it was in fact impossible.

As in the other Cossack hosts, the host ataman, together with his deputy (esaul) and secretary, were chosen by the popular assembly (the krug) that met in the capital; these appointments were changed or extended regularly, exactly how often is not known. The men who filled these posts were usually men respected for their judgement, experience, ability and bravery, for the ataman and his council had powers of life and death in judging and punishing crimes that were committed on Don territory, though in serious cases, in time of peace, the krug would be convened to confirm judgement and sentence; in war or on campaign the ataman could order the death sentence, death being by drowning or by shooting.[7] When important matters were being discussed that concerned the whole of the Don territories, representatives from outlying areas were called in to Cherkassk, or officials were sent out from the capital to sound out opinion. If an outlying stanitsa did not, without good reason, comply with a host order, then it could be made to do so, if need be by force of arms. Settlements that were habitually troublesome, were 'nests of thieves' (presumably thieving from the host), or had been set up without the sanction of the centre, were usually set on fire by an armed party sent out from Cherkassk.

When an ataman or member of his council gave up office he was frequently retained as a starshina or elder, not only as a mark of recognition and respect but also to be available to form a consultative body, should the ataman need its services. Each outlying stanitsa similarly had its own krug that elected the stanitsa ataman and his officials who were responsible for the local government.

The Don Cossacks were not really unified into a single host until the end of the seventeenth century, and a formal recognizable pattern of relationship with Moscow did not come into being until then. Before that time the host was divided into the upper-river and the lower-river Cossacks, and although Cherkassk on the lower river was the seat of government for all Don Cossacks, in the early days the ataman of the upper river would disregard those orders coming from Cherkassk that were inapplicable to, or impractical on, the upper Don. There were, however, other divisions, social and religious, within the host, that could not be bridged by time, and these Moscow endeavoured to exploit.

The main social distinction was between the rich (and therefore the influential) and the poor, the established and the new arrivals, 'the housed' (*domovitye*) and 'the naked' (*golutvennye*). Those that had wealth tended to settle in the centre and south, particularly near Cherkassk; those that had nothing were in the outlying areas or on the upper river. Those with great herds of cattle, chattels and money had often acquired them through the warlike activities of their immediate forbears; yet in course of time their descendants often became traders, financiers or usurers, and, over the generations, lost their fire and became settled in their existence; in the next century they began to acquire house and farm property as well as moveable goods, servants and dependants and, in the final outcome, land. The other less fortunate and more numerous part of the host was the 'ragged' poor, a radical core that could be easily swayed to support any insurrections, whether directed against its own host leadership or against Moscow; among the poor late-comers were many thieves who raided caravans and towns and caused difficulties both inside the host and with Moscow. It was the support of the poor and radical *golotsy* that started the rebel Don Cossack Stenka Razin on his path of conquest in 1669: but when Razin was finally beaten by the tsarist *voevod* on the Volga and fled back to the Don, it was the Don ataman Kornilii Iakovlev who, with an armed band of the conservative and wealthy *domovitye*, hunted him down at Karalnitsk and handed him over as a captive to the Moscow government.[8] Following the Razin uprising the tsar Aleksei Mikhailovich demanded an oath of allegiance from the Don, and this time it was given because the ruling and influential Cossacks had been frightened by the destructive lawlessness within the community that threatened their own lives and interests and the discipline and integrity of the host. This oath of allegiance was renewed without question at each subsequent coronation of the tsar.

The other deep division that was to occur on the Don, as elsewhere in the Cossack hosts and in Russia, was caused by the schism in the Muscovite Greek church. The Russian advance to the Dnieper had brought to Moscow Ukrainian religious influences that caused the Patriarch Nikon to revise the form of prayers used by the established Muscovite church: the revision in itself, viewed at a distance and at a later age, appears to be without great importance, but at the time it caused such a *furor* of dissent that it gave rise to a permanent division that exists to this day, the dissenters or Old Believers (the *raskol'niki*), being persecuted, even executed, for heresy, while they themselves proved ready to take up arms against their oppressors, against what was henceforth to be known as the Orthodox church.[9]

The persecuted *raskol'niki*, after the *sobor* of 1667, sought sanctuary from Russia on the Don and with many of the other Cossack hosts. On the Don they founded a number of monasteries, mainly on the Medveditsa where they preached with such zeal that they soon gathered converts among the host, including the starshinas Samoila Lavrentev and Kirei Matveev, and plans were apparently made by them for a general insurrection together with the Yaik Cossacks in favour of the old faith. Other Don Cossacks, including the ataman Frol Minaev, opposed the Old Believers. Matveev went to Moscow with a deputation to put his case to the tsar, but there he was arrested, and Russian troops were sent to the Don in 1688 'to support the true authority'. Some of the Old Believers fortified themselves in the Medveditsa settlements that had to be taken by storm; the remainder went to the Kuma and, after asking the Crimean khan for protection, entered the Kuban, where many suffered cruel attacks from Kabard or Circassian Cossacks.[10] Others went to the Terek.

The locally elected system of clergy on the Don was changed at this time in that the host was removed from the direct, though very distant, control of the Moscow patriarch, and was put under the nearby Voronezh episcopy, the bishop there henceforth having the responsibility for vetting church appointments. Christianity was later to become an important part in the lives of most Cossacks and in the social structure of the host, and from this was to be born in the next century a child-like trust in the head of the church, the Moscow little father, the *tsar-batiushka*.

The Dutch ambassador to Russia noted in 1660 how absolutely independent were the Don Cossack rank and file, and this was, in part, bred in them by their environment and way of life. For their upbringing was not the same as that of the Russian peasant; the Great Russian patriarchal family group was already strong on the upper Don, but the Cossack elders and the parents differed from the Russian in that they went to great pains to educate the young, not only in horsemanship and in the use of arms but in matters that were applicable mainly to the steppe, awareness and observation, caution, initiative and resourcefulness, endurance, and above all in method, the keeping to a regular system of work and to a basic social and military organization. This had also been a characteristic of Tatar

Cossackdom, for the dangerous life on the steppe demanded it. The Don Cossack was already a scout and soldier long before he reached manhood and when the time came for him to join the military force of the host he was ready to take his place in the ten-man section, reasoning in the same way as his fellows and seeing the steppe through the same eyes as his section ataman, so that collective action became instinctive and military orders were unnecessary. Not for nothing did the Cossacks have the saying, referring to their ataman, 'where your gaze rests, there our eyes follow.'

In the Don host the ten-man section was called the kuren, and these messed together from a common *suma* (saddlebag) or *kasha* pot. Ten sections made the Russian hundred (*sotnia*) or squadron, this taking its name from that of the commander (the *sotnik* or esaul); sometimes half squadrons of fifty men were used for detached tasks and these were commanded by the squadron second-in-command, the *khorunzhii*, derived from the Mongolian word for an ensign; the regiment was known by the Russian description of *polk*, originally of ten squadrons, and was commanded by a colonel (*polkovnik*). The weapons used were those of the Tatar and the steppe, lance, sabre or scimitar, pistolet, arquebus or musket, and sometimes a few light cannon. Generally Don Cossacks rode Tatar fashion except with a much longer stirrup leather, and this was sufficient to give their riders a very different appearance that was noticeable on the steppe at a great distance. The horse equipment, bridlery and saddlery were entirely Tatar. The host did moreover make some effort towards improving the original breed of Mongol-Tatar ponies and increase their size by introducing foreign stallions from the Caucasus, particularly those of a Turkish or Arab strain, but with only indifferent success since large numbers of good horses were not easily to be found even in the Caucasus. It was only in the nineteenth century that a distinctive and improved breed of Don horse could be recognized.

In the first half of the seventeenth century foot service was as attractive to the young Don Cossack recruit as horsed, the majority of the foot being river and sea mariners, although they could always be called upon to fill the role of campaign infantry. But in 1660 the host informed Moscow that their lack of success in steppe skirmishing against the Tatar had convinced them that all Don Cossacks must be horsed, and from then onwards until the end of the century the Don Cossacks converted themselves into a completely horsed cavalry army. They began to concentrate even more on the mobile steppe warfare used by the Tatars, favouring surprise, speed and darkness, with the sudden scattering and concentrating, and the single line *lava* attacks, enveloping flanks and causing panic, using 'the fish-trap' (*venter'-zasad*) decoy to lure the pursuers into ambushes. They tied dried reed-bundles to their ponies for camouflage and to assist them in swimming rivers: they were expert trackers and their strength was in their elusiveness and in their ubiquity. It was probably as a result of this incessant patrolling and the putting out of a permanent outlying protective cavalry screen that life in the Don hinterland, from 1675 onwards, began to take on a less turbulent pattern. Don Cossack cavalry tactics were imitated and adopted by the other horsed hosts.

Life was often hard and wretched for these cavalry soldiers, and more so for the dependants they left behind them in the homesteads or guarding the stock. Yet they themselves rarely thought so. Rigelman, describing them as he saw them about fifty years later, said that they were 'of swarthy or ruddy complexion, bold, merry, cunning, careful, brave, proud, independent, pushing and given to mockery', and he added that 'they know little sickness, the greater part of them succumbing to accident or old age.' They liked to drink and some would squander their campaign earnings or plunder on bouts of dissipation, but habitual drunkenness was rare. When campaigning, any drunkenness could be harshly punished. Much of their valuable booty became the property of the host and part was donated to decorating their churches. In 1730 Christopher Manstein, writing just after the death of Peter the Great, said of them that 'those who had once been fugitives [from Russia] now made excellent soldiers living in a form of republic;' and, even after tsar Peter's campaigns and repressions against the Don Cossacks, Manstein could still say that 'Russia behaves towards them with circumspection— sometimes even with some meekness.'

\* \* \*

By the end of the seventeenth century the southern borders of Muscovy were steadily drawing closer to the Don territories, having reached Belgorod, that had once been wild steppe, so forcing the population there to move south to avoid serfdom. And conditions in the northern Don lands were becoming more settled and the population more numerous due to the many new arrivals. Whereas the old communities there had lived nomad lives, the new could not do so and were forced to live by agriculture and the plough, and they began to sow cereals in the upper Don valley and on the Khoper and Medveditsa. In 1690 the krug at Cherkassk sent the last of its prohibitions of agriculture 'under penalty of firing and death', and this was again ignored by the upper Don, since without a grain harvest the population would have starved. In the next century agriculture spread everywhere, even to the middle and lower Don, and land acquired a new significance; that which was not used for common pasturage began to be allotted for individual use, allotments being made by size according to the Cossack's position, influence and sometimes his wealth. And although the land still remained the property of the host, this allocating of land proved to be the first step towards the conversion of some of the larger allotments to personal holdings and, eventually, private ownership. For the rich acquired land and began to build up vast estates or *khutora*; some were like cattle ranches; other *khutora* were mixed farms or produced cereals, fruit and grapes; but all were worked by hired hands engaged from the poor or the newly-arrived. Whereas in earlier days the newcomers had been accepted, almost as a matter of course, as Cossacks and had their names entered on the rolls, so that they and their descendants would remain Cossacks as long as life lasted, a restriction began to be placed on entry into the host; many of the new arrivals had to be content with remaining peasants on Cossack lands and in Cossack employ. In this way the Don Cossacks were soon to become an exclusive and often a privileged class.

Under Peter the Great, Moscow's demands for Don Cossack military aid increased in that the Cossacks had to furnish troops for the tsar's two expeditions against Azov and then, when Azov had been taken, provide a military garrison there. But since Azov had for long been a thorn in the Cossacks' side, this service was not displeasing to them. When, in 1705, mutineers in Astrakhan wanted help from the host, the Cossacks were doubtful about supporting the insurrection; and when tsar Peter sent the Don Cossacks 20,000 rubles, then that decided the issue, and the Cossacks speedily suppressed the rebellion, receiving in 1706 a *bunchuk* standard and regalia from the monarch as a token of his esteem and affection.

In reality, however, the taking of Azov from the Turks marked the beginning of a new phase in the relationship between the tsar and the Don. For when Azov had been taken by the Russians with the aid of

Don and Ukrainian Cossacks, the immediate Turkish threat had been removed, and Moscow felt that it was in a better position to bring the Don Cossacks to heel. In 1700 there came a new Muscovite encroachment on the northern Don territories, and those Don Cossacks that lived in the northern areas of the Khoper and Medveditsa valleys were ordered by Moscow to leave their lands and resettle near Azov. In 1702 Don Cossacks were forbidden to catch fish in the lower Don and, in 1703, they were commanded to 'make a present to the state' of all stocks of dried fish: those in need on Cossack lands were ordered to take allotted work. The Cossack lands in the north continued to be crumbled away by the border boyars and by the Moscow government; in addition the starshina of the Izyum regiment (of the Slobodsk Cossacks) in the north-west was trying to get Moscow to allot him Don lands. All this the Don host suffered. But when Peter decided that he was going to revoke one of the most important privileges of the host, that of not giving up its refugees, and further demanded the return of all who had fled since 1695, the host refused to comply.

Russia was at this time fighting the Great Northern War against Sweden, and Peter was threatened by the possibility of the defection of the Ukrainian hetman Mazeppa, who was playing a double game; the Zaporozhian Cossacks, too, were of doubtful loyalty. In spite of this, Peter decided on armed action against the Don host and despatched a Russian force under Prince Iurii Dolgorukii to the Don to enforce his orders and collect runaway serfs and other fugitives. These Russian troops behaved with the greatest of brutality, particularly to the Old Believers among the Don population, and committed a trail of outrages. Many Don Cossacks left their homeland and moved on to the Terek or the Yaik.

A Bakhmutsk starshina, Kondratii Afanesevich Bulavin, with a band of Don Cossacks shadowed and attacked the Russians on the banks of the Khoper and killed Dolgorukii. Bulavin then fled to Kodak, among the Zaporozhians, and from there sent messengers to the Ukraine and the Don calling for an uprising against the tsar. The Zaporozhians could not come to a decision whether to support Bulavin, but they ignored the Ukrainian hetman Mazeppa who wanted Bulavin to be given up to the Russians. Soon there were widespread uprisings and fighting, not only among the Don and Zaporozhian Cossacks, but also in the Ukraine, and the disorders spread to Russia at Tambov, Voronezh, Borisoglebsk, Kozlov, the

Slobodsk Ukraine, and to the valleys of the Volga and the Yaik. Maksimov, the ataman of the Don Cossacks, was soon besieged in Cherkassk by rebels from his own host.

Although the Bashkir Cossacks on the middle Volga declared for Bulavin, Bulavin's uprising was doomed in that he failed to win over the Kalmyk Cossack host.[11] Bulavin had moved on Cherkassk where Maksimov had been killed, and Bulavin was elected ataman of the Don host in his stead; Cossacks were then sent north to besiege Saratov and aid the Bashkir host, but this met with failure as the Bashkirs had already been routed by a detached force of 20,000 Kalmyks that had been sent out by the great khan. Bulavin's men returned south down the Volga and took Astrakhan. Meanwhile about 1,500 Zaporozhians, defying their hetman, had left the sech in Bulavin's cause, but they were opposed by Nogai and Kalmyk Cossacks that had been won over by the tsar's envoys with presents and subsidies. The tsarist *voevod* Bakhmetev, together with the Slobodsk Cossacks and the Kalmyks, defeated Bulavin on the river Kurlak, while the Zaporozhians were driven back by the Slobodsk Cossacks to take refuge in Cherkassy in the Ukraine. Bulavin died, either by suicide or in a fight with some Zaporozhians. In 1708 Prince Vasilii Dolgorukii, the brother of the slain, moved into the Don territories with Russian troops, and the killings and burnings began again, over 7,000 Don Cossacks being executed. Some of the Don rebels under an ataman Ignata Nekrasov fled to the Kuma and then to Taman and put themselves under the protection of the Crimean khan, and from this base Nekrasov raided the Don lands. Nekrasov's men were later moved by the Turks to the Danube delta.

The Bulavin uprising and the destruction of the Zaporozhian sech in 1709 saw the end of the Don Cossacks' total independence from the tsar, and from this time onwards many of the old freedoms were marked down for destruction. The Don host lost its northern territories to Russia, and a Russian fortress called *Anna* (later *St Dmitrii*) was built on the site of Rostov on Don not far from Cherkassk.[12] The election of the host ataman was done away with and the tsar appointed Petr Romazanov as ataman 'for as long as the tsar should see fit to leave him there'. On Romazanov's death in 1718 the host was permitted to chose the ataman for the tsar's confirmation (*po vyboru voiska do ukazu*), and Vasilii Frolov was appointed; on his death in 1723 the host chose Ivan Matveev, but this selection was displeasing to the tsar, who appointed Andrei Lopatin. This policy of confirming or rejecting nominations continued under Peter's successors, and in 1738 the empress Anne appointed Danilii Efremov, a Don Cossack who was immensely rich and who owned great *khutora* throughout the territories; it was said of him that he rarely lived on the Don or went to the capital except when his duty demanded his attendance to select subordinate atamans. After fifteen years he petitioned the monarch that he be relieved of his duties and be replaced by his son Stepan.

Stepan Danilovich Efremov had an eventful tour of duty as ataman in that he had to contain the ground swell of mutiny among the Don Cossacks that was finally to erupt in the Pugachev rebellion; and Efremov was remarkable in that, rich and privileged though he was, he was not entirely out of sympathy with the aspirations and fears of the poorer Cossacks nor indifferent to the welfare of the host. His third wife Melanie Karpovna was certainly a woman of the people, for, before her marriage to Efremov, she had kept a market stall in Cherkassk; she, too, was a woman of some character. Stepan had originally been a loyal supporter of the usurping empress, the German Catherine II, but eventually he came to reject the claims and repressions of the central government. In 1772 Catherine sent General Cherepov, the oppressor of the Yaik Cossacks, to Cherkassk and he addressed the krug in the presence of the ataman. But as the address was not to the krug's liking, for the Cossacks feared that they were going to be inducted as Russian regular troops, the delegates attacked Cherepov and he had to flee for his life; this apparently amused the Don ataman. Shortly afterwards, however, Stepan Efremov was kidnapped at night from one of his outlying *khutora* by squadrons of Russian dragoons from the fortress of *St Dmitrii*, it was thought with the complicity of some unfriendly and ambitious starshinas. Efremov was spirited away to St Petersburg to stand trial on charges of treason and peculation and sentenced to death and the loss of property, this sentence being commuted by the sovereign to imprisonment for life. Efremov was sent to Pernov where he remained for many years in chains and fetters and never saw the Don or his family again. Melanie Karpovna's six children were subsequently prominent in the life of the host, one of them, Nadezhda, becoming the wife of the ataman Count Platov. Within two years of Efremov's removal the Pugachev rebellion broke out.[13]

Not only was it the policy of the Russians to remove the powers of the ataman (and the atamans themselves if they proved recalcitrant), but the position and significance of the starshinas had been radically altered when the title, that had formerly been granted by the host for life to former atamans and men of ability and substance capable of advising the serving ataman, was changed to an honorary rank that could be bestowed only by the St Petersburg government. From 1754 the allocation was decided by the military collegium that acted as an honours board.

Step by step the administration of the host territories was restructured to bring it into line with that of the empire. The Pugachev rebellion of 1773–4, much more serious and dangerous to the régime than that of Bulavin, caused the empress to revise any earlier ideas she might have had of liberalization.[14] In 1775 she reorganized the empire into provinces (*gubernii*) and districts (*uezdy*) on the basis of population strength; she patched up her earlier quarrels with the nobility and gentry, since Pugachev's rebellion had taught her that these were the only classes on whom she could rely in emergency, and she did this knowing that an improvement in the standing of the gentry could only mean the spread of serfdom. In the Ukraine peasants were already being tied to the land and by 1796 serfdom was to find a footing on the Don; this widened the gap between rich and poor.[15]

Potemkin, the favourite of the empress and the pre-eminent statesman of the time in Russia, had taken over the responsibility for all Cossack matters; in 1775 he had prepared a plan, that was agreed by Catherine, to separate the military from the civil government of the Don host. The military direction was to remain in the hands of the host ataman nominated by the central Russian government, while the civil was to be entrusted to a civil control board consisting of the ataman, two Russian-nominated starshinas, and four elected starshinas chosen for a year. The Don territories had already been divided up into *okrugi* controlling the stanitsas in the region and these were to have appointed atamans—only in the stanitsa were an elected ataman and council to remain. In each of the *okrugi* regions a starshina was appointed whose task it was to seek out Russian fugitives. All host starshinas and colonels commanding regiments were to receive Russian army ranks and the regular pay of those ranks. The central St Petersburg government at first even tried to create classes of society among the Cossacks conforming roughly to those of the empire based on the carefully segregated system of rank (*chin*) created by Peter the Great.[16] Catherine II took from the Don host the right of choosing the clergy from among their own Cossacks, and from this time onwards the clergy were kept apart as a separate group responsible to the outside bishopric.

The law of 1799, in the reign of Paul, equated all host military ranks with those of the Russian Army and introduced the principles of nobility, by which token those non-Cossacks already settled on the land were secured to it as peasants; by 1811 the larger Don landholders had about 76,000 serfs on their estates.

When Paul ascended the throne in 1796 he cancelled the Potemkin reforms on the Don and restored to the host ataman and his chancellery all its former functions. But this relative freedom was not to last for long, for from 1800 the Russian government added to the chancellery of the ataman three officials appointed by the sovereign; to this number was shortly added yet three more St Petersburg-appointed officials, to handle criminal, civil and treasury matters, so that the ataman retained only the semblance of office. In 1802, after the accession of Alexander I, the host chancellery was again re-formed on the lines of Potemkin's civil government of 1775. The reign of the mentally unbalanced Paul was long remembered on the Don, however, for his decision to send the Don Cossack secret expedition, 20,000 strong, under ataman Orlov, overland by way of Orenburg across the Kirghiz steppe to Khiva and Bokhara, to invade British India, taking with it three million rubles of state funds; every Cossack had to go, 'so that the churches were left without readers and the offices without clerks.' After Paul had been murdered the order was rescinded and the expedition, that still had not crossed the Russian frontier though it had travelled 600 versts, was recalled.

During the eighteenth, as in the seventeenth century, the Don Cossacks were used by Russia as a reserve of troops and auxiliary police. The Bulavin uprising had failed largely because of the intervention of the Kalmyk Cossack host, but by 1727 the Kalmyks were themselves unsettled and dissatisfied so that the Don Cossacks were called upon to assist in quelling disorders there. Between 1750–60 Don regiments were sent to the Yaik because of unrest. Between 1755–8, 4,000 Cossacks left the Don to deal with a Bashkir uprising. In 1767 Don Cossacks were in Saratov because of civil disorders and in 1775 in Voronezh, and they were used, together with Russian troops, to occupy and disperse the second Zaporozhian sech. In 1771 occurred the mass migration of the greater part of the Kalmyk host from the land of the lower Volga eastwards into Asia back to their Mongolian homeland, moving from Russian to Chinese soil, killing such Russians as got in their way. The Russian hosts were called to arms in a vain attempt to turn them back.[17]

When Catherine the Great died in 1796 the kingdom of Poland had disappeared following the last of the partitions in 1795. In 1783 Russia, on the pretext of restoring order, had occupied the Crimea, and, according to the British reports at the time, had massacred a considerable part of the Tatar population: much of the rest fled to Turkey. The last of the khans was forced to become firstly a Moscow pensioner, and then, when the promised pension was not paid, to take refuge with the Turks.[18] In 1787 there followed another of Catherine's wars against the Turks resulting from Turkish intrigues with the remnants of the Crimean Tatars and from Russian designs on Georgia and the Caucasus: by the treaty that ended this war, concluded in 1792, Russia received Ochakov and a frontier with the Turkish Balkans that ran on the Dniester river, while in the eastern Black Sea area Russian troops were already established on the Taman peninsula and eastwards on the north bank of the Kuban river. With the annexation of these new territories the Don Cossacks, like the Ukrainian and Zaporozhian Cossacks before them, were no longer a frontier force, since the borders had passed them by. Already the St Petersburg government was considering the forcible transportation of thousands more Don Cossack families to the Kuban.

The opening of the nineteenth century found Russia with new frontiers to be consolidated, frontiers in the south that ran along the Kuban and Terek rivers, to be defended against hosts of warlike and turbulent peoples, most of them Cossacks since time immemorial.

\* \* \*

According to the official estimate made in 1763, the Don host could raise 19,000 troops. By 1801, however, this figure had been increased to 40,000, for there was already a framework of forty-one horse and two artillery regiments in existence, although these were not necessarily held at full strength in time of peace. During the Napoleonic Wars the Don Cossacks actually put eighty-six regiments into the field totalling over 50,000 men, of which 20,000 are said to have been killed or died on campaign.[19] All the other hosts provided Cossacks for the war, though their total numbers did not come to more than a third of those found from the Don, and it was for this reason that the overall command of the Cossack corps during the 1812 winter campaign was given to Platov, the ataman of the Don Cossacks.[20] Platov commanded, in addition, numbers of other Cossack regiments made up of Tatars, Nogai, Kalmyks, Bashkirs and Kirghiz, all of which ended the war in France as part of the army of occupation.

Napoleon invaded Russia with an army of 420,000 men, crossing the Niemen in June 1812 and taking Vilna before beginning his advance on Smolensk and Moscow. Barclay de Tolly, the Russian commander-in-chief, fell back without offering battle, leaving the Cossacks to cover his withdrawal, and it was for this reason the French were unable to make any contact with the Russian main force. The Cossacks kept all movement under observation, and, as the French march was necessarily restricted to the main highway going east and did not cover the broad farm and forest area to the north and south, many Cossack vedettes and patrols were soon far in the rear of Napoleon's advance and astride the French line of communications.

The French march was rapid, reaching Vitebsk, nearly half-way to Moscow, in July; but by then serious difficulties had arisen in rationing the force. Napoleon had intended that the larger part of this vast invading army should live off the country, but provisions, stores and shelter on the line of march were being systematically fired and destroyed by Cossacks who, according to the reasoning of Caulaincourt, Napoleon's master of horse, 'cared little for Russia or its people;' the Russian inhabitants were driven out eastwards and what the Cossacks could not carry off they burned, so that the French came upon nothing but smouldering ruins and a devastated and deserted countryside.[21] Because of the large numbers of Cossacks in the French rear it became difficult to bring up those few French supply columns that had been made ready for the war; nor could the unit foragers and sutlers that fanned out from the main road in search of food bring in victuals, since they were cut to pieces by the Cossack detachments hidden in the woods and gullies. Already, in the height of summer, the French were to find that not a single soldier or a solitary wagon could be left behind.

The Cossacks generally melted away when faced by strong French forces, only to return as soon as they had passed. But even by August the French cavalry was tiring and might, on occasions, be challenged by Cossacks; for Caulaincourt noted that the Cossacks took better care of themselves and their horses than the French did, in that they did not wear their mounts out by endless skirmishing, patrolling and movement. The Cossacks spent their time standing and observing, and their horses were comparatively fresh when wanted for action; and the Cossacks proved so elusive that it was virtually impossible to capture any of them.

According to Caulaincourt, the first Cossack prisoner was taken near Gzhatsk, a little more than a hundred miles short of Moscow and not far from Borodino. The event was considered of such importance that the Cossack was brought to Caulaincourt for interrogation in Napoleon's presence. The Cossack, who was Russian-speaking and, presumably, from the Don, had lost his horse and had been found by French cavalry asleep under a tree; he was in his thirties, small—not more than five feet high—dark, with quick eyes and a very intelligent face, but not at all informative as he was distressed to find himself a prisoner, and even more so at the loss of his horse and what he called his 'little package', which the French imagined to be his plunder. Napoleon had several gold coins given to him and had him taken to the stables so that he could choose a horse that would be 'lent' to him. Thereafter the Cossack returned to Napoleon's presence, a transformed man, cheerful and talkative.

Napoleon and Caulaincourt were surprised not only at this simple Cossack's lively intelligence but also at the extent of his observation and knowledge, for he was particularly well-informed. The Cossack did not recognize Napoleon and was inquisitive as to who the stranger was, and, having been told, he was himself surprised 'that the emperor was so close to the vanguard and so exposed.' This Cossack had a very high opinion of his own value and that of his fellows, and he told Napoleon that 'in the Russian Army the Cossacks did all the fighting,' and that 'the Cossacks watched while the Russians slept.' 'The French', he thought, 'fought well, but were slack and unobservant' and that 'if the French had had Cossacks in their army, Napoleon would soon have been in China!' Napoleon was delighted with this Cossack's observations, particularly when the Cossack told him that two days previously Kutuzov had just relieved Barclay de Tolly as Russian commander-in-chief. This was news to Napoleon, who told his staff that he thought the change most probable and that Kutuzov, from the Russian point of view, would have been the obvious choice; it was a change that Napoleon welcomed because he foresaw that the Russians would soon halt their retreat and give battle. When the Cossack was pressed to explain his knowledge he said that his unit had just been visited by a Russian staff officer who had brought the news to the Cossack regimental commander.

After the taking of Moscow in mid September there was much fraternizing between that outstanding leader of French cavalry, Murat, the king of Naples, and officers of the enemy Cossacks; for these quick-witted fellows plied the Frenchman with flattery, using him as a dupe, and, as Napoleon rightly suspected, took advantage of their meetings to see what was going on in the French camp, at the same time giving Murat false information about a Russian withdrawal to Kazan. To add weight to their words these Cossacks, in addition to ringing Moscow, actually deployed a cavalry screen east of the city as if they were covering the eastward withdrawal of the main Russian army; in truth Kutuzov's main body had started to move west of Moscow on Kaluga where it was poised to prevent a French withdrawal. And while the Cossacks beguiled Murat with their tales, Napoleon himself understood the nature of the Cossack little better. For he was planning to overcome the poor rationing of his troops in the capital by forming foraging companies of Russian civilians who, armed with French looted gold and provided with carts, would go out into the surrounding countryside and purchase provisions for the *Grande Armée*. There were no civilian volunteers for this particular duty since the Russian population knew exactly what fate would await them at Cossack hands.

Meanwhile, for many hundreds of miles to the west, all French supply trains, escorts and couriers ran the gauntlet of the Cossacks. On 22 September, only fifteen miles outside Moscow, the Cossacks surprised and captured a convoy of artillery wagons together with its escort of two cavalry squadrons; two days later they took prisoner eighty dragoons of the French imperial guard near Vyazma. The French emperor lived in a twilight world of his own, refusing to allow that the couriers using the Smolensk road needed a cavalry escort; it was perfectly safe, he said, 'for he himself rode along it'. The couriers were sometimes taken and sometimes chased by Cossacks right into the suburbs of Moscow; and, thought Caulaincourt, if the Cossacks had realized the importance of their quarry they would have been more determined in keeping up the chase, but they sought only gold and, ignorant of the value of their capture, they scattered the despatches along the wayside like so much waste-paper, so that the French were sometimes able to recover them intact from the ditches.

Eventually the steady loss of the couriers and of the official letters to and from Paris made a stronger impression on Napoleon than any other reverse, and brought home to him the extent of his isolation.

As the Cossacks grew in daring they began to enter the capital by night to capture men and horses, and Napoleon became convinced that the only defence against them would be to use other Cossacks, that is to say Polish or Lithuanian-Tatar Cossacks, and he considered putting up a line of infantry blockhouses round the capital until these foreign Cossacks should arrive. Then, quite suddenly, Platov, the Don Cossack ataman, supported by 6 Russian Corps, attacked Murat at Vinkovo on the Nara and inflicted on him significant losses, the marshal being lucky to have escaped capture. Napoleon censured the swashbuckling Murat for passivity and lack of vigilance, for, said Napoleon, 'the Russians [the Don Cossacks] were much more alert and active than the French.' By this time, Napoleon had already decided to withdraw from Moscow; on 19 October began the retreat and the destruction of the *Grande Armée*.

Two Englishmen, Sir Robert Ker Porter (who had been invited to Russia by the tsar and who, in 1812, married princess Shcherbatov) and Major-General Sir Robert Wilson, in 1812 the British military commissioner with the Russian army in the field, have both left very informative descriptions of the Don Cossacks at this time. Porter described the peacetime Russian-fashion parade uniform of the dark blue jacket and very full trousers with the broad red stripe on the outside, and the high black sheepskin or lambswool cap with the red bag hanging from its top, ornamented with a chain of white worsted lace and tassels. The Cossacks' arms, said Porter, consisted of a light sabre on a broad leather belt, a pike, a pair of pistols, and a black belt across the left shoulder mounting a tin cartridge box with a pistol ramrod attached. 'An uncouth saddle was bound to the horse somewhat like a double pillow, under which was a square of oilcloth painted in various colours [to serve as a shabrack].' Porter continued: 'the Cossacks' persons, air and appointments, and the animals on which they are mounted, seem so totally at variance that you can hardly suppose a reason for so unequal a union. The men are robust and fit for service; their horses seem completely the reverse; mean in shape and slouching in motion, every limb speaks of languor and every moment you expect to see them drop down dead under their heavy burthen; but so false are these shows that there is not a more hardy animal existing: it will travel incalculable journeys and remain exposed to the heat or cold, day and night, without manifesting any sense of inconvenience. Their sustenance is of the most scanty sort.'

General Wilson's descriptions told of the Don Cossack at war, 'mounted on a very little, ill-conditioned horse that could walk at the rate of five miles an hour with ease, or dispute the race with the swiftest, the Cossack carrying a short whip on his wrist [the nagaika], for he wears no spur.' Wilson continued: 'they act in dispersion, and when they do reunite to charge, it is not in a systematic formation but *en masse* [the *lava*]. Dexterous in the management of a horse that is guided only by the snaffle, they can twist and bend their course through the most intricate country at full speed.'

This, too, was Caulaincourt's opinion, for he said of them that the Cossacks were certainly the finest light troops in the world for guarding, scouting and skirmishing; but 'when we faced up to them boldly they never offered resistance—even when [we were] outnumbered two to one; but if one should attempt to attack them singly, or charge them in scattered formation, then one was lost, for they could turn back as quickly as they could withdraw.' Caulaincourt continued: 'being better horsemen and being mounted on more responsive horses than the French, they could escape when necessary or turn back on their pursuers when it suited them. They were careful of their horses, for although they sometimes raced them or set them to long and exacting rides, they generally spared them the futile running to and fro by which we wore out our own.' Such descriptions have been used countless times about the earliest nomads and the Tatars and the Cossack hosts that followed.

Meanwhile the retreat of the *Grande Armée* continued, closely followed by Platov's Cossack corps, while Napoleon still put his faith in the expected arrival of Polish or Lithuanian-Tatar Cossacks. At the beginning of November very severe weather set in. The Cossacks pointed out to General Wilson with some satisfaction that none of the enemy's horse, except those of the Polish corps, had been rough-shod, and told him that it augured badly for the French in winter.[22] And so it transpired. The Cossack horses on the other hand were for the most part unshod; and, as a Frenchman who was fortunate enough to secure a Cossack horse noted, the point of the unshod and unfiled hoof grew downwards in the form of a claw so that the animal had a good foothold and was 'as nimble as a dog across the icy slopes'.

Cold, lack of food and cover, and sickness soon caused the French and their allies to disintegrate; those who fell out were dead men, either to cold or to the Cossacks. Platov's corps, that had been heavily reinforced from the Don, became bolder as the enemy weakened, and about a thousand Cossacks actually came by night into Napoleon's general headquarters short of Vitebsk, 'among the lines where the imperial guard were bivouacked, so that the plain and the main road became alive with Cossacks.' It needed several French squadrons to drive them off and, said Caulaincourt, 'if the Cossacks had attacked in silence, without their usual shouting, the alarm would not have been given so soon and Napoleon would certainly have been captured.'

Caulaincourt described the pitiful fate of French prisoners in Cossack hands, saying that he himself saw what stragglers had reported but what 'we had hitherto refused to believe.' The Cossacks soon tired of taking prisoners whom they would be obliged to march to the rear (and thus deprive themselves of the opportunity of taking further booty), so they merely robbed everyone, taking even the clothes they stood up in: all of these Cossacks had piles of old clothes panelled over their horses; and they carried their loot in nomad fashion, cushioned under their saddles, so that 'they could never have been so high on their horses either before or since.'[23]

General Wilson was on close terms with Platov who told him very much the same story: the Russian Cossacks were more interested in booty than killing, and in one Cossack regiment the plunder taken had amounted, on distribution, to the equivalent of eighty-four pounds sterling for each Cossack, a very large sum in those days. A Tatar Cossack regiment on the other hand had different, even quaint, standards of honesty, and was diffident about keeping captured gold and silver melted down by the enemy from church ornaments, and had offered it to Platov for return to its owners. Cossacks of the Bug, said Wilson, showed no such nicety, and were not averse to the massacring of prisoners.[24]

In this way did the Don and other Cossacks plunder their way across Europe; an immense booty found its way back to Cherkassk and its surrounds. In France, particularly, the Cossacks were blamed not only for looting but for other atrocities on the civil population, even by the historian Henri Houssaye, and probably with justification, although it is to be noted that Houssaye lays similar charges against the Prussians.

Napoleon owed his defeat in Russia to his own folly in entering unprepared upon such a gigantic task, when his own fortunes were on the wane. The *Grande Armée*, an allied force that eventually exceeded half a million men, was largely destroyed because it had not been kept provisioned, equipped or housed against the bitter winter; other than at the engagement at Smolensk, it had fought the main body of the Russian Army only once on the bloody but inconclusive field of Borodino; but it had met the Cossacks everywhere, from the opening of the war until its close, and it was principally to the Cossacks that the tsar Alexander owed his victory.

## CHAPTER 5 NOTES

1  It did not trouble the Don Cossacks that, occasionally, the Zaporozhians were in league with the Tatars or the Poles: the Zaporozhians were always assured of a welcome on the Don and many of them set up their *yurt* there, particularly in the area of the Manych and the lower Don.

2  In 1618, for example, Iurii Zakharevich Bogdanov, the tsar's envoy, brought in a great stock of goods, but wanted in return 'the loan' of 5,000 men.

3  In 1620, for example, only 100 horsemen (out of the 400 that had set out) returned from a raid against the Kazyev *ulus* of the Nogai; and in 1622 the Black Sea expedition under ataman Shilo, originally 1,500 strong, returned with only 700 men. The 1625 raids on Sinope, Trebizond and Samsonov, in which 10,000 Zaporozhians and 2,500 Don Cossacks took part, cost about 1,300 Don Cossack casualties.

4  Another envoy to Moscow, ataman Nauma Vasilev and his stanitsa of seventy, were also put in prison at this time.

5  After trying unsuccessfully to take the towers by storm, the Don Cossacks, ever resourceful, eventually, so it is said, dug a shallow canal capable of taking their boats, and so circumvented the towers and reached the sea.

6  Cherkassk, founded about 1570, was in a marsh and was often inundated by the Don, so that its roads and thoroughfares became like canals; for this reason its houses were raised above the water on stilt-like piles.

7  A campaign ataman was usually appointed for expeditions that did not involve the whole host or require the presence of the host ataman. The campaign ataman similarly had powers of life and death over the members of his force.

8  Stepan (Stenka) Razin was the ataman of a band of poor Don Cossacks who in 1667 became pirates on the Volga, Caspian and Yaik and who returned to the Don in 1669 with enormous booty from Persia. In 1670,

at the head of a large rabble force, he moved up the Volga on his way to Moscow, taking Astrakhan, Tsaritsyn, Saratov and Samara and bringing the very powerful Kalmyk Cossacks (who had just arrived from Mongolia) over to his side. Officials and landowners taken by him were tortured to death and the poor were conscripted into his Cossack army until it numbered a quarter of a million. Razin was a master of lies and propaganda and he pretended that the tsarevich and patriarch were with his forces. He was defeated at Simbirsk, fled back to the Don and was finally put to death in Moscow in 1671. His brother, another petty Don ataman who had served in the war against Poland, had been hanged by Dolgorukii in 1665 for returning to the Don without permission.

9 The Greek Orthodox church existed in Russia from the ninth century, the Russian Orthodox from 1582; the *raskol'niki* were the true orthodox, but here we will call them 'Old Believers'. Differences became very deep, the Old Believers having a fundamental objection to state control and the state appointment of clergy.

10 Most of the hosts continued to accept Old Believers and disregarded the exhortations of the Moscow government and patriarch not to do so; Old Believers that openly professed their faith were always numerous among the Cossacks; in addition there were many others that had themselves listed as Orthodox but continued to pray in their homes in the old way. Even at the end of the nineteenth century a St Petersburg-directed office existed in the Don Cossack capital 'to combat the influences of the Old Believers'. Old Believers on the Don sometimes had their own settlements or lived in a separate quarter of the stanitsas; marriages between Old Believers and Orthodox were not infrequent, however.

11 From 1616 onwards there had occurred what was in effect a second Mongol invasion of the west when part of the Kalmyk people under their own great khan, numbering perhaps half a million in all, moved out of their ancestral mid-Asian homeland in Dzungaria on a fifty year migration, cutting a path through the Kirghiz and Bashkirs, attacking the Yaik Cossack host, and eventually arriving on the lower Volga and west Caspian where they displaced the Nogai as the principal nomadic power in the area. By 1675 they were plundering the Don Cossack territories from the south-east. The Kalmyks were lamaist Cossack nomads, great warriors and excellent horsemen who brought with them the distinctive 'Roman nosed' Kalmyk pony. Short of stature and bow-legged, no Kalmyk man, woman or child would walk 200 paces if there was a pony within that distance, and they had their own distinctive manner of riding, different from that of the Tatar or Don Cossack. This Kalmyk horde was so powerful that the tsar and the Don Cossacks had to treat with it, and the Kalmyks were eventually willing to come to an agreement with Russia since they regarded the Kirghiz, Bashkirs and Tatars as their natural enemies.

12 The north Khoper was taken into Voronezh while the area of Aidar went to the Ostrogozhsk regiment.

13 Other sources of grave disquiet in the Don host were the frequent demands from St Petersburg for the resettling of Don families: e.g. 1,000

to the Terek in 1724 and 1,000 to the Volga in 1732; by 1799 3,000 families had been sent to the Kuban, this causing another uprising that had to be put down by troops.

14 Pugachev was a Cossack born on the Don who had moved to the Terek. When arrested as a trouble-maker he escaped to the Yaik where he raised a rebellion, proclaiming himself to be the tsar Peter III (Catherine's murdered husband). Like Razin, he reserved his hate for the nobility, gentry and government officials, the landowners, the rich and the owners of serfs or slaves, and their families, thousands of whom were murdered at his hands. His early successes were due to the skill with which he appealed to the masses, promising freedom to Cossacks, serfs and minority peoples and religions, and this gave him a great following among the Bashkir and Tatar Cossacks, and among Moslems and Old Believers. Pugachev's short-lived empire with its capital at Orenburg stretched from Kazan to Tsaritsyn and up the Yaik river to the Urals. Because of the support given to Pugachev by the Yaik Cossacks, Catherine decreed that the name Yaik should thereafter be obliterated; the Yaik host and river were renamed the Ural.

15 By the end of the eighteenth century it was said of the ruling class of the Don Cossacks that 'indolence, a fondness of the pleasures of the table, and debauchery in both sexes, luxury and the pride of rank, have, in great measure, banished the ancient simplicity ... all, who are able, purchase exemption from military service' (Ackermann). Pallas added that 'these people, naturally well-disposed, who furnish Russia with excellent light troops, are, notwithstanding their free constitution, crushed by the aristocracy of their chiefs and manifest more and more aversion for the service; while the wealthy and the great live in the most voluptuous indolence and debauchery.'

16 Alexander I had this modified, however, when it was realized that a widespread granting of nobility to officer ranks would break down the structure of the hosts.

17 The Kalmyks returned to Dzungaria to help their Mongolian countrymen against the Chinese; about 300,000 are said to have reached China, although countless numbers were lost on the way. Of the 100,000 that remained in the North Caucasus and on the lower Volga, many served the Russian empire in the nineteenth century in Kalmyk cavalry regiments, and numbers formed a Kalmyk component of the Orenburg and Don Cossacks. Others were assimilated as individuals or as families by the Orenburg, Ural and Don hosts.

18 This last khan Shahin-Girai found his final home in Turkish Rhodes where he was murdered.

19 Don Cossack horse regiments at this time had been reduced to either five or seven squadrons a regiment. The Don population in 1800 was reckoned at 230,000.

20 Platov had been a field ataman before the secret expedition and thereafter he became the host ataman. During his tenure of office the Don capital was moved from Cherkassk to the new town of Novocherkassk about 15 miles north of the Don.

21 Although this was the normal Cossack way of campaigning on their own account, the incendiaries were of course acting under Russian orders, as Caulaincourt was eventually to find when he came upon the proof of the Cossacks' diligence and ingenuity in laying out inflammable materials long before a Russian withdrawal.

22 The rough-shodding of horses was the fitting of metal shoes with the nail-heads protruding, so that the animals could keep their footing on ice.

23 Although the Don Cossacks became sated with killing, the fate of the wretches that they robbed was no different, either from cold or at the hands of the civil population.

24 It is uncertain whether Wilson meant the Bug or the Budzhak host.

# 6 Caucasian Cossacks

At the beginning of the eighteenth century the southern frontiers of the Russian empire were little altered from the borders of Muscovy as they had stood in 1584 at the time of the death of Ivan the Terrible, except that Peter the Great had annexed to Russia the territories of the Zaporozhians. The Crimean Tatars and the Turks still ruled over the Crimea and the broad steppe to the north of the Black Sea running from Edisan in the west through the Tauride to the estuary of the Don. In the Caucasus, the Crimean and Nogai Tatars occupied the broad plain between the Don and the Kuban rivers and roamed as far east as the Terek estuary; and the Ottoman empire claimed suzerainty over all the mountain peoples between the Black Sea coastal fortress of Anapa in the west and the Caspian in the east, although this overlordship was challenged not only by many of the Caucasian hill tribes but also by the Persian empire that bordered on the west coast of the Caspian against Erivan and Daghestan. In reality the Turkish control did not extend beyond the coastal towns.

The Russian empire at this time ended at Astrakhan except for its tiny foothold on the Terek on the west shore of the Caspian, a narrow strip of the Terek and Sunzha basins that reached hardly more than 100 miles inland. Between the Terek Cossacks and the Don Cossacks, nearly 400 miles to the north-west, lay the open steppe of the Nogai and the Kalmyk, so that the easiest and surest route between Moscow and the Terek was by the Volga and Caspian waterway through Astrakhan. The Russian emperors were frequently at war against both the Turks and the Persians as they probed cautiously southwards into the Caucasus, with the Terek Cossacks on the one flank and the Don Cossacks on the other, repeating the old

Muscovite tactic of encroachment and colonization and using the semi-dependent Cossack hosts as their instrument. St Petersburg also put out its own agents, military, civil and even religious, to win over the diverse nations and tribes in the south, seeking alliances, offering protection, promoting discord, and trying to prise loose the Caucasian territories from the hands of the Tatar, Turk and Persian. Russia made alliances with these Caucasian peoples, at first secretly and then openly; then it fought the Turk or Persian in defence of these alliances; and its peace treaties with the two Moslem empires usually confirmed conditions that already existed and gains already made. Finally the territories were annexed to Russia; the annexations were then consolidated by colonization by Slav settlers while many of the native peoples were transported away from the border into the Russian interior.

In 1721, however, the only territory firmly in Russian hands was on the lower Terek.[1] Peter the Great had hoped that this distant settlement would provide Russia with a market and trading *entrepôt* in the middle east, but, by 1724, the town of Terek had already fallen into decay and its citizens were said to have numbered no more than 200 people. The tsar then ordered that a new settlement should be sited further to the south at the mouth of the river Sulak, where a branch of that river, the Agrakhan, separates from the main stream, it being intended that this colony should replace Terek. A fort, the *Sviatoi Krest*, was built near the new town that was to become Sulaksk; what was left of the old Terek garrison was transplanted, and 1,000 families were brought in from the Don, these forming the basis of the new Agrakhansk Cossack host, a host that was further reinforced from the Don territories of the Medveditsa, Khoper and Buzuluk, these latest immigrants setting up five stanitsas on the middle Koisu and on the south Sulak in north Daghestan. These stanitsas were to be repeatedly moved according to the whim of the central government.

The St Petersburg war office made energetic efforts to encourage the expansion of the Agrakhansk host and paid it substantial subsidies, much to the discontent of the surviving remnant of the Terek Cossacks that remained near the river mouth, and also of the Grebensk, who regarded themselves as the faithful defenders of the hill border, for which service they were paid little or nothing. The St Petersburg *voevod* also encouraged the native peoples to move into the valley of the Sulak and join the host, and numbers of Georgians,

13. A Siberian Cossack.
14. A Nogai Cossack
wearing the summer
melon hat without the
fur surround.
15. A Kirghiz Cossack.
Contemporary sketches
made in France at the
end of the Napoleonic
Wars of the Cossack
troops in occupation.
16. Caucasian Tatar
Cossacks (from an early
19th-century photograph).

17. A Tatar Cossack from the Caucasus armed with sabre and *kinzhal* (long dagger). The horse, bridle and saddlery are typically Tatar, with the short-stirrupped rider perched high on the mount due to clothing (and often plunder) being stowed between the saddle and numnah (from an early 19th-century photograph).

18. A Circassian Cossack with *nagaika* (flail whip), *kinzhal* and the distinctive cartridge pockets worn by most Caucasians; with the development of more modern rifles these cartridge pockets became merely ornamental.

19. A Circassian in a *burka*, the waterproof cloak of goat-hair or camel-hair, worn for centuries by Tatar, Caucasian and Russian host Cossacks.

20. Two Kabard Cossacks with a Kabard woman, the blood brothers of the Circassians (an early 19th-century photograph).

21. An early photograph of a Kalmyk Cossack family, a Mongolian ethnic group found in the Caucasus and lower Volga as well as in Central Asia.

22. A Lezghian Cossack in Daghestan (from a contemporary painting c. 1850). Caucasian horses were generally of finer appearance and breed than the Tatar ponies. The carrying of the rifle in a leather case was common to all Caucasian hillmen and Terek Cossacks.

23. *above* The *Dzhigitovka*—the display of equestrian skill that eventually became the fashion in all the Russian hosts. Here the display is by the originators, the Dzhigity, a Caucasian hill people forming part of the Abaza group living near the Black Sea coast between Sochi and Gagry (from a 19th-century painting).

24. *left* Infantrymen of the (Kuban) Cossack infantry belonging to the Caucasus Corps c. 1860.

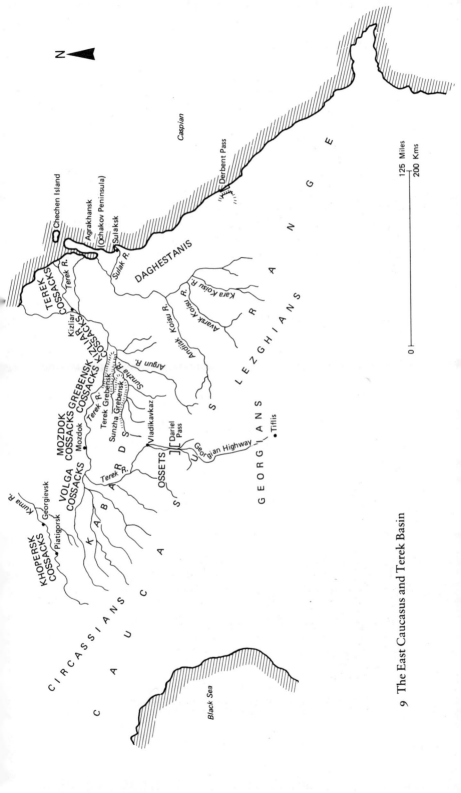

9 The East Caucasus and Terek Basin

Chechens, Armenians, Kumyk and Little Nogai did in fact do so. But the original Don Cossack settlers did not prosper because the siting of the Agrakhansk host had been done in haste; the living conditions were unhealthy and the settlers were under continual attack from Chechens and Daghestanis. By 1730, only 450 of the original 1,000 families moved by Peter the Great remained. What was left of the Agrakhansk host was then uprooted once more and moved about fifty miles from the Caspian to occupy the space between the Grebensk hill and the Terek estuary communities, where, for want of a better name, they were first known as the 'Terek family host'; they were to continue to be a charge against the Russian exchequer, not only for serving Cossacks but also for their families, as the chronicler said—'right down to the last orphan'.

In 1735 the town of Kizliar was founded in the centre of the new community and this became the capital of the transplanted Agrakhansk host that, giving up its name of 'the family host', henceforth became known as the Kizliar Cossacks. Until 1830 Kizliar was a thriving economic and political centre and had a big Armenian, Georgian and Kabard population; goods imported from Russia were sold free of tax in Cossack towns and once again the central Russian government tried hard to populate this corner of the northern Caucasus with settlers.

The defence of the outpost line south of the lower Terek river fell on these three small hosts, the Terek, Kizliar and Grebensk, but, in spite of the quickening commerce, the actual material situation of the Cossacks worsened when additional obligations were imposed on them by the Russian *voevod* or his representatives; so it was that they came to be regarded as the unpaid auxiliaries of the regular forces, for it was their duty to act as couriers, maintain roads and bridges, man the ferries and, at their own cost, find the carts and draught animals for government transportation.

In 1762 the Russian defence line on the river Terek was extended upstream to a point about 150 miles due west of the Caspian where the ruler of the Little Kabards, an ally of the Russians, had founded the new settlement of Mozdok, a Russian-subsidized colony to which a number of Kizliar settlers were sent. Three years later Mozdok became a Russian fortress and was eventually more important than Kizliar, but of the 1765 Mozdok garrison of 100 Cossack riders most were Kabards, Kumyk or other hill Caucasians, so that the St Petersburg government considered it prudent to settle more

Russian families in the immediate area. Mozdok formed the western extremity of the Russian Cossack line, for from there to Azov, about 350 miles to the north-west, was open country unsecured by fort or fortress.

Some time before, in 1732, the Don Cossacks had been ordered by the St Petersburg senate to send 1,000 families to the Volga to protect the Volga town of Tsaritsyn; only one year later these were moved to the area between Tsaritsyn and Kamyshin and became known as the Volga Cossack host. But in fact this host was not to remain long in the area of the Volga since it was to form a reserve from which the central Russian government began to draw Cossack settler cadres for transfer to the river Terek and elsewhere.

Between 1765 and 1770 over 500 Volga Cossack families were moved to the Mozdok area to form the mountain (*gorskii*) Mozdok Volga Cossack regiment in stanitsas sited along the Terek river connecting Mozdok with the downstream area of the Grebensk; this was the first of a number of independent regiments on the upper Terek and upper Kuban, outside of the existing hosts, its leader being known as the regimental colonel and not the ataman. But such was the need for numbers that 200 local Kalmyk families were also recruited into the new regiment together with large numbers of Ossets. The Mozdok regiment was probably the last to be formed that was largely Caucasian in its racial composition: east of Mozdok the Cossacks in the Russian service spoke basic Russian and prayed according to the Orthodox or Old Believer faith, yet they remained indistinguishable in their ways, their dress, their appearance and indeed in blood from the Caucasian Cossacks and mountaineers to whom they largely owed their ancestry. To the west of Mozdok, on the other hand, there were to appear new regiments of Cossacks of a markedly different type, some of them from the Don but most of them newly raised by the central Russian government from Great Russian or Ukrainian peasants or from former Ukrainian or Zaporozhian Cossack communities.

The Caucasian native peoples at that time were made up principally of four main groupings: the Circassians in the west and centre between Taman and Mozdok consisting of the Circassians proper —the Adighé, and their relatives the Abaza and the Kabards; in the centre, south of Mozdok, were the Ossets (or Osetins), the Ingush and the Chechens; further to the south-east and east lived the Avars, Kurins and other tribes that were often called collectively the

Lezghians; and finally the Daghestanis occupying the end of the Caucasus range against the Caspian coast. Together with these peoples were many lesser tribes and groupings of Tatars; for even among the Circassians and Kabards there were old Tatar family names to be found among the nobility, although the Tatar influence there was no longer strong.[2] Most of these peoples on the northern slopes and crests were of the Moslem faith, though there still remained among them numbers of Christians and heathens. From the foothills north of the mountains roamed the nomads and the semi-nomads, tribes of Moslem Nogai and Crimean Tatars, Christian Don Cossacks, and, in the north-east, the powerful lamaist Mongolian Kalmyk Cossack host stretching far and away over the lower Volga. To the south of the central Caucasus range were the Christian kingdoms of Georgia, at enmity with the northern hill peoples and with the Turks and Persians, and already looking to the Russians for help.

In the first half of the eighteenth century it was the Little Kabards north of the Terek who had borne the main brunt of the Crimean Tatar incursions and these, too, turned to St Petersburg for aid. The Great Kabards to the south, however, remained aloof until 1767 when, suspicious of the extension of the Russian line on the Terek westwards to Mozdok and of the Don Cossack deep patrols as far south as the Kuban river, they joined the Circassians and the Nogai in a Turkish-inspired conspiracy to drive out the Russians. The Don and Terek Cossacks and the Russian imperial forces in the south would have been too weak to have withstood such a coalition, and so the St Peterburg agents turned for assistance to the great khan of the Kalmyks who detached a horde of 20,000 of his riders to repulse, in 1769, the Circassians and the Kabards. The khan then withdrew his Cossacks, since he was reluctant to become committed in a Caucasian war that might have left his home *yurt* nearer the Volga vulnerable to Kirghiz attacks from the east. Whereas the Circassians retired unmolested to their mountain fortresses south of the Kuban river, the Kabards, who lived on the open northern slopes in the centre, could not do so and were obliged to come to terms with Russia. It was here that St Petersburg wanted access, for it was planning a military highway that was to run south from Mozdok to a new Cossack garrison settlement of Vladikavkaz, and from there through Osset territory over the Caucasus by way of the Dariel pass—the old Iberian gates—into Georgia. In order to do this the

Russians made local treaties and paid the princes and chieftains subsidies; the highway was, however, pushed through under duress. Before the end of the century a strong Russian force had already been established south of the mountains, and eastern Georgia was annexed to the Russian crown in 1801; from this new territory the Russian empire was rapidly expanded southwards at the expense of Turkey and Persia. Yet the range of the Caucasus, far in the Russian rear, except for the Georgian military highway through the Dariel pass, remained unsubdued for more than sixty years.

When, in 1774, Turkey had acknowledged that the Kabards and Ossets were henceforth to be under Russian control, Russia's main task was to encompass the newly acquired territories by a line of ten fortresses stretching from Mozdok to Azov, for the Kabard centre was essential to Russia not only because it gave access to the Dariel pass but also because it kept the Circassians isolated from the Lezghians and Daghestanis. Ten fortresses were rapidly constructed in 1778–9 on the Mozdok-Azov line. The Nogai and Crimean Tatars were still forces to be reckoned with, however, for they attacked the line and penetrated as far east as Mozdok and Kizliar, storming those fortresses in 1790. But in 1794 the political and territorial situation altered once more in Russia's favour since the Russians had already occupied the Crimea and, by the Treaty of Iassy that ended the Second Turkish War, had been ceded Taman and the north-west Caucasus north of the Kuban river. The old Mozdok-Azov defensive line was abandoned north-west of Stavropol and rerouted to the line of the Kuban river, and another line of forts was begun opposite the Circassian bank. Don Cossack regiments continued to patrol the north shore of the river, as they had in fact done since 1783, but they were too few to do this effectively; the pressing need was for more Cossack regiments to be sited in the border area and, in particular, for new military settlers to populate the area under the Russian flag.

West of Mozdok the frontier was virtually undefended, except by Cossack patrol activity between the weakly garrisoned fortresses, until the arrival in 1777 and 1778 of a newly formed Volga Cossack regiment of five stanitsa squadrons, in all 4,600 men, women and children, former Don Cossacks transported from the Volga who were given an area between Mozdok and Georgievsk.[3] They were followed by the Khopersk Cossacks, a five-squadron regiment exceptional in that it had its own integrated dismounted artillery unit of

160 cannoniers; the Khopersk had originated on the Don a century before but was now made up of Ukrainians, Great Russians, Kalmyks and Persians and accompanied by its 2,000 family dependants; arriving in the area of Stavropol from Azov, the regiment took up position to the west of the Volga regiment in the general area of Stavropol, the town and *guberniia* centre established by Catherine the Great in 1775.

To the north-west of Stavropol the frontier, that subsequently became known as the *Old Line*, was empty of people, though the pasture lands and forests were fruitful, with wild horses, antelope, deer, boar, hare, bear, wolf and fox; even the Nogai nomads were rarely in the area. From 1794, however, settlers began to arrive, mainly from the area of Voronezh, predominantly Great Russians though there were many Ukrainians among them, peasants, state peasants and serfs, coming in families and small communities of their own free will, without government subsidies or encouragement, in search of freedom and land. They organized themselves into settlements and chose their own headmen; there they prospered and multiplied in a way that the Cossacks had never done, so that at the turn of the century their total population exceeded 20,000, greater than that of the Black Sea host to their west. In the early days they were virtually undisturbed by Tatar or Circassian, largely because of the Khopersk regiment to their east and the Don Cossack patrols to their south; indeed the only interference they suffered was from the depredations of wandering Russian Cossacks. But eventually, before the turn of the century, these Russian peasant settlers were transformed by a St Petersburg decree into border Cossacks, being based on Don Cossack cadres brought into the area; there these peasants formed the original Kuban Cossack regiment, and they took their place in the cordon line beside the Khopersk; their senior officers and starshinas were usually Don Cossacks.

The last of the *Old Line* regiments, for the *Old Line* was merely a collection of regiments and had no parent host, was the Kavkaz (Caucasus) Cossack regiment, that was raised from the old Ekaterinoslav Cossack host in the Ukraine, sometimes known as the New Don host. The Ekaterinoslav host had been formed originally in the Ukraine in 1785 from volunteers, former Ukrainian Cossacks, peasants, serfs and slaves. In 1788 it was joined temporarily to the Bug Cossacks by which time it numbered ten regiments, each of about a thousand men, and totalled 50,000 men, women and

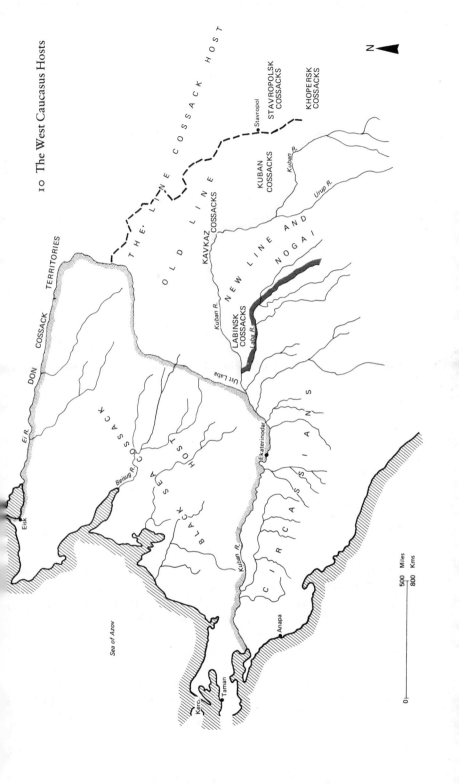

10 The West Caucasus Hosts

children. Its senior officers and starshinas came from the Don host. But the St Petersburg government had been uncertain of the use that could be made of this large Ukrainian host, particularly since the imperial frontier had moved rapidly southwards beyond the Caucasus. It was originally intended to retain the Bug Cossacks, and disband the Ekaterinoslav. But since many of the Ukrainians applied to the senate for a restoration of their Cossack status, even though this should mean transportation to the Kuban, it was agreed in 1801 to reform a part of the old Ekaterinoslav host as a new five-squadron Kavkaz regiment and move it, together with its families, to the north bank of the Kuban river, east of Ust Laba and west of the Kuban regiment, with its headquarters at Tiflisk stanitsa.

By this time the right (or western) flank of the *Old Line* was well forward at the junction of the Kuban river and its tributary the Laba, and hard against Circassian territory; but the left-flank regiments of the *Old Line*, the stanitsas of the Volga and Khopersk Cossacks, were sited in what had become the settled rear area of Stavropol: Ermolov, the Russian commander-in-chief in the Caucasus, directed that the left flank be moved southwards in 1827 to the real frontier of the upper Kuban and upper Kuma.

In the forty years from 1790–1833, the *Old Line* also numbered two detached Don Cossack regiments that rotated in turn on the Kuban cordon line forward of the *Old Line* Cossack stanitsas.

\* \* \*

The defence of the Kuban river on the west Caucasian flank between Ust Laba and the sea had meanwhile been allocated to an entirely different Cossack host, that of the Black Sea Cossacks, a reconstituted host based on the former second sech of the Zaporozhian Cossacks.

In 1783, shortly after Russia had annexed the Crimea, it became obvious that war with Turkey must break out again; in July of that year Potemkin issued a proclamation, only eight years after the dispersion of the second sech, asking for 1,000 former Zaporozhians to rejoin for service in the Ukraine, a half of them to form a boat flotilla and the remainder as squadrons of horse. A number of starshinas of the old sech were given army rank and pay in order to have them available should St Petersburg consider it expedient to reform the complete host. Then, in 1787, when war with Turkey was inevitable, these same starshinas were marshalled by Potemkin into a deputation to wait on Catherine II at Kremenchug and ask for royal assent to reconstitute the Zaporozhian host.

When Sweden entered the war as Turkey's ally there was an urgent need in St Petersburg to embody the Zaporozhians for what was to be the third time. But the former sech had become widely dispersed; many of its one-time members were in Turkey; of those that remained in the empire, some were now traders, seamen, barge-haulers, even serfs, for the old sech territories had become part of the Ukraine or of New Russia and had been broken up into landed estates and crown property. Potemkin intended to reform the host on the new style of the Don Cossacks with a ready-made aristocracy and a gentry, somewhat on Russian lines, a ruling class that would be beholden to the empire; willy nilly, he began to enlist Ukrainian and Russian landowners and their retainers, irrespective of whether or not they had once been Cossacks or Zaporozhians, adding these to the existing cadre of starshinas to form the governing framework of the new host.[4] To these were joined as many of the old Zaporozhian *seroma* that could be collected; since it was originally given out that the host would be formed in the Kherson coast area of the Black Sea, volunteers came in readily from all sides, officers from the Bug Cossacks, former Ukrainian Cossacks from the right and left banks, Great Russian fugitives, Moldavians, Bulgarians, Serbs, Albanians and Greeks, together with men from Turkey, the Danube, the Volga and Azov. At first the need was to make up numbers, but these came in so rapidly that, by September 1789, Potemkin had to issue an order for vigilance 'to exclude fugitives, serfs and army deserters'. Although the field of recruitment was so wide, probably more than fifty per cent of the total accepted were in fact former Zaporozhians.

The new host, that came to be known as the Black Sea Cossacks, was originally given an extensive area on the northern coast of the Black Sea between the Bug and the Dniester in what had, until recently, been Crimean Tatar land. Its first ataman, Sidor Belyi, was a rich starshina and former Zaporozhian. Belyi was succeeded in 1788 by Chepega, appointed by Potemkin 'for his bravery and his services and by the common wish of prominent Cossacks'. Chepega rose to the Russian rank of major-general and, on his death in 1797, the emperor Paul selected Anton Golovatyi from a list of four candidates to be ataman. Golovatyi died, however, that same year and Paul then chose Timofeev Kotliarevskii; and, in announcing the appointment, the emperor deleted the words 'by choice of the host' and changed the old traditional Zaporozhian title of *koshevoi hetman* to that of *voiskovoi ataman* to conform to that used on the Don; there was no longer any question of the Cossack hosts electing their own ataman.

The end of the war with Turkey and the terms of the 1792 Treaty of Iassy gave to Russia the western Caucasus north of the Kuban river. From this time onwards, although St Petersburg did not yet know it, Russia's main foe in the area was to be the Caucasian Cossack and mountaineer rather than the Turk. Meanwhile there was a pressing need to settle and fortify this newly acquired territory on the north bank of the Kuban river from the Black Sea to Ust Laba, a distance of about 200 miles.

The Azov coastline was well known to the Zaporozhians as they had once fished regularly from the mouth of the Kuban river to the Eisk lake, and it was decided in St Petersburg that this newly gained area should be occupied and settled by the Black Sea Cossacks; and it followed that the southern province of New Russia, that included the Tauride and the Crimea, should be extended eastwards across the Taman peninsula into the Kuban.[5] The host esaul Mokii Gulik was sent to reconnoitre, and then, in August 1792, the first party of 3,800 former Zaporozhians landed in Taman. The move was not, however, a popular one, for the starshinas and officers owned property in the Ukraine and many of the simple landless Cossacks disapproved; when a vote was taken in the settlements on the Bug, 3,300 of those who voted were said to have been in favour of the move to the Kuban, while 3,100 were against it. By the end of the year, however, 12,600 Black Sea Cossacks, including families, were already in the area.

The Black Sea host was put under the governor-general of the Tauride for civil affairs but was responsible to the Crimean-Khersonese inspectorate for military matters. The new host capital Ekaterinodar was built on the northern right bank of the Kuban river in the forward area close to enemy Circassian territory, and this was the seat of the appointed ataman and his council, that consisted of two members of the host and a legal procurator and a military 'observer' who was usually a Russian general, the two latter being appointed by St Petersburg. Then, in 1802, the host council was reconstituted according to the latest Don pattern, the two St Petersburg nominees becoming the two permanent and most important members, the rest of the council being made up of four host 'assessors' who were elected by the vote of the 150 officers (that were stationed within reach of Ekaterinodar) from prepared lists of candidates approved by the host chancellery. The Cossack other ranks took no part in the subsequent radas of the host.

The Zaporozhian kurens had been resuscitated under their old Ukrainian and Belorussian names and twenty-seven of them were in existence in the Bug-Dniester lands; these were moved to the Kuban, still called by their original names, and the number was gradually increased to the thirty-eight of the old sech. But the kurens were spread, dice-board fashion, throughout the whole of the Kuban territories from the Kuban to the Ei river more than 100 miles to the north, much too far away to be of any use in the emergency manning of the new line of fortresses and forts (cordons) that were being built along the north bank of the Kuban. Each of these kurens had an elected settlement (*sel'skii*) ataman and an 'observer' responsible for the day to day administration and defence of the area, but the control of the kuren was particularly complicated in that each settlement had another kuren ataman who lived permanently in Ekaterinodar. For the Black Sea Cossack host had reverted to the Zaporozhian sech system of holding a large garrison at the host headquarters made up of the unattached or unmarried and the unemployed (the *seroma* of former days). These lived in the usual barrack blocks, a barrack for each of the kuren, while they awaited employment or accommodation in their linked, though distant, kuren settlements, and they formed the horse squadrons or infantrymen that manned the cordon line. The kuren ataman was voted into office for a period of one year by the barrack-room Cossacks from a short list of candidates approved by the host ataman.

The kuren ataman was, in theory at least, the superior officer of the settlement ataman; in reality the two rarely met and their duties were of an entirely different nature, for the first was a soldier with no ties or responsibilities to the kuren settlement, while the second was a soldier *and* a town mayor or village headman.

This system of colonization was in stark contrast to that on the Terek or on the *Old Line* where the stanitsas were usually clustered within thirty miles of the frontier, where the stanitsa ataman or starshina was undisputed 'god and tsar' in his own domain and from where all men could reach the front from their homes or fields at very short notice. In order to rationalize the position within the Black Sea host the barrack kuren ataman was removed from the chain of command and administration during Alexander's reign, and in 1838 the kuren setttlements were renamed—Don fashion—as stanitsas, eventually increasing to about sixty in number; these were grouped under five *okrugi*, Taman, Beisug, Ei, Ekaterinodar town and Ekaterinodar province. To have solved the problem of the northern stanitsas that had been sited too far from the front would have involved redistributing the population, and this was never attempted: in consequence many male Cossacks in the north were forced to leave their homes and farms for eight or nine months in the year in order to man the cordon line.

Life in the Kuban proved to be one of poverty, hardship and danger. Whether the serfs that had been transported against their will made good settlers is open to doubt; certain it is that senior Russian officers found it distasteful to rely on indifferently trained peasants to form the backbone of the cordon defence against the wild and daring Circassian Cossacks. The military demands made on all the newly arrived colonists were very heavy, for in 1794 a string of forts had to be built along the river and mountain line, and each blockhouse required a permanent garrison of about fifty men. Soon nearly two thirds of all available male Black Sea Cossacks were always under arms. Then, in addition, further troops had to be found to go campaigning in the 1794 Polish and the 1797 Persian wars. In 1796 there was a plague and many deaths in the Kuban. Once again, as had been the case on the upper Terek and upper Kuban, the pressing need was for more settlers to occupy and open up the country and provide the men for frontier defence, and the St Petersburg government hastened to transport people, usually from the Ukraine but occasionally from Great Russia, often whole communities that were in no way Cossack, from landowners to state peasants and serfs. By 1802 the Black Sea host population numbered 23,500 based on fifteen horsed regiments and ten infantry battalions; between 1808–11 another 41,500 immigrants arrived from the Ukraine and in 1820 a further project was undertaken to find an additional 25,000 settlers.

In 1821 Major-General Vlasov (a Don Cossack) had emphasized in a report to Ermolov, the theatre commander, the wretchedness of the people; and the tsar's military favourite, Paskevich, after a tour in the Caucasus, told Ermolov what he had seen of the Black Sea Cossack poverty—a lack of basic necessities, horses, arms, even clothes on their backs, with comfortless dwelling places and untended fields, in all 'a beggarly existence'; and the main reason for it, so Paskevich considered, was the crushing weight of host military service: the population, he thought, could only decrease. Ermolov and Paskevich, who were both considered military reactionaries even in their own time, tried to organize government assistance for the immigrants.

The burden of military service was indeed heavy, particularly for the poor and the newly arrived, partly because of the disproportionate number of men that were being kept under arms and partly because many who could afford to do so found a substitute and did not serve at all; and a poor man who was under arms for long periods could only get poorer. All serving Cossacks, other than the substitutes, had to furnish their own uniform and equipment, items that became very expensive following the emperor Alexander's redesigning of Caucasian Cossack uniforms on the Russian pattern.[6] And although by law every Cossack had to belong to a kuren/stanitsa, only those with some property, that is to say the established, enjoyed a share in the division of community land; the newcomers or the absent poor who were on service, very often went without. No real improvement in their fortunes came until after 1833 when the practice of substitutes was forbidden throughout the Cossack hosts.

Another social and economic ill that grew up in the Kuban from a very early time was that of the large and wealthy estates—the *khutora*, the former *zimovniki* of the Zaporozhians and the Bug. These could only be founded, according to Cossack law, with the permission of the host, but in practice this permission was not always sought or obtained. Some of the host *khutora* were owned, managed and worked by the community, but many new estates were set up by the rich on host land as if they were private property, and these expanded and grew into cattle ranches, great farms or market-garden settlements, becoming major food producers and employers of labour, the workers being Cossacks or fugitive serfs. In 1812 there were 972 *khutora* listed in the Beisugsk and Eisk *okrugi* alone; but although these large agricultural units had great potential and could have added much to the wealth of the host, too often they encroached on other Cossack lands and enriched only a small element of the population who came to regard themselves as *khutor* owners.[7] By 1833 there were in all about 2,000 such large holdings throughout the Kuban area and their prosperity excited the jealousy of the more lawless of the poor, so that, from 1848 onwards, there were renewed outbreaks of *haidamak* violence, night attacks on the rich estates by armed bands, the same disorders that once had plagued the second sech. The refugee serfs and the fishing communities were usually blamed for the robberies, arson and other outrages, although the poorer Cossacks, too, were frequently involved.

The first host ataman appointed by the emperor Paul had been Kotliarevskii, but he, proving unsatisfactory, had been dismissed, to be replaced in 1799 by Bursak, a Zaporozhian warrior since 1764 whose name suggests that he had been recruited from a religious seminary. Bursak could not, however, get on with Paul's Russian military observer, a major-general by name of Kiraev. Kiraev apparently had the interests of the Cossack rank and file at heart for he reported to St Petersburg the many scandals he saw around him—including the 600 starshinas who drew the government subsidy and occupied all the best land but who performed no military service at all: unfortunately the rank-conscious Kiraev considered himself the most important person in the host so that he publicly censured the ataman (who at that time had the Russian army rank of lieutenant-colonel) and actually put the tsar's procurator under arrest. Kiraev was eventually removed by St Petersburg and was replaced temporarily by Dashkov who restored the authority of the ataman and chancellery.

Although Bursak was unable, or unwilling, to rectify the inequalities he saw about him, he was an experienced and vigorous campaigner against the Circassians on the other side of the Kuban river. When he retired in 1816 he recommended Matveev as his successor and this recommendation was approved by the emperor Alexander. Matveev had been a fugitive serf at the time of the formation of the Black Sea host and his mother was still a serf with the Razumovskii family and had no wish to leave their service. Matveev had risen from the ranks to command a Cossack regiment where he had served with some distinction; he was a good-natured man of excellent character, but he was generally unfitted to command the host in action, for he lacked decisiveness and the starshinas thought little of him. And, since he was without his predecessor's aggressiveness, the Circassians soon noted the change and came swarming north across the river.

The theatre command over the Black Sea host was in any event unsatisfactory since it was split between New Russia and the Caucasus; it was only remedied when the control was removed from

Lanzheron (Langeron), the Khersonese military governor, and put under Ermolov, who was both the commander of the independent Russian corps in Georgia and commander-in-chief of the Caucasus. Ermolov soon had Matveev's measure and removed him from the military command of the west Kuban line (but not from the tsar-appointed post of host ataman); Ermolov entrusted the military operations to Major-General Vlasov, a Don Cossack who was the emperor's 'observer' and permanent representative with the Black Sea Cossacks. Vlasov held this difficult post of go-between for six years until he was removed and court-martialled in 1826 by the new emperor Nicholas 'for unlawfully ravaging the lands of the Circassian Prince Sagat-Girai'. Vlasov was replaced by Susoev, another Don Cossack, who in his turn was removed, this time on charges of bribery and corruption. Ermolov thereupon had the west Kuban line, that was manned by the Black Sea host, incorporated into the North Caucasus command and the Caucasus cordon line that ran from Taman to the Caspian under a single cordon line commander, the Russian Lieutenant-General Emanuel; Emanuel was responsible directly to Ermolov. This proved to be the first step in the creation of a new Caucasus line host.

In 1827 a regimental colonel Bezkrovnyi became host ataman and was the first to take the designation 'deputy' (*nakaznyi*) ataman, but during his three-year period of office there were numerous complaints of corruption and abuses, with the members of the host chancellery laying charges and counter-charges against each other before Emanuel and Paskevich (who had succeeded Ermolov as the commander-in-chief in the Caucasus).[8] Bezkrovnyi was replaced in 1830 by Zavodovskii who remained ataman for twenty-three years; Zavodovskii was a self-taught Cossack without education or connections but with considerable political and administrative ability, whose war experience was such that the military command of the Black Sea cordon was restored to the host chancellery. Zavodovskii was a great campaigner and eventually reached the Russian army rank of general of cavalry, dying when on a foray against the Circassians: his chief of staff, Rashpil, like himself, had no formal education or training, having started his Cossack war service in the 1812 Moscow campaign when only thirteen years of age; at twenty-two he was an officer and at forty a major-general.

\*   \*   \*

The only fortresses on the Black Sea line were at Ekaterinodar and Fanagoriia at each end of the sector; in between were the hastily constructed forts (cordons) each with its little garrison, and each putting out the picquets and watch-towers that were dotted along the north bank of the Kuban. To the south of the river the enemy Circassian defences were of the same pattern as those of the Black Sea host, defended villages (auls), watch-towers and patrols; their military organization, their arms and tactics were almost identical; in dress, too, they were alike, and all Caucasians carried the nagaika. But the Circassian Cossacks were generally superior to the Black Sea men across the river since they were better mounted and were generally better horsemen; and they had, moreover, a body of dismounted sharp-shooters—as many as 300 to every 700 horse, jointly forming a 1,000-strong warrior band—and these dismounted men formed the nucleus of the ambushes and the night raids. For days they would lurk in the high reeds on either side of the Kuban river lying in wait for Black Sea patrols or for traffic using the valley road.

The Cossack horsemen of the Black Sea host were by themselves unable to counter the Circassian Cossack raids, and it soon became apparent that there was a need for artillery and good light infantry. The Russian *eger* (*jäger*) rifle regiments had shown that they were quite unsuitable for dealing with quick and unexpected attacks; the Black Sea Cossack infantry—often formed from the poorest who could not afford a horse—did little better. In 1824 it was decided, following Vlasov's recommendation, to raise a corps of infantry sharp-shooters to be recruited from hunters and marksmen with a good eye for ground, who would be trained not as Russian infantry but as skirmishers and outlying picquets, and this led to the formation and training of specialized battalions of *plastuny*—men who did not know what it was to fight in the fashion of the Russian serried ranks but who moved on their bellies and fired from behind cover. These *plastun* units were, in later years, to become a source of great pride in the host.[9]

These improvements were yet to come, for back in the 1830s matters did not stand so well. In the laying out of the kuren settlements the principal object had been to colonize the land, taking no account of how the southern boundary was to be defended. In 1823 Matveev was complaining of a lack of military system in that the regiments in the line were not linked to a single grouping of settlements that might serve as recruiting areas, but were made up of detachments from numerous scattered kurens often more than a hundred miles apart; there was some reorganization to remedy this and it was agreed that men who were on duty more than 100 versts (sixty miles) from their homes should be compensated in that they were to be paid and provisioned at the rates received by the regular army. Even so, there was poverty and sickness everywhere. And both Vlasov and Ermolov complained of Cossack disorderliness and of a complete lack of training and discipline.

In 1843, a German doctor, travelling with St Petersburg government permission and with an official Cossack escort overland along the Kuban on his way to Persia, wrote a graphic description of life on the frontier at this time. One would be lucky, said the doctor, to see twenty people in twenty miles 'in one of the dreariest regions he had ever beheld', and he considered that these descendants of the Zaporozhians could have been far from grateful to Catherine for having presented them with this land. The countryside north of the Kuban was marshy and flat, with not a hill, a rock or a wood to break the monotony of the landscape; it was in fact a vast plain that stretched to the Don, a luxuriant pasturage enamelled with flowers in summer, but in winter an endless field of snow. To the south were the towering Caucasian peaks that climbed from the very bed of the river.

The German travelled in a carriage with a small escort of Don Cossack lancers, all movement being done at a hand-canter for fear of Circassian snipers lurking in the reed beds, horses and escorts being changed about every ten miles. The doctor noted the respect, even fear, with which the Don Cossacks regarded Circassian horsemen; lances, according to them, were useless in hand-to-hand combat with swordsmen, particularly since the enemy riders and horses were more agile and swifter than those of the Don. In event of attack, the Don Cossacks told him, they intended to flee, cutting the traces of the carriage horses after first mounting the doctor on one of them. Under no circumstances did they intend to be benighted on the plain and their main preoccupation was to reach a staging post and the shelter of a fort before nightfall. The doctor, Wagner, condemned the timidity, even the cowardice, of these Don and Ural Cossacks, who, he said, would probably have fought to the death if they had been in their lancer squadrons; but for this type of warfare, when in small groups faced by a Cossack enemy bolder than themselves, they were of doubtful value. And since the Don and Ural regiments were rotated before they had served three years in the Caucasus, they were unlikely to learn the ways of the country.

The doctor had some comment, too, on the Black Sea Cossacks, noting that they had neither Great Russian, nor Tatar nor Circassian features and that they were somewhat moody, lazy, not too vigilant and were little disposed to cross the Kuban and close with the Circassians. Yet compared with the moroseness of the Russian army conscript cantonments, they were positively merry. The Black Sea Cossacks were beardless, had mustachios, wore no item of their blue uniforms except at reviews, had a Circassian cap, a slung musket without a bayonet and a long red-painted lance. Their horses were not well treated, but horses seemed to be in abundance and this seemed to account for the riders' indifference to their mounts. The officers, too, made a poor impression, and 'vodka, dice and cards were their scripture and their morning and evening prayers.' Wagner passed through Ekaterinodar, with its population of about 5,000, its houses of mud and earth (only a few being of wood), all thatched with straw, none with pretensions save that of ataman Zavodovskii; the streets were straight, broad and airy with the gardens and orchards carefully tended, though overall everything was dirty. There was a small fort in the centre of no great strength for use in an emergency, housing 800 horse and 150 foot, and a little Cossack cathedral that served also as the garrison church, 'tawdry and in poor taste and of little wealth'. The outlying stanitsa settlements had the same square form, regular broad streets, white-walled houses of mud-covered wattle and thatch, with a small stone church in the centre that also served as a fort, for there were no other defences except a prickly hedge that could easily be set on fire.

The doctor moved eastwards along the upper Kuban 'with its sentry boxes aloft on four high poles at each of the crossing places'; he then crossed to the upper Terek reaching the territories of the Grebensk, Kizliar and Terek Cossacks, and these made an entirely different and very favourable impression on him. For whereas the Cossack men and women west of Mozdok were Slav, those Cossacks between Mozdok and the Caspian were indistinguishable, apart from their language and faith, from the Circassian, the Kabard or the Lezghian mountaineer, slighter than the Black Sea Cossack, taller, more elegant, agile and supple, bolder and more intelligent; for their women, he concluded, had been Circassian or Caucasian for centuries. Their dress and arms were entirely Caucasian, even to the carrying of the carbine or rifle slung in a decorated leather case—the only Russian Cossacks to do so—and they were generally reckoned, said the doctor, to be as knowledgeable and wily as the Circassian and to be better soldiers than the Black Sea Cossacks; and just as the Don Cossacks and ponies had been superior to Napoleon's 1812 cavalry conscripts and their mounts, so were the Terek, Kizliar and Grebensk (like the Circassian) more able and agile than the Cossacks of the Don.

Tolstoy served as an army officer for a short period in the Caucasus from 1851 and, although his knowledge of the Caucasian enemy may have been limited, his observations and descriptions of the Grebensk Cossacks were exact and colourful. The Grebensk were, he thought, closer to the mountaineer enemy than to the Russian soldiers billetted in their villages, for among the men 'it was the height of style to dress like a Circassian [i.e., Caucasian]' and their Russian speech was interlaced with foreign words. Rarely did the Grebensk Cossack condescend to stay at home, and when he did so he *lounged*. Drunkenness was a rite, not a habit, and a woman was the instrument of the male's well-being; as long as she was unmarried the woman was allowed to make merry and was permitted great freedom, but when she became a wife she was expected to work till the end of her days, for the male was thoroughly oriental in his demands on her obedience and toil. The Cossack, *in the presence of strangers*, regarded it as unbecoming to gossip with or pay attention to his wife, and he professed to regard manual labour as the province of the women and the Nogai slaves. In doing this he copied not only the Nogai and the Tatar, but also the Caucasian, for the Caucasian practised lounging, indifference and nonchalance, and gave himself dignified and imperious airs; and amongst these impressive Caucasian gentlemen the Circassian was the lord of all.

Among the Grebensk Cossacks, however, the appearances did not necessarily signify the reality. The male Cossack worked, however unwillingly, for long hours in the vineyards or fields when necessity forced him to do so. The married woman, though she might keep in the background in the presence of strangers, was the centre and often the power in the household. The work, the farming, the very prosperity of the family revolved around her, and even the married women were generally unrestrained and unrestricted in their behaviour and sometimes in their morals. In the home in summer the woman wore nothing but a single shift; in winter or in the fields her clothes might be Russian or Caucasian; but for the feast days and holidays the woman's clothing was very ornate and almost entirely Caucasian, with silver or gold coin necklaces and bangles, although the Russian kerchief was sometimes worn instead of the high-mitred Caucasian head-dress.

As on the Don and the Kuban, isolated farmsteads or houses were a rarity on the Terek, and the families of the host lived side by side in the closest proximity in the fortified settlements, each day driving their cattle out to graze as they went out to work in the outlying fields where they remained from dawn to dusk, when the deserted villages came to life once more. The stanitsas were rather like those of the Black Sea host, with a main street in the centre and a gate at each end in a perimeter wall or earthworks and thorn hedge. The houses were of mud and wattle with a reed-thatch roof on high ridge poles, and, if there was any danger of flooding, the houses were usually raised on stone piles or wooden stilts.

Tolstoy and Wagner were both keen observers of what was going on around them. For the doctor's comment that the Don and Black Sea Cossack with a lance was no match for a Circassian swordsman, and that the lance was formidable only in mass, was borne out by the experience of the host. And ten years later, in 1853, the lances were removed from the Black Sea host as being 'of no use against hillmen'. The doctor had ample opportunity to mix with the Cossacks, particularly with the Don Cossack escort, and he saw the Cossacks generally as 'full of cunning and dissimulation, remarkable among a people so uncultivated'; amongst themselves Don Cossacks were friendly, courteous and talkative, but always ready to take advantage of and even rob their comrades. They had, he thought, 'a great propensity for theft, being in truth without gratitude or generosity', and being 'a people of degraded character'. Their stealing from the inhabitants of foreign lands was without shame. And yet, concluded Wagner, all Cossacks contributed much to the Russian Army, mobility, resourcefulness and elasticity, 'those qualities that were wholly lacking in the ponderous Great Russian'.

In 1832, about ten years before the German doctor's travels, there had been an extensive reorganization of both the Siberian and the Caucasian Cossack hosts. The Siberian had been reformed as a line Cossack host, of five brigades each of two regiments, in the fashion of the Russian Army: the Caucasus Cossack regiments followed suit. The Terek, Kizliar and Grebensk were transformed in 1836 into a single host and regiment—to be known as the Semein-Kizliar Cossacks; this regiment was then joined with the other independent regiments in the upper Terek and upper Kuban, the Mozdok, the Volga, the Khopersk, the Kuban and the Kavkaz (the last four each having two regiments), to form a composite Caucasus line Cossack host under its own ataman Major-General Verzilin, a Russian army general appointed on Paskevich's recommendation. There were now only two hosts manning the Caucasus cordon line between the Sea of Azov and the Caspian, Zavodovskii's Black Sea Cossacks in the west and Verzilin's line host in the east: both came under the commander of the cordon line who was himself responsible to the commander-in-chief in the Caucasus.

Meanwhile more Cossack regiments were being formed in the centre of the Caucasus line host: two regiments of Stavropolsk, the majority of the rank and file of the regiments being Slav peasant settlers; then, in 1839, two regiments of Vladikavkaz Cossacks were formed from 1 and 2 Little Russian regiments brought from the Ukraine and these were given the task of patrolling the Georgian military highway; two regiments of the Labinskii Cossacks were founded from settlers when the *Old Line* frontier was moved forward in 1841 from the upper Kuban to the Laba river (the *New Line*). Then in 1845 these sixteen regiments of the Caucasus line host were brigaded in eight brigades of two (sometimes three) regiments each, and a further three regiments (3 Labinskii and 1 and 2 Sunzhenskii) began to form that same year.[10] For the emperor was intent on raising regiments of soldiers, wherever he could find them, bracketing them together as part of the Russian military order of battle; and he had little interest in a multitude of tiny Cossack hosts and independent regiments doing guard duty on the frontier. But it *was* Nicholas's policy to attract foreign warriors, and in particular non-Russian Cossacks, to serve under the Russian colours by joining them to the imperial forces, often in privileged positions at his own capital and decorating his own court. A Crimean Tatar guard squadron, with its colourful uniforms, had come into being in 1827; in 1828 there followed a Caucasian mountaineer (*gorskii*) Cossack horse troop (expanded two years later into a guard squadron), whose Circassian dress was to set the pattern for the uniform of His Majesty's own *Konvoi*; these Moslem volunteers were handpicked

from the *gorskii* composite irregular regiment that served the
Russian command in the Caucasus.

* * *

Life in the newly formed Caucasus line host was a curious mixture of
the new and the old. On the extreme left flank the Terek, Kizliar and
Grebensk, now one host and regiment, had a tradition that extended
for nearly three centuries. Some of the regiments of the centre and
right had a history that scarcely covered three years. The line ataman
and his staff were usually army officers appointed from St Petersburg; some had barely seen a Cossack prior to arriving in their
appointments. Verzilin was an army officer; Nikolaev, the second
ataman (from 1837–48), *was* a Don Cossack; his successor
Kriukovskii was a Pole, educated by the Jesuits, a Rizhskii dragoon
officer who had, however, commanded first the Gorskii and then the
Khoperskii Cossacks before becoming ataman. On his death in 1852
he was followed by Major-General Prince Eristov, a Georgian,
educated in Tiflis before going to the imperial guard and the Russian
Army service. Rudzevich, the last ataman of the line host from
1855–60 was a Russian general and the son of a general.

The new host government consisted of the appointed ataman, a
host administrative organization and a host duty watch (*dezhurstvo*
—the operations, planning and executive staff), a military justice
commission and a trade and industry institute. The brigades and
regiments had territorial, military and local government responsibilities. At the lowest level, that of the stanitsas, the ataman or
starshina was still elected by the popular vote at the rada or krug
assembly, but in actual fact these appointments, too, were controlled
by the host ataman, and the day-to-day administration of the
stanitsas could be, and often was, closely supervised by the brigade
or regimental commanders.[11] Even in the newest regiments the
traditional institutions and procedures of the old Cossack hosts were
adopted with the fundamental difference that these had to conform
to a Russian military framework that was imposed on them from
above.

Life was dangerous and difficult on this new mountain frontier
where every male from the age of fifteen to sixty was continually
under arms and worked with his gun at hand. Major-General
Kriukovskii, the line host ataman, met his death at the hands of the
Chechens.

Further to the west, the Black Sea Cossacks, although they might claim traditions that stretched back tenuously over the centuries, were also made to conform to the Russian pattern. Zavodovskii, the last of the old Cossacks and the ataman for twenty-three years, had died on campaign and was replaced by Filipson, a Russian general, an infantryman who had never been a Cossack and who had come from the Russian Olonetskii regiment and the Russian general staff; Filipson brought in his own newly appointed host chief of staff, a Russian cavalry major-general Kusakov from 2 Carabineer regiment, and this officer was to succeed Filipson in 1860 as the last ataman of the Black Sea host. Filipson himself had had, however, considerable experience of fighting, as part of the Russian forces, south of the Caucasus.

The principal reason given at the time for the appointment of the Russian Filipson to command the Black Sea Cossack host was the dangerous position in which Russia found itself in the Caucasus at the time of the Crimean War. Although Turkey might have ceded Caucasian territory to Russia by the terms of successive peace treaties, the lands were not in Turkey's gift and, since the inhabitants recognized neither sultan nor tsar, the mountain ridges and valleys had to be fought for by those who would rule them.

The Circassians, Kabards, Chechens, Lezghians and Daghestanis were the sworn enemies of the Georgians, but were often at war amongst themselves. The Nogai Tatars had once ruled over much of the Caucasus but they were now strangers in an alien land, living among the hillmen and Kabards and often being dependent on them, for neither the Circassians nor the Turks stood on ceremony in their dealings with the Nogai. As early as 1796 the Nogai, almost panic-stricken, had been seeking Don Cossack help to remove themselves and their families northwards across the Kuban. Many Nogai and Circassian defectors, princes with retinues of some thousands of armed followers, frequently sought refuge with the Russians, and it was St Petersburg policy to befriend these fugitives and take them into the Russian or the Russian Cossack service and resettle them on host land. Many, however, subsequently became an embarrassment to St Petersburg since they had no wish to settle permanently or to take orders from a foreign host. Some were in constant touch with their Circassian Cossack relatives south of the Kuban and were suspected of acting as the ears and eyes of the raiding parties that were to follow.

There arose, moreover, a succession of Moslem religious leaders, some in the pay of the Turks and some at enmity with the sultan, but all intent on inciting a holy war against the infidel. The first of these was a Chechen, Sheikh Mansour Mohammed, who was eventually captured by the Russians in 1790; he was succeeded by even more fanatical adherents to the Muridist movement that aimed at uniting the Moslem sects and destroying all non-believers, the Mullah Mohammed and the Gazi Mullah from Daghestan, who stormed Kizliar and Vladikavkaz; and finally the Lezghian Shamyl, the most renowned of them all, who, successfully overrunning much of the Russian Cossack territories and threatening the military highway into Georgia, defied the Russian and Cossack forces for decades. The danger to the Russians became even more acute when Shamyl appointed deputies or 'Naibs' to represent him and co-ordinate the powerful Circassian tribes in the centre and the west, so that it became essential that the Russian should, come what may, retain control of Kabardia and the Dariel pass, with the dual aim of keeping the Circassians separated from Shamyl's followers in the east and of safeguarding the military route southwards into Georgia. When, in 1854, British and French warships entered the Black Sea it was no longer possible for Russia to maintain its forces south of the Caucasus by the sea route. St Petersburg ordered the evacuation of many of its naval strongholds on the Black Sea coast for fear that they should be forced to capitulate either to the allies or to the Circassians.

The Black Sea host provided a number of dismounted *plastun* battalions for the defence of Sevastopol in 1854 and 1855, but the mounted Cossack regiments that served in the Crimea were found by the Don and Ural Cossacks. Neither they nor the Russian cavalry distinguished themselves. Lord Lucan, the commander of the British cavalry in the Crimea, had been present with the Russian Army during the Turkish War of 1829, and he described the regular Russian cavalry as 'being as bad as could be' though he admitted that 'the Cossacks could be damnably troublesome to an enemy, especially in a retreat.' For the Cossack was usually more intelligent, more observant and often better educated than the Russian cavalry or infantry of the line; on the other hand the Cossack was less amenable to the harsh and rigid discipline of the Russian troops, and, notwithstanding Russian efforts to introduce cavalry discipline and order, the Cossack still kept his old frontiersman's ways with a loose and informal relationship with his leaders. On service he wore what he pleased and his mount was an unkempt, diminutive and scrubby pony little improved from those of the Tatar hordes, but still sharing with its rider an extraordinary stamina.

These characteristics, bred into the soldier by his birth and surroundings, separated the Cossack troops from the Russian mass—as the German doctor Wagner had noted just a few years before. The Russian line cavalry lacked dash and initiative; the Russian infantryman was unthinking and obstinate, a formidable foe only in defence; the Cossack, on the other hand, was observant, cautious and independent, with a highly developed instinct for self-preservation, for he saw no virtue in dying where he stood when by removing himself a verst to the rear he could continue the fight. Although the Cossack mounted regiments were organized in much the same fashion as line cavalry, they had little value for shock action since they lacked the necessary discipline and training. But, as Paskevich and Lucan were agreed, there were no better troops than Cossacks for reconnaissance, for raiding, for seeking out gaps, or for pursuit. All this was well illustrated in the Crimea.

The French troops at Evpatoria noted how they were continually under observation night and day by what appeared to be a single Cossack on a distant sky-line. All attempts to capture him or drive him off failed, for he simply withdrew at the approach of French patrols; but as soon as the French returned to camp the solitary Cossack was back at his post. The Cossack invariably had a companion just over the hill top, a spare horse and a bivouac of sorts, for the vedettes always worked in pairs; if the French made a deep raid in strength, more and more Cossacks appeared, always keeping their distance. It was impossible to rid oneself of them and impossible to escape their observation.

Yet as line cavalry the Cossacks were insignificant. On 23 October 1854, at Balaclava, two Russian hussar regiments in the centre, with Don and Ural Cossack squadrons on their flanks, were ordered to attack the thin red line of the 93rd (Sutherland) Highlanders who were standing in open country without the protection of field-works; but all of them failed to close with the Scottish infantry and they were driven off by rifle and artillery fire. Shortly afterwards the same Russian cavalry force advanced against the British heavy cavalry brigade, and Ryzhov, the commanding cavalry general there, described the flank movement of the Ural Cossacks, galloping on with a great hurrahing, still in six-deep column, 'but moving to the right of the enemy and not approaching him'; and the great silence of expectancy that fell on the battlefield (immediately before the charge of the heavy brigade) 'except for the Cossacks that continued their everlasting screaming, though they, anyway, were some good distance off.'

Later that afternoon the Cossacks were indeed engaged by British cavalry, when the British light brigade, due to an error in orders, was sent down the North Valley, without infantry or artillery support, to capture Prince Obolenskii's Don Cossack horse battery. Cardigan's light brigade of about 700 sabres approached rapidly along the valley and it soon became apparent to the Russian observers that neither case-shot nor rifle fire could stop it. Ryzhov, who was present with Obolenskii at the battery position at the valley-head, ordered forward two regiments of hussars and two of Cossacks (in all outnumbering the British by about four to one) to cover the guns. But, said one watching Russian uhlan officer, 'the Cossacks, frightened by the disciplined order of the mass of cavalry bearing down on them, did not hold, but, wheeling to their left, began to fire on their own troops in an effort to clear a way of escape'; then the whole of the Russian cavalry force in the valley fled, the majority of the Don gunners abandoning their guns and making off, mounted on horse teams and limbers.

Another witness, a Russian artillery officer called Kozhukhov, who stood at the end of the valley, said:

> The [routed] hussars and the Cossacks did not come to their senses for a very long time, for they were convinced that the whole of the enemy cavalry were still after them and they did not want to understand that they had been crushed by a comparatively insignificant handful of desperadoes. The first to recover were the Cossacks and, true to their nature, they set themselves to the task in hand—rounding up riderless English horses and offering them for sale, so that expensive blood-horses were sold for three or four half-imperials—or even less.

Ryzhov, a cavalry lieutenant-general, was afterwards censured for sending Cossacks forward to stem the charge of enemy line cavalry, for the limitations, and the strength, of the Cossack forces were well appreciated in the imperial Russian Army. In truth, however, the two Russian hussar regiments, the Ingermanlandskii and the Kievskii, did no better and fared no better than the Cossacks, that afternoon at Balaclava.

\* \* \*

The end of the Crimean War in 1856 and the capture of Shamyl in 1859 removed most of the dangers to the Russian position in the Caucasus, although fighting with the hillmen was to continue for several more years as new Cossack stanitsas were sited on newly occupied lands to the south of the Kuban and Terek. Pressure was continually being put on the hill tribes to force them to emigrate to Turkey or to resettle in the lowlands to the north of the Kuban, and attempts were made to attract the mountaineers and their families into Russian employment in ancillary military works, transport and bridge-building units, in an effort to break up the age-old feudal system and social order of the Caucasian highlands.

But the social order within the Russian Cossack hosts in the Caucasus was in itself changing. In 1848–9 there was a final wave of immigrants from Kharkov, Chernigov and Poltava, in all 12,000 people.[12] In addition, throughout the whole of the first half of the nineteenth century, there came from Great Russia a steady stream of discharged soldiers, state peasants, fugitives and deserters, and even merchants and townspeople with or without St Petersburg authority. In all, more than 100,000 people of Slav race entered the north-west area of the Caucasus between 1809 and 1850, bringing the total Black Sea host population up to 150,000.

This mass immigration gave rise to new problems, for there were no more wars to be fought, and land, once plentiful, was no longer to be had for the asking. In 1828 a census showed only sixty-two inhabitants of the Black Sea host lands who were not registered Cossacks. By 1842 the situation had so changed that very few applicants were being admitted to the Cossack host, and the new settlers, whether they were rich or *bourgeoisie*, Russian, Jewish or Armenian traders, discharged Russian soldiers or Russian and Ukrainian peasants, all had to be content to remain outside of the Cossack hosts, as *inogorodnie*, without the use of allocated Cossack lands. In theory the outlanders were not permitted to own landed property, although in fact there was nothing to prevent them from acquiring property or land by purchase. This 'outlander' population grew rapidly during the nineteenth century and eventually, at the time of the Bolshevik revolution, challenged the very existence of the hosts.

The ownership and allocation of host land even within the Cossack hosts was complicated and led to further dissension and strife. It was traditional that the private ownership of land within the host domain was irregular if not unlawful. St Petersburg, on the other hand, had encouraged the ataman and starshinas to assume the ownership of land for their private use and for that of their heirs. Many of them had taken as their own not only land but the means of production, *khutora*, mills, dams, horse studs, fish stews and the extensive brick factories to be found in the area of Ekaterinodar. Then there were the Russian and foreign merchants, contractors and prospectors who were arriving in the Kuban intent on buying up these industries and even obtaining St Petersburg granted monopolies. Oil had been found on the coast of the Azov Sea in 1834.

Agrarian and social reforms were urgently needed to relieve the poverty and sickness and remedy the many abuses. Officially there was no serfdom on the Kuban or the Terek; yet, though the numbers of serfs were not large, serfdom did exist in that Russian slaves had been purchased in Russia and transported to the Kuban by the Black Sea starshinas to become serfs on their privately-owned estates.[13] In 1838 the serfs numbered only 1,258, but their plight was often a very unhappy one.[14] Between 1842 and 1847 there was some attempt at regularizing the allocation of host land, but on the first 1842 distribution a Cossack was to have thirty desiatinas (about eighty acres) while a general was to have fifty times that amount; by 1847 these allocations had been halved as there was insufficient land to go round. In 1862, at the time of the abolition of serfdom when many of the freed serfs had, by law, to be given land, the land was reallocated by giving to each stanitsa its own *yurt*, a land reserve to be allotted to all enrolled Cossacks; this time the size of the family was taken into account when the division was made. The land hunger continued, however, not only among the Cossacks but also among the landless and moneyless outlanders for whom there was no prospect of relief.

In 1860 the two Caucasus Cossack hosts were reorganized once more and their active regiments were reduced in number, since there was no longer any need to keep large forces under arms. The Black Sea host was renamed the Kuban host and took over the western group of the Caucasus line, what had been the *Old* and the *New Line*, and included in its new peacetime order of battle the Kavkaz, the Khopersk, the Labinsk and Line regiments. The Volga, the Gorsko-Mozdoksk, the Kizliar-Grebensk, the Vladikavkaz and the Sunzha Cossack regiments went to the eastern host that was redesignated as the Terek host; the capital of the Kuban host remained at Ekaterinodar while Vladikavkaz on the Georgian military highway became the new garrison centre for the Terek host. This was the format that was to remain without significant change until 1914.

## CHAPTER 6 NOTES

1  In 1721 the Grebensk and Terek Cossacks were removed from the Russian foreign office and were put under the war office (the military collegium).

2  Some of the names of sub-tribes or clans among the Circassians were the same as those found among the Nogai: they may have originated from former Tatar chiefs or may have been political groupings.

3  The Volga Cossacks had been promised that they would be allowed to retain their old name, organization and privileges in their new homeland where they were to have the full use of all the land in their allotted area.

4  Part of the Ekaterinoslav gentry and even some of the landowners in the north along the Moscow-St Petersburg highway were listed for transfer. Many of these went most unwillingly.

5  The Black Sea Cossack area yet to be settled was bounded by Taman, the Azov Sea, the Ei river in the north and the Kuban river in the south.

6  Alexander I introduced expensive, complicated and impractical uniforms for the Caucasian hosts that came to be worn only for ceremonial parades but not for normal day-to-day duty (when the soldier wore simple Circassian dress). The cost of a foot soldier's uniform and equipment in 1833 was 111 rubles; that of a horseman with a 'reliable' horse 289 rubles. Eventually a fund-holding *artel'*, on the basis of a stanitsa or host chest, came into being, the community and the Cossacks themselves contributing cash or equipment, in order to fit out the poorest of the recruits.

7  Other unlicensed *khutora* became dens of robbers who plundered and terrorized the countryside until, eventually, armed action had to be taken against them by the host.

8  In 1827 Nicholas had designated the heir-apparent (tsarevich) as 'ataman of all the Cossack hosts'; thereafter the *de facto* ataman of the hosts was known as *nakaznyi* (or *nakaznoi*) *ataman*—literally 'ataman by delegation'.

9  The origin of the word *plastun* appears doubtful; to creep '*po-plastunski*' means to crawl, in the fashion of the *plastuny*, on one's belly using one's elbows for propulsion.

10  Regiments of the same name were grouped in the same brigades, so that the brigades became Kavkazsk, Labinsk, Kubansk, Stavropolsk, Khopersk, Volgsk: 7 Brigade had three regiments, the Gorskii and two of Vladikavkaz; 8 Brigade had the Mozdoksk and the Grebensk/ Kizliarsk.

11  In 1842 for example it came to the ears of the host ataman Nikolaev, that Baron Fitinggof (von Vietinghof), a regimental commander of the Kubansk, was interviewing all Cossack girls before betrothal. Cossack marriages were, admittedly, usually arranged between families, but Nikolaev (himself a Don Cossack) thought this procedure unusual even for Cossacks and he wrote to Fitinggof to ask why he was so wasting his time when he surely had other things to do.

12  They included, as the statistics show, a man called Moskalenko, probably better off than many, who landed in the country with his wife, four infant children under the age of seven, two horses, two carts, some sugar and meal, the clothes they stood up in, and six rubles.

13  For example the ataman Bursak had paid in Kharkov 1,950 rubles for fifty serfs of both sexes (and their progeny for all time) to staff his own privately owned *khutor*.

14  In 1839 there was the notorious case of a colonel by name of Zhivotovskii who had himself flogged to death three of his female serfs. He appears to have escaped punishment except that he was handed over to the custody of the church—presumably because he was considered to be insane.

# 7 Hosts and Hordes in Asia

When Muscovy had conquered Siberia in the sixteenth and seventeenth centuries, arriving at the Sea of Okhotsk on the Pacific in 1647, the territory overrun had been that in the north of Asia where the great rivers had made easy movement from west to east possible, and where the regions were sparsely populated by scattered and primitive peoples that were unable to bar the progress of the Russian troops and Cossacks that claimed the country for the tsar. To the south of this newly conquered Siberian empire the situation was, however, very different, for there the lands were inhabited by numerous and warlike peoples, stretching from Astrakhan in the west to Manchuria in the east, Turco-Tatar and Mongol nomads from the Caspian to Lake Baikal who still covered vast distances in their annual migrations—Cossacks everyone; yet further to the east Chinese cavalry patrolled the frontier of the river Amur to the Pacific. Just as the development of the Russian Terek and Kuban hosts had been profoundly influenced by the Caucasian Cossacks and hillmen, so did the Asiatic Russian hosts take on the life-style of the tribes and nomads against whom they fought and the habits of the indigenous people amongst whom they lived. Russian Asiatic Cossackdom developed into a line of hosts that sprang up across the waist-band of Asia from the Volga to the Amur, guarding the southern frontier of Russian Siberia—the Astrakhan host, the Yaik (Ural) host, the Orenburg, the Siberian (and, after the Russian annexation of Turkestan, the Semirechie), the Transbaikal, the Amur and the Ussuri hosts.

At the extreme west of this line, the immediate threat to Russian security in the lower Volga valley and the counter to Russian expansionism was the powerful Mongolian Kalmyk horde. The

Kalmyks were often allied with Russia and with the Don Cossacks, but the khan's alliances were brittle and their continuance often depended upon regular gifts. Each used the other in the furtherance of his own interests.[1]

To the east of the lower Yaik (Ural) river lived the Kirghiz, a very numerous nomadic people of Turco-Tatar race with some Mongol mixture, most of whom are now known collectively as Kazakhs; these occupied the area between the lower Volga and lower Yaik rivers (a region that they disputed with the Kalmyks) and they grazed for nearly a thousand miles to the east and south-east from the Caspian and the Aral to Lake Balkhash and the Pamirs, that were the home of the true or Kara-Kirghiz. The Kirghiz, the Kara-Kalpaks and the Uzbeks further to the south were part of the hordes of the earlier Mongol-Tatar empire, and the western Kirghiz (who were formerly the Sheibanide horde), together with the Kara-Kalpaks, maintain that they are of the same ethnic stock as the Nogai. In the language of the Kirghiz the name *kazak* or *kazakh*, which they use for themselves, apparently has the same meaning as the *kazak* of the Crimean Tatar or the *kazak* (Cossack) of the Russian. For the Kirghiz were all mounted nomads, with their worldly goods on the hoof or in the *kibitka* cart of the steppe.

In the seventeenth and eighteenth centuries the Kirghiz were in three hordes, the middle and little in the north and north-west, each with a population of nearly half a million, both of these bordering on Russian Siberia, and the great horde further in the interior, about which less was known. Only the great horde was entirely independent of Russia. Among the Kirghiz were to be found Shamanists and Moslems, but in general these nomads paid scant attention to their religion, caring for little beyond horses, fighting, drink and women. They had the nomad's shaved head and topknot, the old among them wore beards and the young sported mustachios, and their breed of ponies was famous throughout the steppe; they were indeed little different from Batu's hordes of four hundred years before except that they had fire-arms. The Ackermann portrait said of them:

> They are a roving and pastoral people and their wealth consists in horses, sheep, camels, oxen and cows: but, in general, they are better pleased with what they derive from pillage. They are always booted and on horseback. They are familiar with the trade of robbery which is constantly practised, and from which

25. Men of the Sevastopol Plastun Infantry of the Kuban host c. 1855 (from a photograph taken during the siege of Sevastopol).

26. A contemporary artist's impression of Kuban Cossacks in action after being surprised by Circassian Cossacks, firing from a square formation known as the *batovanie*.

27. Circassian Cossacks fleeing, after having raided the Kuban Cossack line c. 1850.

28. The Dariel Gorge (Pliny's Gateway through the Caucasus) a natural rift with 4,000-feet high walls through which flows the source of the Terek river. The Russians built the Georgian military highway, the road to the left of the picture, patrolled and kept open by Terek (Vladikavkaz) Cossacks (from a 19th-century lithograph).

29. The Georgian highway at the summit of the Dariel pass, guarded by a Vladikavkaz Cossack fort. On the flat rock high above the fort stands the remains of the legendary Georgian Queen Tamara's castle that once controlled the gap (from a 19th-century photograph).

30. An early photograph of a *telega* cart crossing the steppe south of the Don, with the Caucasus in the distance.

31. The main square in Vladikavkaz, a Terek Cossack capital and garrison town (19th-century photograph).

32. A Kuban Cossack post on the Kuban river c. 1850 (a 19th-century photograph).

33. Cossacks in Tashkent, probably Orenburg and Kuban Cossacks from the Turkestan Cossack Cavalry Division c. 1895 (from an early photograph).

34. 'The alarm' sounded by a watchman on the Kuban river by smoke signal, gun and galloper, warning of Circassian Cossack raiders (from a contemporary sketch).

35. Cossack and Russian infantry take the Daghestan village stronghold of Leturi 1858 (from a painting).

even those who live under the protection of the Russian government do not always abstain. The Kirghiz take good care not to commit any act of hostility on the frontiers of Russia when their herds are foraging there; but no sooner are their cattle in safety, than they seek quarrels, and conceal themselves in ravines, whence they sally forth upon caravans, or upon neighbouring villages.

Their enemies were any whom they could catch unaware, whether Kalmyk to the west, the Mongolian tribes to the east, or the Russian and Bashkir to the north. It was the Kirghiz peoples, occupying what are now the provinces of Uralsk, Turgai, Akmolinsk, Semipalatinsk and part of Turkestan, who formed a barrier to Russian expansion in the area north of the Caspian Sea for more than a thousand miles to the east.

The Bashkirs were another Turco-Tatar race of nomads speaking a Turkic tongue allied to that of the Kirghiz and the Meshcheryak, and they also were kinsmen of the Nogai. The Bashkirs occupied the southern area of the Ural mountains about Ufa and Orenburg, and they numbered less than half a million at that time. Like the Kirghiz they were in part Moslem, their nomadic culture and habits being those of the steppe; they made good cavalry soldiers, electing their own troop and squadron commanders in the usual horde fashion. Although in appearance much like the Kirghiz, they were, however, called by them *istaki*, or 'the dirty', and, according to Ackermann, 'it must be acknowledged that they completely justified this epithet, their character, too, being none of the best, for on a summer evening it would be hard to find a Bashkir that was sober.' But whereas Kirghiz females appear to have been little more than chattels, Bashkir women, like those of the Kalmyk, seem to have occupied a more privileged position in the social order of the family and the clan. The Russians made good use of the Bashkirs as mounted troops in their forays against the Kirghiz.[2]

To the east of the Kirghiz the population was largely Mongol, numbers of whom lived within the border of the Russian empire, the Buriats in the area of Irkutsk and Transbaikal, and the Tungus that were scattered in small groups from the Yenisei river to the Pacific ocean. The Buriats were nomads, occupied with their herds and flocks, said to be indolent and not particularly distinguished for their intellectual qualities, but hospitable, good horsemen, and

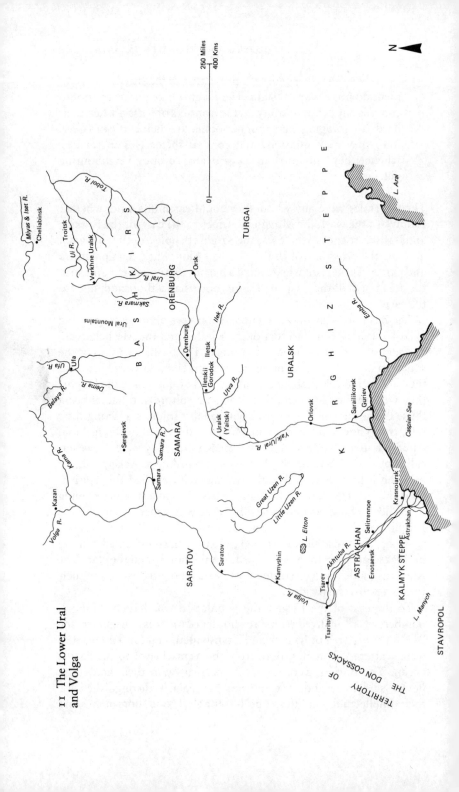

11 The Lower Ural and Volga

possessing an almost incredible stamina. The Tungus, on the other hand, were highly intelligent and resourceful and were mainly hunters, trappers, boatmen and fishermen, although there were nomads and shepherds among them. The Tungus, like the Buriats, had the same astonishing powers of endurance and, in addition, were apparently noted for their high moral qualities.[3] The majority of these Mongols were Shamanists. Both of these peoples were recruited into the Russian eastern Asiatic Cossack hosts and many of the Russian Cossacks and exiles took Mongol wives, from which sprang the cross-bred race, the *karimki*, speaking both the Russian and the Mongol tongues, claiming Russian nationality as part of the host, but displaying in their countenance the stamp of the Mongol.

All of these Asiatic peoples, principally the Buriats, Tungus, Bashkirs, Kirghiz and Kalmyks, had a pronounced effect on the growth and development of the Russian Cossacks in Siberia, since many joined the Russian hosts voluntarily, bringing their families with them. Sometimes whole squadrons, even regiments, were non-Russian; many Russians in the hosts took their wives from among the Turco-Tatar native peoples as well as from the Mongols, and this set most of the Asiatic hosts apart from the other Cossacks in their methods and customs and in their social order and values.

\* \* \*

There were Cossacks on the Volga in the area of Astrakhan from a very early date, but these were either the Volga pirates who were dispersed in 1577 by Ivan the Terrible's *voevod*, or Cossack adventurers from the upper or lower Don. By the early eighteenth century, however, the Russian settlements on the left bank of the Volga began to suffer from Bashkir penetration from the area of Orenburg, and it became obvious that the eastern frontier of Russia was open to nomad attack all along the river line Astrakhan-Tsaritsyn-Saratov-Samara and then along the Kama, since the Don and Terek Cossacks were too far away in the south to give any protection, while the Yaik Cossacks formed no more than an isolated outpost to the south-east, giving some security only against the Kirghiz. Across the Volga estuary and in the steppe to the south-west lay the Kalmyk horde; and, although its khan was kept friendly by regular payments, he was not a vassal of Russia and no reliance could be placed on him as later events were to show. For the time being St Petersburg had to be content with using the Don Cossacks and the Kalmyk horde as counter-balances to each other.

Meanwhile action had to be taken to cover the undefended Volga area against Bashkir attack by putting out an outpost line, and between 1730 and 1733 St Petersburg ordered the Don Cossacks to move 1,000 families to the north and resettle them on the Volga in the area of Tsaritsyn and Kamyshin, with patrol responsibilities stretching as far north as Saratov; from this Don Cossack nucleus the new Volga Cossacks were born. In addition, in 1737, an Astrakhan Cossack regiment was formed by decree of the senate; its strength was barely more than three squadrons, about 100 Russians and 200 Kalmyks. A few years later, in 1742, all the Kalmyks deserted in a body, taking with them their equipment and government-owned horses; to replace them all sorts of local riff-raff (sbrod) had to be taken in, and the unit became no more than an unreliable mercenary free corps without ballast since it had no cohesion, land or family settlements.

From 1750 onwards, however, steps were taken to reorganize the Astrakhan regiment on the basis of Cossack stanitsas, and the first of these was sited at Kazachebugrovsk, formed in 1757 just outside the city of Astrakhan; the unit was then expanded to 600 men and re-equipped, it being forbidden to recruit any more 'vagabonds or fugitives'. In 1764 the St Petersburg military collegium gave the regiment land for new stanitsas on the right bank of the Volga above Astrakhan reaching as far north as Enotaevsk, and from 1784 the allotment was extended yet further to take in the areas of Chernoiarsk and Krasnoiarsk. The regiment manned the steppe military posts and provided escorts for government officials and caravans.

Meanwhile the Volga Cossacks had built six stanitsas between the Volga and the Don from Kamyshin to Tsaritsyn. But the situation on the lower Volga changed radically when, in 1771, the larger part of the Kalmyk horde departed from its grazing grounds and began its long march back to Dzungaria in Central Asia, in order to aid its Mongolian kinsmen against the Chinese, leaving a trail of devastation behind it. With most of the Kalmyks gone and those that remained being either in Russian Cossack service or friendly to Russia, the future need was to contain or subdue the Bashkirs, and this could be done more effectively by reinforcing the Russian Cossack military presence in the Bashkir home territory of Orenburg. The Volga Cossacks, some of whom had come under St

Petersburg suspicion of supporting the Pugachev insurrection, were then moved by Catherine the Great to the south where they formed the Volga Cossack regiment on the upper Terek and also reinforced the Mozdok regiment. Other Volga Cossack remnants were taken into the Astrakhan regiment.

Although, with the departure of so many of the Kalmyks, there was little immediate danger on the Caspian north shore since the Yaik (Ural) Cossacks there were responsible for outpost security against the Kirghiz, the Astrakhan Cossacks were kept in being, from 1803 at a strength of three cadre regiments, finding detachments to police the Kalmyk steppe and, in addition, providing units for Russian service in Europe in 1812, against Persia in 1813, in the Caucasus in 1823 and at Baku in 1827. The Astrakhan regiment was required, also, to man a cordon patrol line that stretched from the Caspian to the Akhtubinsk river (near Tsaritsyn), from there northeast to the Elton lake and onwards connecting with the Yaik Cossacks on the Uzensk river. When the danger from the Kirghiz eventually receded, this patrol responsibility was done away with and Astrakhan Cossacks were then used to support the Caucasian line host in the south by manning a new Kuma-Manych line. In 1864, after the capture of Shamyl, this task, too, was abandoned, and the Astrakhan Cossacks became a regional patrol and police force and a Russian reserve for war.

In 1816 the peacetime regiment had been given a mounted artillery half-company of six guns, and the following year the regiment was transformed into a Cossack host, its first ataman, Skvortsov, being an Astrakhan Cossack. The new host (*voisko*) that consisted of two *okrugi* or *otdely*, had its headquarters in Astrakhan and, from 1833 onwards, came under the military governor of Astrakhan, this appointment being combined with that of host ataman. In peace only one four-squadron regiment was kept in being, with two squadrons in the capital, one out on the Kalmyk steppe with the nomads, and one being stationed at the Kalmyk khan's court. In war three regiments could be put into the field.

Towards the end of the century the Astrakhan host numbered about 26,000 souls, of which a number were Christian Kalmyks (though only 160 Moslems and 720 Old Believers were listed); in addition there were 2,800 *inogorodnie* outlanders. The whole were distributed between Astrakhan and forty-two settlements, of which eighteen were stanitsas and thirteen *khutora*. The host wealth lay in horses, cattle and sheep, fishing and salt exporting being the only other main industries.

* * *

The origin of the other host on the north Caspian shore, that of the Yaik Cossacks, is uncertain though it is generally assumed that they came from the Don in the sixteenth century as pirates, probably by way of the Volga. From 1580 they settled on the right bank of the Yaik river, from the Ilek tributary to the Caspian Sea, founding the main settlement of Yaitsk (Uralsk). The Yaik Cossacks received their first *gramota* decree from Moscow in 1591 and this is generally accepted as the date on which the host was founded. The internal structure of the *voisko* and its customs were similar to those of the Don Cossacks.

During the times of the troubles the Yaik Cossacks joined with those of the Don in their march on Moscow, and together they caused more damage within the borders of Muscovy than any of the other foreign armies. From the reign of Mikhail Fedorovich, the Yaik Cossacks began to have regular dealings with the tsar. In 1614 the rebel Cossack Ivan Zarutskii and Marina Mnishek were seized on the north Caspian by tsarist forces and the Yaik ataman Baloven, who had given them shelter and support, was hanged. In 1623 Moscow put the Yaik host on the same official standing as that of the Don, the Russian foreign office being responsible for its affairs, but from 1670 the Yaik Cossacks were subordinated to the government of Kazan, and from this time onwards the host began to provide military detachments for Russia's European wars.

In 1719 the responsibility for the host was transferred back briefly to the foreign affairs collegium and then, shortly afterwards, to the military collegium; then in 1720 it was put under the governor of Astrakhan. Three years later it was ordered that the appointing of the elected host ataman must be confirmed by the St Petersburg government.

From about the year 1700 the situation within the host had been a very unhappy one in that there had been a social split between the rich starshinas and their adherents on the one side and the poor Cossacks on the other. The starshina party included those who had wealth and influence; many of them were those whose fathers and forefathers had at one time held positions of honour or responsibility, being the loyal servants of the St Petersburg government

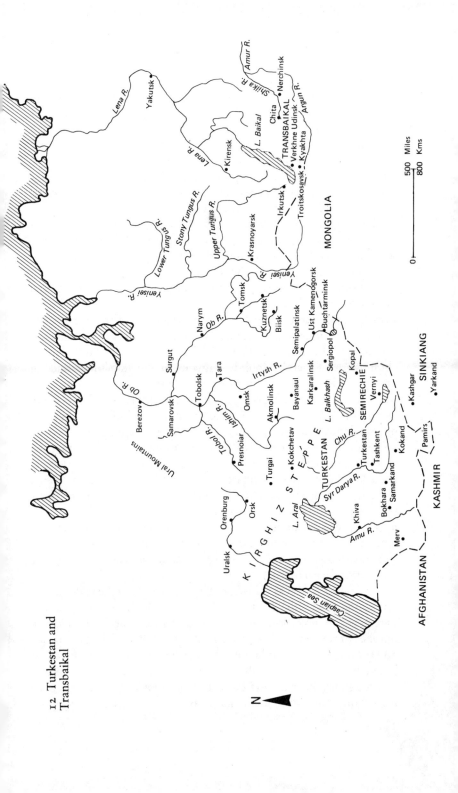

12 Turkestan and Transbaikal

from whose ranks the ataman was usually chosen. This party used host funds to their own advantage and imprisoned any who questioned their right to do so. A similar situation existed at this time on the Don. But on the Yaik the rank and file were poorer than 'the naked' on the Don and felt themselves to be more oppressed, and this had given rise to the fierce hatred between the factions. The ataman Rukavishnikov complained, in his turn, to St Petersburg about the arrogance of Russian officials: eventually he was arrested and executed by the order of the tsar.

The new ataman Merkurev was disliked by Peter the Great's foreign office collegium and had been accused of harbouring fugitives from Russian law and serfdom; the starshina party, too, had come under suspicion in the Russian capital. A number of investigators were sent from St Petersburg, one of them, a Colonel Zakharov, compiling the register that included only 3,000 names as Cossacks; but these commissioners served to exacerbate the problems since their arbitrariness and exactions caused even more bitterness among the rank and file Cossacks. Moreover the investigating commissions generally found in favour of the starshinas, and, in 1723, Merkurev was confirmed as ataman. In 1738, however, Merkurev was in trouble yet again because of more complaints made against him; the Cossacks tried to vote him out of office and in 1740 he was deposed by order of the crown; he was replaced by Prytkov and then the two brothers Borodin; the military collegium tried thereafter to alter the system of electing a single ataman, preferring the selection of three candidates, one of which would be confirmed by St Petersburg; and they proposed to introduce Russian bureaucratic and accounting methods in order to give order and stability to the host. This was not done, however, and the power was returned to the ataman, except that he was to rule through a consultative and executive council consisting of two starshinas, two esauls and a secretary-general (pisar).

In 1744 the host was transferred to the custody of the *guberniia* of Orenburg where the host had the good fortune to come under Nepliuev, an able and enlightened governor who carried out a number of reforms and improvements after having taken the host's and the *inogorodnie* outlanders' wishes into account. The governor built a line of outposts on the lower river forward of the left bank to guard against Bashkir and Kara-Kalpak attacks and had the two important but independent stanitsas of Gurev and Iletsk, both originally settled by *inogorodnie*, taken into the Yaik host; he also had the fishery regulations revised and river barriers constructed as an aid both to fishing and to the conservation of fish; and he reorganized the salt farms that were the other important source of Yaik revenue.

The country between the Volga and the Yaik rivers consisted of half-barren steppe and many salt lakes, the reddish sandy soil being more strongly impregnated with salt the further south one travelled. Except in the mud deposits of the river valley there was little agriculture, and corn had to be brought in from Samara. The steppe could, however, support livestock, and the rearing of cattle and sheep should indeed have provided great wealth, except that the Cossacks could only keep what they could protect, for all herds had to be guarded day and night from Kirghiz and Kalmyk raiders; yet some rank and file Cossacks owned as many as two or three hundred horses, the same number of horned cattle, and even more sheep, these being a mixture of the European with the large-tailed Tatar breed. Some Cossacks became traders, but most preferred the habits of a half-nomad people, the rearing of cattle, the collection of wild honey and the hunting of boar, beaver, wolf and fox and, above all, fishing.

The fisheries were controlled by strict laws and regulations since they were the main occupation and the source of the real wealth of the host; for the Yaik river was teeming with belugas of up to 800 pounds in weight, sturgeon of up to 150 pounds and white salmon in abundance, these ascending the river from the Caspian as far as the settlement of Yaitsk where they were stopped by netted booms, booms that were frequently broken by the weight of the shoals of fish in the river. The fishing season was divided into four annual fishing periods, licences to fish being given out as tickets to all Cossacks on the military service register, the ataman receiving four, the starshinas three, civil and military officers two and the rank and file one, one ticket giving one man the right to fish for a year; unwanted tickets were sold to those not on the register.

The richest fishing season was the winter one during January, usually over a 200-mile stretch of the frozen river, and it was carried out after sled races to the areas set out for the day's sport. Many hundreds of men would assemble for the fishing, all armed for fear of Kirghiz attack. On arrival at each fishing place each man would stake out his area of ice, but had to await the firing of a starting gun before sawing a hole in the surface and dropping his hooks into water said to be up to fifteen fathoms deep; many men would catch up to ten sturgeon each in the course of a day. When that area was fished out, they would be lined up to race off to the next fishing spot. The spring fishing was different, for it was done with boats and nets at the river estuary between Antonovsk and Gurev, but this was generally less rewarding than the first, even though the nets were often so weighted with fish that there was difficulty in drawing them out of the water. The October fishing harvest was meant for the Cossacks' own winter supply of food. Most of the catch of the December fishing was taken as a present to the St Petersburg court, from which the deputation commonly returned with 'a present in exchange' of a thousand rubles. Large quantities of salted fish, caviare and isinglass were exported from the Yaik.

The Yaik Cossacks had many traditional social similarities with the hosts of the Don and the Dnieper, but there were other customs that were more akin to those of the Nogai, the Bashkirs and the Kirghiz. At the great religious and political festivals the people assembled after church service and regaled themselves with brandy, dried fish, caviare and bread, using the bark of trees for plates.[4] The ataman and starshinas then drank the health of the sovereign and his family and prosperity 'to the Cossack nation', and these toasts were the signal for the commencement of drinking bouts and general drunkenness. With them, as with the Zaporozhians, any creditor might seize his debtor, tie a cord round his left arm, drag him home, tie him to a post and maltreat him until the contributions of the charitable or of his friends enabled him to discharge his debt. But, if the creditor happened to bind the right arm of his debtor, the creditor forfeited all claims, and was even liable to punishment for having prevented his prisoner from making the sign of the cross. Weddings were celebrated with Tatar dances, feasting and debauchery of every kind; and it was not uncommon for the husbands, soon after the ceremony, to sell their wives for a trifle at public auction. This barbarous practice, according to the Ackermann account, was not put down until the end of the eighteenth century. In this the Yaik differed particularly from the Don host where the strong family and marriage ties formed communities within communities, each family becoming a social and working unit made up of successive generations.

By the middle of the eighteenth century the host was receiving an annual subsidy of 7,900 rubles a year in return for which it was expected to maintain seven horsed regiments each of four squadrons. The *naemka* military conscription system on the Yaik was, however, very different from that of the other hosts, in that active duty was in the main voluntary, volunteers being reimbursed by a host fund into which all males of military age who had not volunteered for active service had to pay a graduated tax. Only when sufficient volunteers were not available was conscription applied to make up the shortfall, and then by lot. This system seemed to suit the needs both of the non tax-paying volunteer and of the taxed stay-at-home, and it was flexible according to the needs of the soldier, his family, the season and the host: the number of men unfit for service was the lowest of any host, because every Cossack made sure that his neighbour was pulling his weight either by bearing arms or by paying tax. The *naemka* system found little favour in St Petersburg, partly because the system was seen to be unfair in that each Cossack excused service paid the same rate of *naemka*, whether rich or poor (this generally meaning that only the poor served), but more particularly because large numbers of the reserve were indifferently trained since they had not been under arms long enough to have acquired any skill. The Cossacks of the host liked the *naemka* system, however, and they fiercely resisted any outside attempts to alter it.

Under Nepliuev's careful control the host knew a brief period of stability and contentment, in spite of the interference of the Bishop Luki Konashevich of Kazan who had been made responsible for religion within the host. The clergy, as in the other hosts, had always been chosen by the Cossacks from among their own number, and these were confirmed in their posts by the bishop. But, since the influence and numbers of Old Believers were strong in the Yaik as elsewhere, the bishop tried to insist that he should choose, as well as confirm, the clergy; he also prosecuted the Cossack Old Believers: this persecution was only called off in 1755 when the St Petersburg government became worried about the unrest in the Yaik host, particularly since there were also widespread disorder and violence among the Bashkirs at that time.

No sooner had the influence of Nepliuev been removed than the old hostility between the starshinas and the people's factions flared up again, aggravated because of the abuses of ataman Borodin and other officials in the spending of the host monies. In 1761 Loginev challenged the authority of the ataman and was deported. Once again investigating commissions were sent from Orenburg and the capital to hear complaints, but these, in the view of the Cossack party, were won over by starshina bribes. The government agent, Major-General Cherepov, ordered Russian troops to fire on the assembled crowds. In 1771, when the Yaik Cossacks were ordered to arms by St Petersburg to bar the progress of the march of the Kalmyk hordes eastwards to Central Asia, the Cossacks refused to obey, and a Cossack, Kirpichikov, raised a revolt. In 1772 a Russian detachment under General Traubenberg, the military commander of Orenburg, was attacked by Cossacks and Traubenberg was killed; and there were other bloody uprisings during which the ataman Tambovtsev was lynched and many starshinas were murdered. Four months later tsarist troops, that included 1,000 Kalmyks among their number, arrived under General Freiman and the rebellion was mercilessly put down with hangings, quarterings, imprisonment and exile. A Russian *kommandantura* was substituted for the host government and a garrison was put into the capital of Yaitsk; and this was the situation when the rebel Pugachev arrived in the Yaik territories. Pugachev, a Don Cossack who could neither read nor write, came to the Yaik by way of the Terek, and proclaimed that he was Peter III, the husband of Catherine II and the rightful emperor. During the three years of rebellion that followed, Pugachev campaigned against Kazan and Orenburg, but failed to take the Yaitsk capital that held out against him: he set up his own capital and court at Orenburg and, in a general reign of terror, he had scores of thousands of those whom he judged to be his enemies murdered, the wealthy, the educated and any in positions of responsibility; hundreds of towns and settlements were destroyed.[5]

Following the capture and execution of Pugachev, in 1775, the name Yaik was held to be so infamous that it was obliterated from all records and maps, the river becoming known as the Ural and the capital settlement as Uralsk. Those among the Cossacks that had remained loyal to Catherine petitioned the monarch that the host should be reconstituted as the Ural Cossacks; since these Cossacks were needed to protect the line from the Ilek river to the Caspian Sea against the Kirghiz, the petition was granted on the condition that the host should continue to be ruled by a Russian *kommandantura* aided by a starshina council, a council that was to become a collection of advisers and officials rather than the representatives of a wealthy class. The artillery was removed from the host, never to be restored, and the Russian garrison remained permanently in the territory.

Following the 1803 military reforms of all the Cossack hosts, the Ural establishment was set at ten regiments, each of five sotnias, although this was raised to twelve regiments during the 1812 war. Exact military organizations and establishments were laid down and the Russian military jacket (*mundir*) was introduced; from 1803 all Ural Cossacks were called up for service and no paid substitutes were to be allowed, but this caused such an outcry that in 1806 the *naemka* system was restored. By 1835 the Ural host conformed generally to a common *voisko* pattern except for its own traditional system of recruiting; there was, however, one further difference that set it apart from other Cossacks in that the administration of its funds and resources were concentrated at host level, none being controlled by the three districts (*otdely*) or the thirty stanitsas. The reason for this lay in the uneven distribution of resources, particularly in fisheries and good arable and grazing land, over the whole of the Ural territory; some stanitsas had an abundance while others were very poor, and the only way to compensate for this was to administer the finances centrally.

The host horses were considered to be among the best in Russia and the campaign mount was usually a cross between the native Kirghiz mare and a Kabard 'Argamakern', although many English thoroughbred stallions were also imported. The cross between the Kirghiz and the 'Argamakern' appeared very ill-looking and awkward even by Tatar standards, but was in fact superior in performance, hardiness and stamina to other Cossack pony breeds, and herds each up to 3,000 strong roamed the steppe.[6] Unlike most of the other Cossack communities the Ural *voisko* had a small surplus of horses that they sold to the other hosts.

\* \* \*

The Orenburg Cossacks did not share with the Ural a long history or wealth of tradition, for they owed their founding to military necessity and the ingenuity of their patron, Nepliuev, the governor of Orenburg on the upper Ural river. The Orenburg Cossacks were in fact service Cossacks created to continue the defensive line, already manned by the Ural Cossacks, both to the east against the Kirghiz and to the north-east against the Bashkirs. For the upper Ural river had its source in the southern end of the Ural range of mountains in the heart of the Bashkir homeland.

The town of Orenburg had been founded as a Russian military centre in 1735, and at that time the nearest Russian settlements were probably at Alekseevsk and Sergievsk, not far from the Volga city of Samara. There were also other so-called Cossack settlers, believed to be remnants of earlier Siberian expeditions, living to the east of the Urals on the Iset river, a tributary of the Tobol; these settlers were, in a 1738 order of the Orenburg military governor, given a military organization and transformed into the Iset Cossack host. Nepliuev then built a west-east line of forts from the Samara river to the Ural and the Ui (a tributary of the Tobol), extending this to the north-east in the upper reaches of the Ural valley to present-day Verchne Uralsk, a line of defensive works that was completed in 1755. The town Cossacks and part of the population from the towns and settlements of Samara, Alekseevsk, Sergievsk, Ufa and elsewhere were moved forward into what was known as the forepost line that stretched from Orenburg to the upper Ural. These settlers, together with the Iset Cossacks and Little Russian immigrants, formed, in 1755, the basis of the new Orenburg Cossack host under a single ataman. That year the original host had a military strength of about 5,000 and this had been doubled by the end of the century. The Cossack's liability for military service was from his twentieth to his fiftieth year, the register showing three categories: those on full service and full pay—the 1,300 men of 'the irregular corps' needed to man the line; then the immediate reserve that was on half-pay; and finally the mobilization or war reservists who were usually the more elderly, and were unpaid. The fact that the immediate reserve received any pay at all was a relic from town Cossack days.

In 1798 there was some reorganization to bring the host onto a more usual Cossack pattern: the irregular corps was left as a single service unit, but the remainder of the host, that is to say all the families and the male Cossacks on the half-pay or unpaid reserve, were divided into five territorial cantonments, each with its own ataman who was made responsible for both local military and civil government. That same year the male population of the city of Orenburg was formed into the Orenburg regiment, eventually expanding into four foot battalions for service in the line.

The cantonment idea was not entirely successful, however, since Russia was already extending its influence into the territory of the

Kirghiz, what is now Kazakhstan, and the cantons became too far away from the forward line. There followed a thinning out of the population of the cantons both forward to the line and further to the west to the river Ilek, to join up with the Ural Cossacks and protect the salt mines there. In 1803 the host chancellery was reformed on the pattern of the Black Sea Cossacks and the Ural Cossacks, and the irregular corps of Orenburg Cossacks on full-time service was reformed as a single regiment on the Russian regular army pattern. In 1826 and 1827 more than 13,300 discharged soldiers of the Russian Army, together with their families, were transported to join the host, and from these numbers further line battalions were raised; the host continued to grow apace by the enforced conversion of peasants and the transporting of immigrants of all types. In 1840 the armed strength of the host elements in Orenburg, Cheliabinsk and Troitsk numbered 42,000, to which were shortly added another 25,000 peasants and 10,000 discharged soldiers and, in 1842, a Kalmyk regiment of 1,700 sent from the horde at Stavropol. By this time the Orenburg host numbered ten horsed regiments, six foot battalions and two artillery batteries.

This increased Russian presence on the line of the upper Ural served to quieten the Bashkirs and the Kirghiz and, from 1845 onwards, the Kirghiz steppe was relatively peaceful. In 1835 a new forward Cossack defence line had been built from Orsk connecting up with the Berezovsk redoubt, and the former Cossack line then became known as the inner rearward line and was taken over by Russian line regiments. In 1866 the host, still subordinate to the governor of Orenburg, was divided into three *okrugi* or *otdely*, each with an ataman at its head, preparatory to being made ready for further Russian expansion into Turkestan.

The Kirghiz hordes were in fact being encircled from the north by the Russian Cossack cordons and outpost lines, all of them continually encroaching on the Kirghiz pasture lands, and this encirclement was like a great horned moon with the Ural Cossacks forming the western horn against the Caspian, with the Orenburg host joining them as part of the centre arc. The rest of the arc and the eastern horn pressing in on the Kirghiz were to be found by the Siberian Cossacks, Cossacks that were settled mainly in south-west Siberia behind the Ural mountains.

\* \* \*

The original Siberian Cossacks had been those companions of Ermak who had fled from the Volga in 1577 and who, in the service of the Stroganov brothers, had overthrown the Tatar Siberian khanate. Eventually these Cossacks had been forced to withdraw, but the movement eastwards into Siberia and across Asia had been taken up by other bands of Cossack adventurers and tsarist detachments that had founded Berezov, Surgut and Narym on the line of the Ob, arriving, at the beginning of the seventeenth century, on the river Yenisei, settling Kuznetsk on the Tom above Tomsk in 1617, Krasnoyarsk on the Yenisei in 1628, Kirensk on the Lena in 1655, Nerchinsk on the Shilka in Transbaikal in 1656 and finally arriving in the Kamchatka peninsula in 1696. In 1649, Khabarov with seventy Cossacks followed the Lena upstream from Yakutsk, arriving on the Amur where he founded the settlement of Albazin. This was destroyed by the Chinese in 1685. Four years later, by the 1689 Treaty of Nerchinsk, the Russians gave up the line of the Amur to the Chinese but continued to hold on to the Transbaikal.

At the beginning of the eighteenth century Russia's attention had been drawn temporarily towards Mongolia and Sinkiang, the Siberian governor Prince Gagarin having told Peter the Great that much gold could be found in Yarkand. The easiest approach to the area of Mongolia was upstream along the Irtysh, and new Cossack settlements were sited along its banks, at Omsk in 1716, at Semipalatinsk two years later, and, in 1720, at Ust Kamenogorsk near the Altai mountains not far from Mongolia and the Dzungarian khanate. It was this string of early Cossack settlements along the line of the Irtysh that eventually became the Siberian Cossack host. These early Siberian Cossacks differed radically from those of the Don and Yaik in that originally they had had no host and lived in widely scattered and small settlements, often in government pay as individuals, so that their status was little different from that of service or town Cossacks; even hunting and trading rights were allotted to individuals rather than to communities.

During the eighteenth century the Chinese in Manchuria and in Mongolia were regarded as the principal Russian enemies in the east, and the Irtysh line was strengthened to withstand a Chinese attack. In 1745, five Russian dragoon regiments were brought into the line and many town Cossacks in Tara, Tobolsk and Tiumen, settlements that were now rear areas, were uprooted and resettled along the upper Irtysh valley. The Irtysh between Omsk and Ust Kamenogorsk at that time formed the southern frontier with the Kirghiz: the lands to the east and south-east of Ust Kamenogorsk were under the control of the Chinese.

From 1750 onwards a line of forts was built that ran from the Irtysh valley, north-east to the Ob and then on to Kuznetsk, in order to cover the mines there from Chinese interference. In 1757 Russian attention was drawn to the area further to the south when the Chinese invaded the Dzungarian khanate, the same invasion that was to draw the Kalmyk horde back to its homeland; in consequence another defensive line was built from Ust Kamenogorsk to Biisk and a new fortress of Buchtarminskaia was constructed in 1781 in the Irtysh valley, forward and close to the Chinese frontier, and this was garrisoned with Cossacks together with a reinforcement of 2,000 discharged soldiers, who, by a few strokes of a Russian official's pen, were reclassified as Cossacks.

By the end of the century the active military strength of the Siberian Cossacks stood at only 6,000 men, and its 1808 establishment was ten regiments of five sotnias each, with a single artillery company of twelve guns. There were, admittedly, town Cossacks of Russian extraction to be found in some of the main towns and settlements in the rear areas, principally in Nerchinsk, Selengensk, Yakutsk and Okhotsk, but their numbers were not great. Because of the shortage in the Cossack strength the St Petersburg government authorized the raising of Mongolian Cossack regiments in Transbaikal for use, if necessary, against the Chinese, a Tungus regiment in Nerchinsk in 1761 and four Buriat regiments in the Transbaikal in 1764, regiments that nearly ninety years later would form the Transbaikal Cossack host.

But to return further to the west, to the Kirghiz steppe and what is now Kazakhstan. In the latter part of the eighteenth century the Kirghiz were ringed to the north-west by the Ural and the Orenburg Cossack hosts, and to the north-east by the Siberian Cossacks that lined the north bank of the Irtysh river above Omsk. Yet another cordon line had been constructed in 1752 connecting the Irtysh at Omsk westwards to Presnoiar on the upper Tobol river where the Siberian Cossacks linked with those of the Orenburg host.

From about 1822 the piecemeal annexation by Russia of the territories of the Kirghiz hordes gathered momentum, Orenburg being the co-ordinating centre of operations and the Siberian Cossacks the main instrument. For it was held that Kirghiz raids against the empire gave ample cause for the Russian counter-raids; new Cossack settlements were established further and further to the south, at Kokchetav, Karkaralinsk, Bayanaul, and Akmolinsk. In 1831 there was a Cossack detachment at Sergiopol, in 1841 the Cossacks were at Kopal, south of Lake Balkhash, and at Turgai. In 1839 Perovskii, the military governor of Orenburg, sent a Cossack expedition against the khanate of Khiva south of Lake Aral, that was unsuccessful. But, nothing daunted, the governor, soon to become a governor-general, continued the steady Russian encroachment. By 1854 the Russian empire extended to Lake Aral, the Syr Darya and the Chu, bordering on modern Turkestan. The Russian frontier was steadily moving southwards and the need was for more men to settle the new areas: there was a transfer of 5,600 northern colonists to the south and several thousand Russian peasants were brought in from other provinces. In addition, Kirghiz were taken into the hosts.[7]

In 1846 the whole of the border territories occupied by the Siberian host was divided into ten regimental areas, with the artillery recruiting over the whole of the region. In 1861 the host was reinforced by units of the Tomsk and Tobolsk horse, foot and town battalions of service Cossacks that brought it up to the strength of twelve horse regiments and three half-battalions of foot.

This continued Russian expansion was not the forced result of the pressure of population, for the vast territories that Russia controlled in 1850 were only thinly settled. The main motive for Russian aggrandizement was political, the desire for international power: the secondary motive was to acquire outlets for trade. Russia's defeat in the Crimean War hardly retired the empire's frontiers—it merely held them temporarily in check. By 1860, within four years of the end of the Crimean War, Alexander II secured by conquest all the lands between the Black Sea and the Caspian and then, by breaking a treaty with the British covering the neutrality of Turkestan, Russian troops and Cossacks crossed the Syr Darya and the Chu and overran that territory, taking Tashkent in 1865 and Samarkand in 1868. The emirates and khanates of Khiva, Kokand and Bokhara had already submitted to Russian suzerainty, and Turkestan became a Russian *general-gouvernement* with its capital at Tashkent. In 1867, after the formation of the Turkestan military district, the Semirechie Cossacks were formed from the Siberian Cossacks in the seven-river district to the south-east of Lake Balkhash. They consisted of only two regiments of horse.

The defence of the border areas of the Siberian empire stretching eastwards from the Siberian Cossack outposts near Biisk on the upper Ob, to the upper Amur and Ayan on the Pacific coast, was the responsibility of what were called 'border Cossacks' and these were commanded and administered centrally from Troitskosavsk; they included all Cossacks in the Russian service on the borders against China, particularly the Russian detachments in Transbaikal and the foreign regiments of Mongolian Tungus and Buriats. Meanwhile, in 1822, the town Cossacks, that formed the second line of defence in the interior, had been reformed so that they remained under the civil administration and acted as the citizens' reserve. This reserve was divided into two categories: the regimental town Cossacks, including those of Tobolsk, Tomsk, Yenisei, Irkutsk, Yakutsk, Transbaikal and the Siberian-Tatar, that could, if needed, be moved away from their base; and the stanitsa Cossacks who were used only for local guard duties.

The Treaty of Nerchinsk, signed with China in 1689, had forced Russia away from the Amur and restricted its borders to the Yablonovoi range in the north, where they had remained for the next 150 years. Even so, the Chinese still accorded Russia a relatively favourable position vis-à-vis the other European powers in that the Russians were permitted to send a land caravan to China through the Mongolian crossing place of Kyakhta south of Lake Baikal once every three years. The nineteenth century, however, saw a change in Russo-Chinese relations after China had fought an unsuccessful war against Britain in 1839–42, for thereafter other European powers began to encroach on its sovereignty; Chinese power was on the wane; Russian strength in Siberia, on the other hand, had increased considerably in the last hundred years by conquest and by colonization. The one governor-generalship of Siberia had been divided into two, one for east and one for west Siberia, and this had the effect of allowing the emperor's representative and governor-general in the Far East, the energetic Nikolai Muravev, some degree of initiative. Nicholas I was, moreover, determined that Russia should re-enter the Amur, particularly since this offered the only suitable access to the sea. In consequence, in 1851, two Russian settlements of Nikolaievsk and Mariinsk were founded at the mouth of the Amur contrary to the agreements with China that existed at that time.

In 1851, following the proposals of Muravev, the Transbaikal Cossacks were formed into a single and separate host, taking in the

Tungus and the four Buriat regiments, all Transbaikal town and stanitsa Cossacks, the Russian 'border Cossacks' in the area of the Irkutsk government, together with all peasants of the Nerchinsk region (these with their families numbering about 30,000 and forming the basis for the new infantry battalions). The host was split militarily into three brigades each of two horse regiments, together with twelve foot battalions and an artillery brigade of two batteries, and it was designed to cover the whole of the Mongolian border.

In 1854 an expedition, made up of a line battalion, a Transbaikal Cossack squadron and a mountain battery, was sent down the Amur to its mouth to claim the river for Russia, and two years later the Transbaikal Cossacks began to colonize the valley, the first settlers being made up of 13,000 exiles and soldiers under sentence that were transported, mostly to the Amur but partly also to the Irkutsk and Yenisei regiments. This forcible colonization continued with the movement of Transbaikal Cossacks to the Amur until, in 1862, there were sixty-seven stanitsas and a population of 11,800 on the Amur, and twenty-three stanitsas and about 5,000 on the Ussuri (the southern tributary of the Amur), these providing three Amur horse regiments and one Amur foot battalion together with one infantry battalion on the Ussuri. The pace of colonization then slowed down because of the difficulty in maintaining the numbers in the harsh conditions and frequent flooding in the country.

In 1857 Alexander II ordered the founding of a new Russian province north of the Amur, and as the Chinese had just begun a war against Britain and France they were in no position to resist. The Russians proclaimed themselves to be the friend of China and the enemy of the British, but at the same time were determined to profit by Chinese weakness, and in 1860 demanded, and obtained by the Treaty of Peking, the region between the Amur and Ussuri rivers and the Pacific ocean. This partially encircled Manchuria with its warm-water harbour of Port Arthur, that was to be occupied by the Russians after 1900 until they were forced by the Japanese to relinquish it in 1905.

In 1879 the Amur Cossacks were finally split from the Transbaikal and formed a separate host, and that same year 390 Ussuri families were moved to the south Ussuri region near the Pacific coast and Vladivostok, and this gave rise to friction with China. Then, five years later, the Ussuri outpost was included in the general-governorship that took in the Transbaikal, Amur, Ussuri-Maritime and Sakhalin in order that the Mongolian-Manchurian border should be under a unified command.[8] Finally, in 1888, the tiny Ussuri host was separated from the Amur and its half-battalion was transformed into a half-regiment of horse.

The Amur and Ussuri, both the offspring of the Transbaikal, were thus the last Cossack hosts to be raised.

CHAPTER 7 NOTES

1 In 1688, Galdan, the great khan of the Kalmyks, was proposing to the tsar that he should be provided with Russian artillery (to be served by 2,000 Cossacks) to enable him 'to ravage all the borders of China outside the Great Wall'. This request was apparently not met. The khan on more than one occasion loaned the tsar as many as 20,000 riders for his wars against the Circassians, Kabards, Bashkirs and other rebel Cossacks.

2 In 1825 the Russians raised regiments of 'Bashkir-Meshcheryak Cossacks' totalling about 10,000 men (out of a Bashkir population of 345,000) for service against the Kirghiz. They outnumbered the Slav Cossacks in the Orenburg area and because of this they were mistrusted by the tsarist authorities: an attempt to restrict the numbers under arms, when they were no longer needed for service against the Kirghiz, led to a Bashkir mutiny and the final disbandment of the force in 1845.

3 The Manchus themselves were a highly civilized off-shoot of the Tungus.

4 In tsarist Russia the religious festivals were those normally associated with the religious calendar such as Christmas, Lent and Easter, and, in addition, the many named Saints' Days: the political feast days were the tsar's birthday and battle and other anniversaries.

5 For further information on Pugachev see chapter 5, note 14, page 125.

6 As on the Don, the imported foreign blood-stallions had to be kept under cover during the winter, otherwise they would not have survived; the mares and foals wintered out on the steppe.

7 In 1869 numbers of Kirghiz that had been inducted into the Orenburg Cossack host rebelled: order was not restored until after the Khivan campaign of 1873.

8 In the next century the Transbaikal was removed to the East Siberian Irkutsk general-governorship.

# 8 In the Service of the Empire

During the eighteenth and the early nineteenth centuries the whole social structure of the Russian Cossack hosts had been changed by the St Petersburg sovereigns, and the task of bringing the Cossack under Russian control, started by Peter the Great in 1695 and continued by Catherine II, was finally achieved by Nicholas I in 1835. Yet, in enforcing his restrictions, Nicholas made them appear as though they were honours graciously bestowed by a thankful monarch. From 1827 the tsarevich was the hereditary ataman, and from this time onwards the host atamans were known as the deputy or delegated atamans, acting on behalf of the crown. Everything was progressively Russianized, government, civil and military organization, ranks, equipment and military uniform. The hosts were regarded as a frontier defence corps and a reserve of settlers and cheap soldiers that could be moved about at will; and the Russian government had begun to increase hosts and raise new ones from any elements to hand; when there was no longer any need of the Cossacks in the homelands in which they lived, the emperor had them moved on or disbanded them.

In the Ukraine the Slobodsk regiments had long since disappeared into the Russian Army and this was the fate, too, of the Ukrainian Cossacks. During the Napoleonic Wars some Ukrainian Cossack regiments had been raised, but more often than not regular Russian regiments were merely redesignated as Ukrainian Cossacks in deference to nationalist opinion. By 1816, when the danger was passed, these regiments were returned to the army lists as Russian uhlans. In 1831, at the time of the renewal of the Polish troubles, eight 'Little Russian Cossack' regiments were formed, each of four active and two reserve squadrons, but by 1842 they had been transplanted to the Caucasus or phased out once more.

Many of the hosts were artificial in that they had no real Cossack roots, and this applied particularly to the new Ukrainian hosts as well as to the Danube, the Azov, the Caucasus and Siberian lines, the Orenburg and, eventually, the Transbaikal, the Amur and the Ussuri.[1] The intention, first put in hand by Potemkin in 1775, was to apply Russian organization and methods, firstly to the Don host, and then, using this as a pattern, to all other hosts, so that they should be uniform throughout. Officer ranks were to conform with those of the Russian Army and the host government and social order were to be brought closer to those that existed in Russia. Nicholas's final achievement was the last link in the chain, the 1835 decree that laid down the new structure and liabilities of the Don Cossack host that was intended to provide the template for all other hosts; by this decree all Cossacks and their descendants were permanently locked into the *voisko* by law with no way out, unless of course the host should itself be dissolved by St Petersburg.

In 1843 the German doctor Wagner stayed overnight with a Don Cossack regiment in the Caucasus and was part of the company that listened to the tales of one Igurov, a Cossack major, himself a veteran of the 1812 war, concerning the exploits of his grandfather, a renowned cattle-thief, and of his night-raids and fights with the Nogai on the open Tauride steppe. Among Igurov's audience was a Russian general staff officer of education and intelligence whom the German doctor afterwards cross-examined as to the likely truth of Igurov's account; to which the Russian staff officer had replied:

> In essentials his account is true. Wild beasts like his grandfather who would butcher Tatar women and children may have lived on the Don during the last century, but now they have all died out, for they are no longer tolerated by military discipline, and the inhabitants of the steppe have all become much tamer. A giant like Igurov [the grandfather], if he appeared among the Cossacks today, could no longer play the same part, for he would be thrashed like any other Cossack. The Don Cossacks are now admirably disciplined but it is only since they have been recently reorganized by the emperor [Nicholas I] that they have become a really valuable military force. Ten years ago a few necessary modifications and reforms, such as the abrogation of

useless privileges that interfered with discipline, occasioned some ill-blood. But now all changes are tolerated without opposition and the Cossacks soon became used to them.

Major Igurov's son, a foppish young officer of the Don Cossacks, had been among the listeners. The Russian general staff officer had something to say about him to the German doctor:

From old Igurov to his great grandson, you can distinguish three epochs in Cossack history, three transitions in the development of these remarkable horsemen. The grandsire is a representative of the blunt old spirit of the sons of the steppe that Peter the Great began to bridle with his iron hand. This was a difficult task at that time; but now a check is kept on everything so that the chastising hand of our emperor can smite the Cossacks with the speed of lightning. The major himself is the type of a transitional generation. He [as the equivalent of a Russian regular army major] would by no means relish the old equality and anarchy of the steppes. He has seen and tasted the beauties and delights of Western Europe [in the Napoleonic Wars]. Yet he has one foot in the past and sighs and longs for the freedom of the good old days. His son is quite a creature of modern times, coming from the cadet school with the vices and the advantages of large cities, elegant in his manners, superficial and empty in mind and heart. The [Don] Cossacks now answer the purpose of trained elephants to tame the wild ones so that the warlike hordes of the Siberian steppes are taught to obey the command from the banks of the Neva. All these hordes are regarded as suitable recruits and thousands of drill-sergeants from Moscow and the Don are now engaged in teaching them.

Although the Russian staff officer stressed that the Cossacks were broken to discipline, the German doctor meditated whether this had not been achieved at a certain cost. For although Wagner noted the very wide difference that still existed between the 1843 Cossack discipline and the servile obedience of the Russian soldier, he thought also that the free manly Cossack spirit was probably broken and gone, so that the Cossack of his day was neither Cossack nor soldier.

By the early nineteenth century, the Don Cossacks, that were to serve as the pattern for the other hosts, were no longer a closely knit community and were already in part Russianized according to the St Petersburg mould.

*    *    *

When Peter the Great finally succeeded in having the letter of his order obeyed that no fugitives should be admitted into the Don host, the Cossacks circumvented his order by allowing fugitives and other Russian migrants to settle on the Don without being admitted to the Cossack register, in this way creating a further problem in that these new arrivals became the outlanders (*inogorodnie*) who, even as early as 1763, already numbered 20,000 males. From 1768 there was in existence a rich Cossack hierarchy together with a numerous petty nobility whose status was not associated with host function, and these were beginning to seize on land and the peasants who lived there, sometimes with the tacit approval of St Petersburg. Meanwhile officials and petty nobility were also bringing in serfs from Russia, and, by the time that this practice was forbidden, in 1811, there were already over 76,000 serfs in the territory. That same year the 20,000 peasants that had been settled on the Don since 1763 were reclassified as Cossacks, but meanwhile many other outlanders had arrived. There were numbers of Nogai and Kalmyks, too, on the Don, some of them nomads and some settled in their own stanitsas, both within and outside of the host.[2] Land was becoming scarce and in 1816 a law was passed forbidding peasants to settle on host land. Meanwhile the proportion of Don Cossacks to the total inhabitants in the Don province continued to fall, particularly since large numbers of Don Cossacks (10,000 between 1846 and 1848) were continually being moved to the Caucasus by order of the St Petersburg government.

Other of Peter the Great's ordinances were to sow trouble for the Don Cossacks. When Peter had forbidden the Don Cossacks to sail the Azov and Black Seas they had become primarily landsmen rather than seamen, and their energies had been directed to extending their territories to the south and south-east. But, to ensure that his orders were obeyed, Peter had created a new settlement at Troitsk (Taganrog) and built a Don river fortress of *St Dmitrii* (Rostov) that he peopled with agriculturists and artisans. Potemkin, as Prince of the Tauride, went further in that he removed the strip of Azov Sea coastline and the Don estuary from the host 'by agreement with [his protégé] the Don ataman', and peopled it with Russians, Little

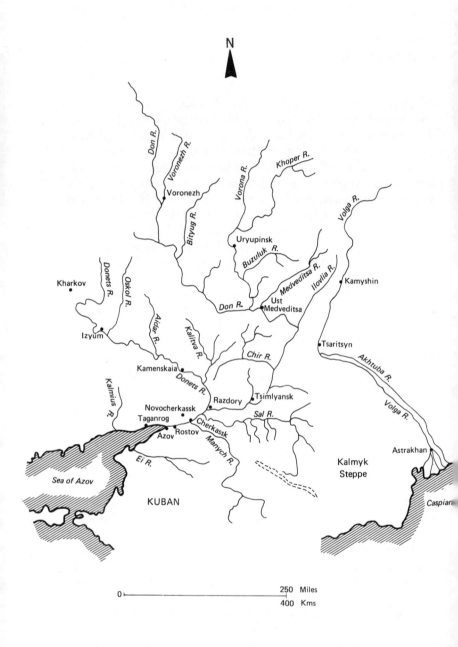

N

13  The Territories of the Don Cossacks *c.*1820

Russians, Greeks from Morea and Armenians from the Crimea. These territories were lost to the host and the Cossacks did not like it. In 1795 Rostov was taken into the Ekaterinoslav *guberniia* and Taganrog became a city; these cities eventually became great trade and industrial centres entirely foreign to the Don host. Nearly a century after the event the host still continued to petition the tsars for the return of the ceded lands and, in 1887, the emperor agreed by a special dispensation to this return, so adding 325,000 inhabitants to the numbers of the Don Cossacks, mostly town dwellers and industrial workers who had nothing in common with Novocherkassk, as the events of the 1917 revolution were yet to show.

In 1775, at Potemkin's instigation, the Don Cossacks had been given a government administration to deal with military and civil affairs, and the whole territory had been divided into five *okrugi* (or *otdely*) to which the stanitsas were made responsible. But no government assistance or advice was given on service liabilities, the division of land or on finances. The burden of the 1812 war had fallen most heavily on Platov's Don Cossacks who provided sixty regiments for operations, with a further twenty-six regiments in reserve, as against only twenty-five regiments provided by all the remaining hosts; and in 1819 the Don ataman Denisov had asked St Petersburg for guidance on this and other matters, presumably because he thought that the Don Cossacks had an unfair military burden. Nothing was done, however, except to appoint commissions to look into the problem and these failed to produce an acceptable solution.

The 1835 decree set the Don peace and reserve contribution at fifty-six regiments and at last regulated military organization and service, so that the same rules might be applied to the other hosts.[3] Nor were the Don Cossacks excluded when Nicholas I began to appoint serving Russian generals as atamans, generals who had never been Cossacks; such was Khomutov, a Russian general who was nominated Don ataman in 1848.

Notwithstanding this, the Cossacks, in 1856, at the beginning of the reign of Alexander II, were still a state within a state: once a Cossack always a Cossack, and death was the only exit from the host; in the Caucasus line host no Cossack woman could marry outside the host without the ataman's permission, and those that married within the host were often subjected to official inquisitions —and host as well as family coercion; no non-Cossack, at least according to Cossack law, could own houses or immovable property on host lands; the whole Cossack male population had a war liability for as long as they were fit to sit a horse or shoulder a rifle; nor did military service necessarily excuse them from taxes, for they usually paid taxes on the host land allotted and, if not under arms, a poll tax in addition.

Alexander II was inclined to the view that Cossacks had outlived their usefulness and he and his advisers regarded their conditions of service as antiquated and oppressive. Reform was the order of the day and at long last, between 1861–3, serfdom had been abolished, it having been made obligatory for the governments to compensate, usually by a grant of land, those former serfs who had been tied to the land and relied on it to eat and live. As early as 1866 Alexander had a reviewing committee examine the plight of the Cossacks and recommend alterations aimed at permitting Cossacks to leave the hosts and reorganizing military service so that this might be reduced and, if possible, be carried out by volunteers. Alexander required, in addition, that the military and civil government and the judiciary within the hosts should be entirely separated, and considered that 'the hosts should be brought up to date so that they might continue to give good service in a modern age as they had done in the past.' It was necessary to bring the hosts into the civil administration and make them accountable to Russian common law, fitting them into the existing political framework of governments or provinces. The reviewing committee was so slow to produce recommendations, however, that the war ministry, at Alexander's bidding, took it upon itself to introduce changes.

Between 1867 and 1869 new laws were passed allowing Cossack officers to leave the host at will, while other ranks could do so in certain circumstances. Action was taken to regulate the position of the outlanders living on the host territories, for their grievances were many: some resented the property-owning restrictions that some of the hosts tried to enforce on them; others that they were taxed by the host but had only a very limited voice in its affairs; others that they were not permitted to become Cossacks. Yet the 1840 Orenburg host solution to its outlander problems—that all outlanders should either join the host or depart—had found no favour either. Many of these outlanders already possessed landed property on host lands, whatever the old Cossack laws might have decreed, but they had no security of tenure. The Don Cossack host had a further problem in that it had a very large number of imported serfs who had been resident for generations and, by the emancipation laws, many of these serfs, who were henceforth to become outlanders, had to be given plots of Don land, so that the ancient host laws regarding land ownership could no longer apply.

Between 1867 and 1870 there was a reversal of the position of the outlanders in that the new St Petersburg laws tended to favour them to the detriment of the hosts; from that time onwards outlanders could no longer be forbidden to settle on Cossack lands, and Russian subjects were given the right by law to own immovable property within the domain of the hosts, subject to some rather vague safeguards that lands owned by outlanders could not be held in perpetuity but should, at some time in the undefined future, revert to host ownership. From 1870 the outlanders were permitted to have some say in local community affairs.

Such reforms, in retrospect, might be considered equitable, but they struck a severe blow at the exclusiveness of the Cossack society, a society that was privileged and yet, at the same time, burdened by enormous military commitments. The reforms gave rise, in addition, to incongruities in that in some Kuban stanitsas the outlanders outnumbered the Cossacks, and the Cossacks regarded as unreasonable that the outlanders should have any say in service obligations that they were not called upon to perform. Moreover the new laws permitted Russian and Little Russian landowners, merchants, speculators and colonizers from the Russian interior to enter and settle host lands at will at any future date, provided that they had sufficient funds to buy or rent accommodation there. This could only lead to a further dilution of the hosts.[4]

\* \* \*

Under Peter the Great the hosts had been controlled by various departments of the government in turn, the foreign office, the senate and the war collegium and ministry. In 1774, during the reign of Catherine the Great, Potemkin, as Cossack ataman, had controlled the hosts directly. Throughout the nineteenth century the hosts were the responsibility of the war ministry: in the early 1850s they came under the former department of military colonies, from which they were transferred in 1873 firstly to the administration of irregular troops and then to the main administration of Cossack hosts, all of these administrations being within the war ministry. Matters of importance were considered by a committee formed principally of

Russian military officers and civil servants and chaired by the chief of this main administration, and its orders were sent out for implementation to the Russian generals commanding the military districts in which the Cossack hosts were situated.

Towards the end of the nineteenth century the hosts had been reorganized in such a fashion that they could be fitted into the political, military and civil organization of the Russian empire. The Don Cossacks were considered to be sufficiently large and important to justify their being classified as a general-government and independent military district, although the size of the territories was insufficient to grade them above that of a Russian *oblast'*. The ataman of the Don Cossacks in Novocherkassk who had a Russian general's rank and who might, or might not, be a Don Cossack born, received his orders, military or civil, direct from St Petersburg. This applied, too, to the ataman of the Siberian Cossacks who, at his headquarters in Omsk, also had the status and rank of a Russian governor-general and general commanding a military district, for, in addition to the Siberian host, he commanded also the Russian troops in Western Siberia (the Steppe), covering the government of Omsk and the oblasts of Akmolinsk and Semipalatinsk. With the other hosts, however, the situation was different in that they were all responsible to subordinate Russian military headquarters. The atamans of the Kuban and Terek Cossacks ranked as governors of the oblasts that they controlled from their capitals at Ekaterinodar and Vladikavkaz, but in all military and civil matters both came under the viceroy and governor-general of the Caucasus in Tiflis, who, from 1888 onwards, was given the honorary title of deputy ataman of the Caucasus Cossacks. The ataman of the Astrakhan host was also the governor of Astrakhan, although his Cossacks were often dispersed between the governments of Astrakhan, Saratov and Samara; the ataman of the Orenburg host was also the governor of the Orenburg *guberniia*; the ataman of the Ural Cossacks was the *military* governor (that is to say the commander of troops) of the Ural oblast, though not the *de facto* governor. But all three hosts, the Astrakhan, Orenburg and Ural, were subordinated to the commander-in-chief of the Kazan military district. The Semirechie Cossacks at Vernyi similarly came under the commander-in-chief and governor-general of Turkestan at Tashkent, while the ataman of the Transbaikal Cossacks at Chita, the Amur Cossacks at Blagoveshchensk and the Ussuri Cossacks at Vladivostok came under the commander-in-

14 The Russian Cossack Hosts c.1914

chief and governor-general of the Amur (later Pri-Amur) at Blagoveshchensk (later Khabarovsk).[5]

The responsibilities of the ataman depended not on their titles, weighty and sonorous though these often were, but rather on the military establishment of their hosts and on the presence or absence of other Russian army formations within their borders. The ataman of the Orenburg Cossacks, one of the larger hosts, was the governor of the Orenburg *guberniia* (though he need not necessarily have been born a Cossack). The ataman of the tiny Ussuri host, on the other hand, though he was titled the *military* governor of the Maritime oblast, in fact commanded only his own Cossacks; the Russian troops in the oblast were either under the command of the Vladivostok fortress commander or else under the Russian army headquarters in Nikolsk.

In 1775 Potemkin had introduced a uniform government (*pravitel'stvo*) in all the hosts to handle civil and judicial affairs according to a Russian pattern, and this had been modified by Paul's chancellery, a modification that remained in force until 1835. After 1835 each host had a double administration, one for military and one for civil affairs, and the size and type of these administrations were again set according to Russian patterns of military and civil government and the tasks that each ataman had to perform: the Siberian host had a full military district staff; the Don, Kuban, Terek and Orenburg had the equivalent of a corps staff; the Ural, Amur and Transbaikal had the skeleton Russian headquarters that would normally be found with the oblast in the interior.

The ataman remained an all powerful figure, even more so in that he was no longer accountable to a Cossack electorate. By now the hosts were far too dispersed to enable the representative host assembly, the krug or rada, to be constantly in being, and its powers were in any case now so restricted that it had fallen into disuse since the eighteenth century, except for ceremonial or state occasions. The starshinas had enjoyed a brief spell of authority, but after 1769 they took no part in government unless summoned by the ataman for consultation. And so the ataman remained in effect very much the equivalent of his Russian counterpart, the governor-general or governor of a *guberniia* or oblast, the sovereign's representative, appointed and removed by the emperor and with his first responsibility to St Petersburg.

Below the level of the host ataman the Cossack territories had,

36. Tatar Cossacks, firstly in Lithuanian, then Polish, and finally Russian-Lithuanian service. This picture clearly shows the effect of Russianizing, since by 1850 their uniforms were identical with those of Uhlans. Kalmyks, too, wore an Uhlan pattern of uniform and were issued with a general-service Russian sabre.

37. Terek Cossack of the Guard.

38. The streets of tsarist Warsaw being swept by Cossacks while a police officer (at the extreme right) stands rigidly at the salute. The picture would suggest they were Caucasian line, possibly one of the two Kuban squadrons stationed in the Polish capital. The artist has depicted the flailing *nagaika* silhouetted in the centre against the sky.

39. Although these Ural lancers are of the Guard, their horses appear to be of coarse steppe or Siberian origin; and although the regulations provided for horses of the Cossack Guard to be ridden (on ceremonial occasions) with curb and spur, the bridle and saddlery generally used was of the age-old Tatar-Cossack pattern—a jointed snaffle, leather headgear generally free of buckles, billets and even stitches, a standing martingale, breast-plate and crupper, and the stirrup irons secured together by a strap under the horse's belly.

40. Trumpeters of the Don Cossacks of the Guard c. 1890.

41. No. 2 Battery of the Don Cossacks (photograph taken at Zhitomir near Kiev).

42. Terek and Kuban Cossacks of the Emperor's Personal Escort (*Konvoi*) Guard Regiment, supposedly on manoeuvres, pose for the camera c. 1890.

44. An officer of the Transbaikal Cossacks c. 1890 whose features clearly show his Mongol origin.

43. Ural Cossacks on *voltige* exercises—the modern equivalent of the *dzhigitovka*. As the 1890 camera was unable to take rapid-motion pictures, action had to be frozen.

45. Lancers of 1st Orenburg Cossacks (photograph at Kharkov c. 1890). The flat-faced features of the lancer on the left indicate a Nogai, Kirghiz or Bashkir origin.

46. A Soviet soldier from the resuscitated Kuban Cossacks in the traditional cap and *burka* watering his horse in a Moldavian village (May 1944).

47. Soviet soldiers from the resuscitated Cossack Corps (in this case 2 Guards Cavalry) water their horses in the Elbe (May 1945).

since 1802, been divided into the *okrugi* or *otdely* districts, and at the head of each was an ataman and small staff. This district ataman was a senior Cossack officer appointed by the host ataman, with the approval of St Petersburg, to co-ordinate and control the many stanitsas that formed the body of the host: the *otdel* ataman was responsible for military and police matters within the district and for the training, inspection, equipment, accommodation and reserve lists of all the stanitsas under his control. The cost of *otdel* headquarters was paid out of host funds. Only below the *otdel*, at the stanitsa level, did the organization of government take on its traditional Cossack pattern.

The Cossack stanitsa, known formerly to the Black Sea Cossacks as the kuren, could be a large town or a scattered rural or steppe settlement; on the Don it might be called a *gorodok* or in Orenburg or Siberia a *krepost'*, *redut* or *vorpost*. From 1870 onwards all settlements except the hamlet (*poselok*) in all the hosts took the name of stanitsa. Any settlement of thirty families or more had to have an assembly of all householders, and each assembly had to elect its own ataman, the election of all stanitsa atamans being confirmed by the oblast, that is to say usually by the host. Each stanitsa had its own ataman, assembly, administrative organization, staff and offices, its own magistrates and its own court. It collected its own taxes and paid its own bills, and it was responsible for the selection of its youth for military service and the examination and recommending of cases for deferment or excuse. The stanitsa kept service and reserve lists and implemented district directions and assembly recommendations, and kept a check of personal and host military equipment. The cost of local stanitsa government was paid for solely from stanitsa funds.

Every stanitsa had property rights of land and water in its own *yurt* or area (except in the Ural Cossacks where the host owned them in common). The stanitsa often assisted in the financing of its churches and elementary schools—some school attendance being compulsory after 1871 for all boys and girls on the Don; it supported the needy families of those on service and the disabled. The stanitsa owned the greater part of the arable and pasture land and the forests and it allocated to each Cossack his *pai* that was to support him and his family, usually reckoned at thirty desiatinas (about eighty acres), although in practice the allocation varied very widely according to what land was available.[6] But since all lands could be reallocated, and the rapid increase in population demanded that this should in fact be done every few years, the Cossack had little interest in improving the *pai* he worked or pastured; this, together with poor husbandry, overcrowding and the deforestation of great areas that were never replanted, led to a general exhaustion of the soil.

Except on the Ural the land retained under host control was small, varying from two to twenty-eight per cent of the whole, and usually comprised the roads, troop exercising land, host forests and a reserve of land or property to be allocated or rented out for a fixed number of years. In addition to the host and stanitsa lands there was also privately owned land to be found on the host territories and some assets that were owned by the state—in particular the Orenburg mines.

The host funds, all of which were strictly controlled by the war minister so that special permission was required from St Petersburg in the event of unusual or unbudgeted requests, acquired their income from state aid (forty-three per cent of the whole), rents, hirings, sales of resources, royalties, and interest on capital. The expenses chargeable to host funds included the cost of the military and civil administration down to the *otdel* ataman (in the Ural host down to the stanitsa), grants and pensions to military and other pensioners, the maintenance of military and civil schools and military accommodation, the purchase and repair of arms and the cost of all troops on active duty. During the 1877 mobilization there had been a further drain on host funds when it came to light that many of the mobilized Cossacks lacked even the personal equipment that they should have provided for themselves. The Don host alone had to find half a million rubles to equip the thirty regiments mobilized from the reserve, and a further 80,000 rubles to purchase additional horses. In 1877 all the hosts, except the Terek, had, however, sufficient funds to assist in making good the equipment deficiencies in all the newly mobilized regiments.[7]

The host government and administration were no longer Cossack in the traditional sense since they were essentially an extension of Russian autocracy. A measure of self-government was possible at stanitsa level in that the ataman was still elected by the assembly, subject to confirmation by the host; and, within the policy limits imposed on him by the *otdel*, the stanitsa ataman enjoyed a measure of freedom. He could and usually did consult with the elders, and,

where wider issues were involved, he summoned advisory committees made up of representatives of Cossacks, outlanders and the
clergy. But he was not obliged to take their advice and, in the final
outcome, he alone was responsible for the course that he set himself.
Yet, all in all, according to the 1891 judgement of the war minister
Vannovskii, the 1870 military and civil reorganization did not work
well, for Vannovskii talked of 'maladministration, corruption, in-
efficiency, unworthy representatives, indiscipline and lack of interest
and, in particular, of a lack of supervision at host level'. On the other
hand it could also be said that this description might have been
applied, and perhaps with equal accuracy, to the tsarist military and
civil administration throughout the empire.

The Prussian officer Freiherr von Tettau, in an admirable 1892
work that was aimed at examining the Cossack organization and
assessing its value for modern war, unconsciously follows the line of
thinking of the German doctor Wagner, some fifty years before,
wondering if even the old and established Cossack hosts had not lost
much of their military value, partly because of the changing conditions of Cossack life and partly as a result of the St Petersburg
insistence on Russianizing and uniformity. With his nomad enemies
already overcome, the Cossack's life and property no longer depended on his powers of observation, his caution, his cunning and on
his valour, on his horsemanship and his skill at arms. Whereas at the
beginning of the century his musket or rifle was his own property and
always to hand, in that his sustenance or life might depend on it, the
latter-day government-issued rifle was kept in a central armoury. At
one time the Cossack had made it his business to acquire the
best-quality blade and the most serviceable horse that he could
afford or steal, but after the pacification of the Caucasians and the
Kirghiz, the same need was no longer there. Nor could excellent arms
be acquired from the Turk or from the Moslem armourers, and the
Cossack turned instead to cheap products from Warsaw in order that
he might fulfil the letter of the law and provide himself with field
equipment. Most had a horse of sorts, but, as the recent mobilization
had shown, a large number of these mounts were rejected out of hand
by the regiments' veterinary surgeons as unfit for service.

Von Tettau believed that the strong admixture of forcibly settled
peasants, even discharged soldiers, had weakened the ability and the
morale of some of the hosts, particularly those that had little original
Cossack element, the Orenburg, Siberian, Semirechie, Transbaikal,

Amur and later the Ussuri, the artificial Cossack hosts that had been created at the behest of the Russian empire, not spontaneously or of volunteers, but of men on whom the stamp of Russian peasantry, even serfdom, was deeply imprinted. Such men might, after the necessary training, have made good Russian infantry. But they would not have been soldier-farmers, warriors who could at the same time provide for themselves from the soil; only too rarely could they have been made Cossacks. Nature and the environment had made the original Cossack what he was, shaped by a hard, bitter and dangerous life, and von Tettau very much doubted the literary romantic notions of the birthright and tradition of the warlike Cossack that were being kept alive by tsarist-designed uniforms and plaintive steppe song.

This view was often shared by the Russian military and by some of the older-established hosts. The Russian commanders tended to regard Cossacks as poor-quality cavalry, which, by the second half of the nineteenth century, is what many of them had in fact become. Large numbers of Cossack regiments were brigaded with Russian line cavalry in cavalry divisions, too often without having had the necessary specialized training to fit them for this role. And too few of the old Cossack hosts could have produced units highly skilled in reconnaissance, observation and harassment, as they could once have done fifty years before. Sheleznov, writing at about this time under the Ural Cossack imprint, doubted that a Russian ploughman, in his gentle heart a man of peace, could ever be converted into a warlike Cossack merely by giving him arms and a uniform; a better alternative, he thought, might be to apply to the fierce Kirghiz nomad horsemen who knew only the barren steppe and the howl of the wolf, in that there 'one might make something out of him,' though that 'something', Sheleznov feared, 'might be an armed robber who would terrify both foe and friend alike.' Of such stuff were the original Cossacks made. But such a warrior would have found little favour in nineteenth-century St Petersburg.

\* \* \*

Until 1835 there was no regular system of military recruiting in any of the hosts and nor was there any definite military establishment. Nothing had been put in writing to define the military duties of the Cossack or of the host and it was merely understood that every Cossack was a soldier who could be called out for service as long as he was fit to bear arms. The Ural Cossacks had developed their own *naemka* system of service; in the other hosts rules were made according to circumstances, it being generally acknowledged that it was the duty of every Cossack to serve as long as the need arose, except that a man might escape this duty by paying for a substitute to perform it for him; these substitutes usually required a cash payment and often, in addition, the provision of an outfit, arms and a horse. The practice of permitting substitutes was certainly not popular outside the host since substitute service tended to fall on the very poor or the unintelligent, or on the otherwise unreliable, dissolute and drunkard element of Cossack society. Some time before 1835 St Petersburg had attempted to suppress it.

The emperor Nicholas tried to regularize Cossack military service in his 1835 orders to the Don; by these orders the term of service for officers was set at twenty-five years while that for the rank and file was to be for thirty years. But these periods represented the total years during which the Cossack would be at call, not the length of his service actually under arms, and there was a genuine desire on the part of the authorities to restrict this period of service under arms by ordering that regiments should be rotated so that they did no more than three active years' service at any one time. It was also ordered (and was indeed already happening at the time) that the youth of the Don should carry out stanitsa duties, mainly those of municipal watchmen and of a labour corps, before entering on full-time military service. The 1835 orders further stipulated that Don Cossacks from any one stanitsa should not all serve in the same regiment together, but should be distributed throughout a number of regiments, it being normal tsarist practice to use widely separated recruiting areas for individual line cavalry and infantry regiments: insofar as the Cossacks were concerned it also prevented a situation arising where all men were removed from a settlement when a regiment went abroad on service. The 1835 orders called, moreover, for the founding of a Russian-pattern Cossack cadet corps to provide a source of officers in order to improve the standard of the Cossack officer entry: for although the Cossack was usually more intelligent and often better educated than the army rank and file in Russia or the Ukraine, the Cossack officer's general and technical education was held to be inferior to that of the officer of the Russian Army. However that may be, the hosts continued to take most of their officers from recommended Cossack non-commissioned officers who could pass a simple examination in reading and writing, were 'acquainted with the catechism' and could prove some basic practical military knowledge in field work.

By 1860 new ideas prevailed in St Petersburg, and the government began to favour a system of military service similar to the *naemka* used by the Ural Cossacks. An experiment was tried by which every Cossack who wanted to serve should be allowed to do so and for as long as he so wished, being under arms for most of his adult life if he so wanted; and special financial rewards were arranged to encourage him to volunteer. Those who did not elect to serve would not be required to be under arms beyond the preparatory period, but they would have to pay additional taxes as the price of this exemption. If there were insufficient volunteers to make up the required numbers in the active regiments, then conscripts would be taken by lot. This experiment was applied firstly to the Don, and then in 1867, to the Orenburg, and in 1871 and 1872 to the Kuban-Terek, the Siberian, the Astrakhan and the Transbaikal; the experiment failed because the burden was shouldered by too few and it led to a drastic reduction in the real military strength of the hosts in that a professional long-service peacetime force could neither create nor maintain the reserves needed for modern war.

The success of the 1870 short-service German Army in the Franco-Prussian War led to an immediate change of views in St Petersburg. A new 1874 law for the Russian Army, and its 1875 application to the Don Cossacks, transformed the imperial army and the Cossacks from long-service to short-service engagements in order that large mobilization reserves of trained men could be created. Indeed, the Russian government became so determined to apply the principle of universal service throughout the empire that, in 1874, it required that even the Ural Cossacks should abandon their old part-voluntary *naemka* system and conform to the new law that was being adopted in all the other hosts. This led to an immediate Cossack uprising on the Ural and the banishment of 2,000 Ural Cossack families to the wilds of the newly conquered Turkestan, a place of exile from which they were only allowed to return in the reign of Nicholas II.

The law that was introduced on 1 January 1875 covering the military liabilities of the Cossack hosts remained in force until 1914. All Cossacks had to provide their own uniform, equipment and arms except for the rifle and the lance, these being found by the government, although a half of the cost of the rifle was charged to the host.

Every mounted Cossack had to have his own horse and horse equipment according to the military specification. A Cossack's service was split into two portions, active and home guard (*opolchenie*), and the active was divided yet again into three classes, preparatory, field and reserve. The preparatory class included all Cossacks between the ages of eighteen and twenty-one under training that was carried out at the Cossack's home stanitsa. The first year was devoted to mustering and ensuring that the Cossack was properly equipped and could take care of his equipment in military fashion, and some time might be spent on individual instruction. In the autumn of the second year collective training began, and this was continued throughout the third year, at the end of which time the Cossack was transferred to the field class and joined an active full-strength Category 1 regiment at home or abroad.

The length of service in the field class was twelve years divided into three categories of four years each. The men in the first category, usually aged from twenty-one to twenty-five, formed the regular regiments and batteries maintained in peacetime.[8] Towards the end of his fourth year the Cossack was sent home and released from full-time service, following which he passed into the second category of field service for the next four years, and then finally into the third category, at the end of which time he would be about thirty-three years of age. The eight years in the second and third categories were classified as 'extended leave', and while the Cossack was on this long furlough he went about his normal daily life but was still required to maintain his uniform, equipment and horse ready for mobilization, and was subject to recall for short periods of training of three weeks a year in Category 2 and one period of three weeks in Category 3. At the age of thirty-three the Cossack left the field force and joined the reserve for five years, after which he went into the home guard *opolchenie*; there he was liable to be recalled only until his forty-eighth year, but in fact he was likely to rejoin, if fit and if the fancy so took him, at any age.[9]

Because of the unrest and disorders on the Ural in protest against the proposed 1875 conscription, the Russian government was forced to modify the application of the law to that host so that it took into account the earlier *naemka* system. From 1875 onwards the preparatory period in the Ural host began at seventeen years of age and lasted for two years only, and at nineteen the youth was a trained Cossack and entered on two years' full-time home service. From the age of twenty-one to thirty-six he was in the field category available for service anywhere, and for five years after that he was liable for full-time home service, after which he entered the *opolchenie* home guard. But the field service was performed, as far as was possible, by volunteers, the shortfall being made good by conscription by lot. Those who were not actually under arms, including the youth who had a postponement of training because of educational or hardship reasons and the more elderly who had formerly spent some years under arms but were now in the *opolchenie*, had to pay a tax graduated according to age and circumstances. All had to serve, however, in the preparatory period for a minimum of one year.

The universal conscription had also been applied to the citizens of the Russian empire, but the law and its application were very complicated. The law applied generally to all Great Russians, Little Russians, Belorussians and Jews, but there were many exemptions elsewhere in that Finns, Moslems of the Caucasus and Turkestan, and the many native peoples of Siberia did not have to serve. Even among the Russian population the conscription was not general in that the army did not require the numbers that became of military age each year, so that these had to be much reduced by deferments, exemptions and by lot. Those conscripted were liable to serve for five years with the colours, although in practice this service was usually reduced to three-and-a-half or four-and-a-half years according to arm of service. In consequence, according to Rediger's 1892 St Petersburg survey, the citizen of the empire was likely to serve a little longer than the Cossack but proportionally far fewer were conscripted.[10]

Until about 1860 the Cossack might serve two or even three periods of three years each in an active unit, and the conditions in the Caucasus and Kirghiz steppe meant that he learned his duties in a war theatre. When Turkestan had been occupied there remained no theatres of operations, and peacetime training became a matter of greater importance than before, with a need for training camps and exercise grounds. In reality, however, there could be no satisfactory substitute for the skirmishing of real war. After 1860 too many of the young officers went to the reserve without practical experience, and those natural warlike abilities that remained to the Cossacks never had a chance to develop because of the lack of service with formed bodies of troops in actual warlike conditions. All this reflected on the abilities of the junior leaders and on the performance of Cossack formations and units. The Polish insurrection of 1863 had already shown that a large number of Cossack officers were ignorant of their duties.

Cossack officers, in common with the officers of the Russian Army, came from all classes of society. It had been the practice until about 1880 to promote a large proportion of Cossack officers directly from the ranks, but, after the creation of the cadet corps, strenuous efforts were made to increase the number of cadet and Junker schools and to make these the main source of Cossack officers.[11] The Don Cossack cadet corps, founded in 1880 at Novocherkassk, prepared the better educated or more favoured Cossack youths from the Don and from some of the other hosts, for entry into the Cossack cadet schools; there they studied for one year before being accepted into the Cossacks of the guard or the Cossack artillery as aspirant officers. The other Cossack regiments were to get their officers from the newly established Junker schools at Novocherkassk, Stavropol and Orenburg, where applicants were enrolled for a two-year course, sometimes directly from school but more usually from the Cossack rank and file. The vacancies in these schools were too few to meet the demand, so a Junker sotnia of 120 Junkers under Cossack officers was formed as a special wing of the Nikolai cavalry school in St Petersburg, a school that was designed to produce young cavalry officers for both the guard and the line cavalry of the Russian Army. A large number of vacancies were also set aside for Cossacks in Russian Army cadet and Junker schools, but these vacancies were not always filled due to the lack of suitable applicants.[12]

Because of the Russian insistence that Cossack aspirants should be qualified before becoming officers there was a constant shortage of officers on the active list, in fact barely enough for the Category 1 regiments, few for the Category 2 regiments and none at all for those of Category 3. In the event of the Category 2 and 3 regiments being called out, and this was done during the 1877–8 Turkish War, nearly all of the officers came from the reserve.

Freiherr von Tettau, who was knowledgeable and well-read on Russian military subjects, thought, in 1892, that the usefulness of the young Cossack officer hardly compared with that of a German corporal. And so it might have been, according to the army standards of the day. But the Russians and the Cossacks had to make the best of what they could get, and the young Cossack officer was undoubtedly better instructed than the rank and file under him. For whereas the German non-commissioned officers were a source of great strength to the army of the Kaiser, the corps of non-commissioned officers in the Russian Army—and even more so in the Cossacks—was weak and inexperienced since the Russian and Cossack non-commissioned officers could rarely be prevailed upon voluntarily to extend their service beyond the initial term of three or four years. Long-service sergeants or sergeant-majors were almost unknown.

In 1888 there were reckoned to be 305,000 men of military age and fit for service out of a total male population of 1,200,000 in all the hosts; of these a little more than half (160,000, or about thirteen per cent of the males) were likely to be called upon in war, partly because of the economic hardship that would be caused to the hosts if greater numbers were removed and, more particularly, because there were insufficient horses to mount them.

There were numerous privately owned studs and horse-rearing establishments within the host territories, but by Cossack standards their mounts were expensive and were sold elsewhere; the Cossack hosts depended mainly on their own steppe herds and those on the stanitsa pasturages, and these were everywhere in decline, except in the Ural. Of the steppe horses that were not either over- or under-age for military service, only a little more than half of them could be broken as satisfactory saddle-horses. The Ural, Orenburg, Siberian, Semirechie and Transbaikal hosts had enough horses to mount all their men and sufficient over for war reserves, but the Don Cossacks had only two riding horses for every three men who were fit and of service age; and although there were enough horses for all regiments of the three categories, there were insufficient for replacements and reserves. Even the short Turkish War of 1877–8 had shown how precarious the horse situation was in the Don host.[13] The Kuban and Terek hosts were even worse off, for they had no more than one riding horse for every three men who were fit and of service age. The quality of the hosts' horses varied widely, too. According to Krasnov, the commander of a reserve regiment in the Turkish War, the Don horse was what it had always been, small, thin, light, hot-tempered with a strong back and firm hoof, rarely sick, impervious to cold and wet and eating almost anything. The Trans-Don horse, that was sold mainly to the Russian line cavalry, was bigger and looked a much better horse, but in fact, according to Krasnov, it was inferior to the Don pony in all respects unless crossed with the

Kalmyk steppe breed. The Kabard and Black Sea Circassian horses were excellent, but there were too few of them in the Kuban and Terek. The Orenburg Cossack horse was of poor quality, but the Ural pony, though a particularly ill-looking and misshapen animal, was by far the best of the Cossack mounts.

At this time Khoroshchin reckoned that a Don Cossack's equipment would cost about 188 rubles; Kuznetsov put it at 250 rubles; much of the difference depended on what the Cossack was prepared to pay for his horse, and in order to encourage the Cossack to get a better animal the government began to pay an annual horse allowance of thirty-seven rubles to those in the guard and twenty-one rubles to the other mounted men.[14] This did not, however, help the young recruit or the reservist who, when called to the colours, had to appear with a horse that was fit for service. And since, in the case of the eighteen-year-old, the horse had to be found by his father, who, like as not, had other sons to provide for, the burden on the whole family was a great one. Indeed the 1877 mobilization showed some of the advantages of the Ural *naemka* system in that whereas so many of the Don Cossacks of Category 3 came into the depots with incomplete equipment, unfit horses or without horses at all, the Ural men reported in cheerfully, well equipped and on good ponies, with some of the Cossacks having had as much as 300 rubles paid out to them or their families from the *naemka* fund.[15]

\* \* \*

The Cossack horseman was almost entirely self-taught as a rider, for most of them had ridden from infancy; but he generally rode in his own nomad fashion, not so high in the saddle as the Tatar, and certainly longer in the stirrup, but often slumped untidily over his pony's withers. On the other hand his elbows and wrists were always at rest. To have taught him to ride cavalry fashion would have been to deaden his natural abilities.[16] He wore no spur and controlled his horse by a simple jointed-snaffle bit and the nagaika whip that, contrary to a Russian Army order forbidding the irregularity, he stuffed in his top boot instead of suspending it from his wrist by the loop. Cossacks in the guard, according to regulations, were supposed to ride their steeds guard-fashion, with curb and spur; but the photographs of the time still show the Cossack guard on manoeuvres spurless and with the snaffle instead of the curb.[17] The Cossack ponies, too, needed little military schooling to improve their agility or handiness, as even in their semi-wild state they were more than a match for the trained Russian cavalry horse. No amount of dressage could have improved their appearance.

Much has been made in Cossack story and literature, particularly in the Caucasus, of the *dzhigitovka*, the daring and skilled trick riding of the *dzhigit*. This riding originated from the Caucasian tribe of that name and was copied by both the Kuban and Terek Cossacks, the word *dzhigit* also being used in a wider sense to describe not only a trick rider but any bold and daring blade. The *dzhigitovka* became an established and almost traditional feature of Cossack festivals and shows, requiring nerve, agility and judgement from both man and horse alike, usually involving a circus-type mounted gymnastic display, firing from the saddle on the flat or over obstacles, and firing from behind a galloping horse. But, in fact, the *dzhigitovka* was not popular with the Cossack hosts or, unless he were a rich man, with the Cossack himself, because of the possible loss of good horses through injury. The Russian Army, in particular, frowned on these equestrian exercises as being without any military value, and they were soon relegated to the occasion of the military display or circus spectacle.

In the army the gallop was little used except in an emergency since it was wearing on the horses, and the Cossacks were required to conform to the usual cavalry practice when carrying out forced marches by moving at an extended trot of 16 versts (10 miles) to the hour; and if some of the smaller of the Cossack ponies had to change to a hand-canter in order to keep up, then that was perfectly in order. And there was a measure of agreement, too, among the Russian Army and Cossack higher commanders in the late nineteenth century that the modern horseman was an insufficiently good marksman to fire with effect from the saddle, even though his horse be stationary. The trend among the Cossacks was to dismount the men and tether the horses in a *batovanie*, that is to say to secure six or more horses by their bridle-reins run behind the girth of a seventh anchor horse; the lances were then put on the ground and the men moved off on foot with their carbines to their firing positions.

In the latter half of the nineteenth century there was considerable doubt in the Russian Army not only as to how the Cossack of the future should be used but also as to the proper role of cavalry. Some thought that the lancer had outlived his usefulness and others went so far as to propose that all cavalry should have a secondary role as mounted infantry, and did so with such success that in 1882 the cavalry gave up its lances; lancer and hussar regiments were transformed into dragoons and armed with the bayonet in addition to the carbine and sword. Some of the Cossacks were armed with lances while others were not. The Don Cossacks, traditionally lancers, were allowed to retain the lance for service in Europe for possible use against the cavalry of the Central Powers where uhlans and even German dragoons had the pike; but by 1894 the number of lances in Don regiments was halved in that they were retained only by the front rank; this applied, too, to the Astrakhan, Ural, Transbaikal and Siberian Cossacks. The Orenburg did not usually carry the lance, but by 1894 lances were taken into use again there preparatory for war service; the Black Sea Cossacks had originally had lances, that were removed in 1853 and then restored twenty years later, but as Kuban Cossacks they no longer had the lance from 1886 onwards. Terek Cossacks had never had the lance, and the Semirechie, the Amur and the Ussuri lost the lance by 1894. The Bashkir Tatar Cossack *divizion* of four squadrons at Orenburg and the Crimean Tatar Cossack *divizion* of two squadrons based on Simferopol were armed with sabres and carbines and were without lances, the Crimean Tatar Cossacks being unusual in that they had a rifle company permanently grouped in peace and war with each pair of mounted sotnias in the fashion of the Circassians. The only other Cossacks to have rifles or infantry were the Orenburg until 1873, the Amur until 1894 and the Transbaikal; and the Transbaikal dismounted men were phased out in peace in 1902. By 1914 the only Cossack infantry remaining were the *plastun* battalions of the Kuban host.

By 1875 the mounted Cossack units were to all intents and purposes regarded as cavalry regiments by the Russian Army commanders and the tactical staffs who decided the pattern of formation grouping, since fourteen Don Cossack regiments formed the fourth regiment of each of the fourteen Russian cavalry divisions, while four other Cossack regiments formed a Don Cossack cavalry division.[18] Kuban and Terek Cossack regiments, together with Daghestan and Osset irregular Cossack cavalry, were brigaded from 1878 onwards with dragoon regiments to form the dragoon divisions of the Caucasus. The Russian high command had already taken the decision to convert much of its cavalry to dragoons because it considered that with the increasing fire-power of modern weapons the days of close-formation mounted shock-action were passing; mounted shock-action, it began to think, could only be possible in the future if the attacking cavalry advanced and charged in extended order, and so it began to train its Russian cavalry to attack in the open *lava* formation, the tactics so beloved of all the Cossack hosts and nomads, the Tatars, the Bashkirs and the Kirghiz.[19]

The tsarist military authorities had attempted to introduce uniformity and a certain tidiness to the Cossack hosts in the matter of arms, equipment and dress, although with only limited success. Since the individual Cossack was the provider, and since he was often a very poor man belonging to a corps that the Russians classified as 'irregular troops', the results could hardly have been otherwise than they were, with little uniformity of pattern or even colour.[20] His rifle belonged to the state and host and, from 1871, was a .420-inch breech-loading bolt-action Berdan sighted up to 1,250 yards, a United States weapon manufactured under licence; the Asiatic hosts still had the .60-inch Krin'ka rifle, a Minié muzzle-loader converted to a breech-loader, each man in the Asiatic hosts usually carrying in addition a Smith and Wesson revolver. By the end of the century the Krin'ka gave way to the Berdan that was itself replaced by the modern three-line (.299-inch) 1891 five-round magazine bolt-action carbine and rifle, the rifle that was to take Russia through two world wars.[21] The rifle continued to be slung Cossack-fashion over the right shoulder (whereas Russian cavalry carried it over the left) except that the Terek Cossacks carried the slung weapon in a leather-tasselled and stitch-decorated Circassian-pattern rifle-case. Rifle ammunition was carried in two pouches and also in bandoliers slung over the left shoulder. Cossacks, unlike the cavalry, were not provided with bayonets.

The lance or pike, the property of the host, was originally of wood and was nine feet long without a pennon, although this came to be replaced by a lighter hollow tubular metal stave nearly eleven feet in length with a leather shoulder loop and another at the butt for the toe. The sabre was supposed to be much the same pattern as was carried by Russian dragoons, with a slightly curved blade that was just under three feet long, except that the Cossack sword had no hilt-guard. The sabre was suspended by a diagonal sword-belt over the right shoulder, except in the Kuban and Terek where it was attached to the waist-belt together with the long *kinzhal* dagger. The Cossack's saddle equipment was different from that of the cavalry in that the bridle was a single-reined bridoon and the saddle a simple tree with a padded cushion placed over it, the whole resting on four felt numnahs with a leather cover over them. Wallets were attached to the front arch of the tree, and a small valise was carried in the rear of the saddle, the Russian Army pattern grey-brown greatcoat and hood being strapped in front of the rider or, in the case of the Kuban and Terek hosts, the folded *burka* being strapped on the saddle-bags in the rear.

Before the end of the century the Cossack military dress had been standardized, more or less on the Russian Army pattern, in that all the hosts now wore the army *mundir* or field service tunic blouse with coloured host shoulder straps (instead of the earlier *chekmen* coat), together with a braided, peaked or peakless, forage cap (except for the Caucasian and Asiatic hosts that wore a sheepskin *papakha* of any natural colour except black or white), wide blue-grey trousers (*sharovari*) with a broad coloured stripe denoting the *voisko*, and high knee-boots. The two Caucasian hosts wore the traditional Circassian Cossack dress, a frock-coat *cherkesska*, open at the front and reaching below the knees, ornamented with cartridge pockets at the breast, and a high conical sheepskin cap. The ancient nomad black or brown felt *burka* cloak was worn in the Kuban and Terek instead of a greatcoat. The Kuban *plastun* infantry uniform was the same as that for cavalry except that the cloth top of the sheepskin *papakha* was black instead of scarlet.[22] When on service in Turkestan in summer all Cossacks wore a light-weight camel's hair tunic or frock-coat (*armiachina*) as protection against the heat, and heavy red leather breeches (*chambary*) to guard against long spear-grass.

Cossack artillery was of no consequence, being sufficient only for the running battles against the Circassians or Kirghiz: should any greater fire-power be required it would fall to the Russian artillery to provide it. In addition to the single Don guard battery, there were nineteen line batteries, seven for the Don, five for the Kuban, three to the Orenburg, and two each to the Terek and the Transbaikal: on mobilization the number of Don line batteries was tripled and those of the Orenburg and Transbaikal doubled. Each battery had six 3.42-inch guns eventually replaced by the 1902 3-inch Quick-Firer gun that fired a 14-lb shell to a range of about 7,000 yards. Battery commanders were often lieutenant-colonels from the Russian service.

\* \* \*

The military organization in peace and in war and the recruiting and mobilization system of the Cossack hosts after the 1875 reforms were standardized and simple. In the Don host, for example, the ataman was a general or lieutenant-general, with a civil administration under a major-general and a military directorate under another major-general who was called the chief of staff. Each of the five districts of the Don was commanded by a major-general or colonel, and each, in 1882, recruited and maintained three Category 1 peacetime regiments, kept the reserve rolls up to date and held the equipment for the six regiments in the Categories 2 and 3 reserve; each was also responsible for the supervision of all reserve training and for the preparation of the intake in their district. The guard and the artillery were recruited by all districts of the host. In war, therefore, the Don Cossacks, like the other hosts, could triple the regiments that they had in peace. Don regiments were numbered in sequence from 1 to 15 for the peace establishment and from 16 to 30 and 31 to 45 for the two reserve categories.[23] Regiments 1, 16 and 31 were linked by association, as were 2, 17 and 32 and so on, since the soldier from Regiment 1 would normally do his four years of reserve service in each of the other two regiments (16 and 31), and the three regiments formed a link (*zveno*), the three regiments of each link being of course based in the same recruiting district.

The military organization in other hosts was similar to that of the Don. The Kuban Cossacks had only three recruiting districts that between them (in 1886) maintained the ten Category 1 peacetime horsed regiments and two *plastun* battalions (increased by 1894 to six) and these could be tripled in war by the addition of a further twenty regiments of the Categories 2 and 3. The regiments were not numbered in sequence as they were on the Don but bore names that were either those of the Caucasus stanitsa from which they originated or had a historical association (e.g. Khoper and Kavkaz); in war the Category 1 regiment became the 1st Khoper while the other two categories became the 2nd and 3rd Khoper, so that the *zveno* link was retained by the name and not by the linking numbers, as was the case on the Don. The Terek, in 1886, had four recruiting districts each of which furnished one regiment in peace and three in war, and these, like those of the Kuban, took their names either from a regimental historical association (such as the Volga), or the region from which they originated (Gorsko-Mozdok or Kizliar-Grebensk). The Transbaikal Cossacks were similarly listed by regimental name, that is to say the Nerchinskii and the Verkhne Udinskii.

There were some additions and some disbandments around the turn of the century, but this generally was the Cossack organization that was carried forward by the empire until 1914. The Ukrainian Cossack had disappeared and the only truly European host was that of the Don, mainly Great Russian but with Kalmyk and Tatar elements: of the Caucasian hosts the Kuban Cossacks were predominantly Slav and largely Ukrainian; on the Terek they were predominantly Caucasian, although the Cossacks there were Great Russian in speech and mostly Orthodox in religion. The Cossacks on the foothills of Asia, the Astrakhan, Ural and Orenburg were largely of mixed Great and Little Russian stock but the further east one travelled the more Asiatic they became in their racial and social composition and in their customs. Of the eleven hosts established by the empire, some, the Astrakhan, the Semirechie, the Amur and the Ussuri, were very small and even when fully mobilized could each contribute no more than from six to twelve squadrons.

In addition to the eleven hosts there were remnants of the town Cossacks at Irkutsk and Krasnoyarsk that continued their existence into the twentieth century, though these numbered only a squadron each in peace and three squadrons in war. And there were other Cossack troops that formed a permanent part of the military forces of the Russian empire, the descendants of peoples who had been Cossacks long before the name was known to Russia, Tatar horse, Bashkir and Turkoman horse, the Daghestani horse and Ossetin cavalry, all of them properly classified as Cossacks and listed as such in the official Russian army lists.

CHAPTER 8 NOTES

1 There were a number of tiny hosts that were formed and disbanded and then reformed according to the tsarist need for troops. The two Danube Cossack regiments were formed in 1829 and 1844 in Bessarabia from the remnants of the former Danube (*Ust Dunaisk*) host, the descendants of the Zaporozhians in exile that had been broken up in 1807, and the Budzhak Cossacks, together with Serbs, Bulgars, Greeks and Albanians that had served against the Turks: in 1856 they became the New Russian host before disbandment in 1868. The Azov Cossack host was formed in the Ekaterinoslav *guberniia* in 1832 from former Zaporozhians returning from Turkey: it was disbanded in 1865.

2  In the mid nineteenth century there were 30,000 Kalmyks on the Don.

3  At the time of the Crimean War in 1853 the Don establishment stood at 53 regiments and 14 batteries as against a total Cossack establishment (all hosts) of 132 regiments, 23 foot battalions and 24 batteries. In fact the Don Cossacks mobilized or embodied a total of 80 regiments, and 30 per cent of the male population was under arms.

4  Out of the total Don population of 1,595,000 in 1887, 683,000 were *inogorodnie* outlanders. The lowest proportion was in the Transbaikal, 4,300 outlanders out of a total population of 168,300; throughout all the hosts the recorded average non-Cossack population was 32 per cent. Krasnov reckoned, however, that the true figure was much higher than this, since generally the new arrivals took care not to report or advertise their presence to the police in case they should be turned away. Much of the trade within the hosts, particularly on the Don, was in the hands of Jewish and Armenian outlanders. Notwithstanding the anti-Semitism in the host leadership (and in that of tsarist Russia) Jews were allowed to settle, though not to own land in the early days. Don Cossack traders did exist, although their numbers were not great, and these could elect for exemption from military service if they paid a 300-ruble fee into host funds.

5  The Transbaikal Cossacks were subsequently transferred to the commander-in-chief of the Irkutsk military district.

6  According to the Land Allocation Law of 1882 each Cossack was to have a minimum of from 10 to 25 *desiatin* according to category while each officer was to have from 50 to 100 *desiatin* according to rank.

7  In 1888 the richest of the hosts in capital per head in rubles were the Astrakhan (63), Ural (32), Don (22) and Siberian (20). The poorest were the Terek (6) and Amur (6).

8  In the guard horse squadrons, and in the Ural, Don and Orenburg artillery, the Cossack served for only three years instead of of four.

9  According to the regulation the Cossack need not go to the expense of maintaining a horse in peacetime when in Category 3 but he had to have one on mobilization. When in the reserve he had to maintain only his uniform and equipment.

10 According to this survey 65 per cent of all male Cossacks bore arms at some time as against 31 per cent of Russians. On mobilization about 5 per cent (2½ million) Russians would be called up as against 13 per cent (172,000) Cossacks.

11 A Junker was an officer cadet usually taken from the ranks: a cadet was in a separate (and usually more favoured) category, coming direct from school.

12 The Cossacks had particular difficulty in finding suitably qualified young officers for the few Cossack batteries, so that Russian Army artillery officers were seconded to fill vacancies in the Orenburg, Kuban and Terek hosts.

13 In addition to having a horse and equipment, the Don men had to report for service in 1877 bringing with them eight days' biscuit: the biscuit proved to be the only item that the Cossacks would be sure to have, for,

determined that they should not go hungry even if they walked to the war, some brought in enough biscuit for a month.

14 A ruble was worth about two shillings in the 1890s; a Cossack's pay when on active service away from home was 3 rubles a year according to the 1886 rates, 6 rubles if in the guard.

15 Ural Cossacks had a reputation, even with Russian military commanders, for reliability and high spirits even under the most adverse conditions; Perovskii, the Orenburg military governor, had the highest praise for those who went on the 1840 Khiva expedition.

16 Russian and foreign riders, however experienced, when they appeared in the Don stanitsas were regarded with amusement or derision by Cossack man and woman alike, while the children would flock behind calling 'Mind you don't fall off!' and worse. The Kalmyk fashion of riding, on the other hand, was accepted and even imitated by the young Cossacks on the Don in an attempt to appear different and gain attention among their fellows.

17 The simplest form of a bit is a straight-bar snaffle, usually of metal, with a ring at each end to which the single bridle-rein is attached; another bit is the broken or jointed snaffle (used by the Cossacks) consisting of two half-bars connected by a ring-joint in the centre and having the usual bridle-rein rings at each end. The curb is a straight-bar bit to which metal side-pieces are attached, used in conjunction with a curb-chain that fits in the groove under the horse's jaw; the side-pieces, to which the reins are attached, exert additional leverage on the horse's mouth, the longer the side-pieces the greater the leverage, this forcing the animal to relax its jaw and bend its neck. Generally, well-schooled horses and experienced riders can perform any equestrian exercise on a snaffle, once the horse is brought 'on to the bit'; in practice, however, European cavalry rode their horses on the curb, since the curb gave more certain control in emergency.

18 The Russian cavalry division had two brigades each of two regiments: the four regiments were hussars, lancers, dragoons and Cossacks, although in the Caucasus the three Russian regiments were sometimes all dragoons. A Cossack cavalry division had four regiments of Cossacks.

19 The object of the squadron or the regimental *lava* was to outflank the enemy, threaten his rear, put him off balance and, if he were cavalry, force him into open order so that the Cossack could engage him in single combat. The advance was done at a trot in two widely separated lines or ranks one behind the other or in echelon, the horsemen continually making ground and opening up from the centre or to a single flank, so that each horseman was at least four paces from his neighbour. The commander was only 200 or so yards behind the advancing ranks, with a staff (*maiak*) of a few gallopers to assist him in giving direction and with a small reserve behind him. When the foremost line was sufficiently close to charge, the leader began to scream, the scream being taken up by the Cossacks of the sotnia. The *lava* was suitable for tribal or colonial actions but it had no place in modern war.

20  Even Viskovatov, the Russian authority on imperial army uniform, was at a loss in attempting to define Cossack equipment and dress. When describing the *élite* Don ataman guard regiment he says, 'all ranks were ordered to wear a belt, of no particular design or colour: but, in so far as it was possible, officers in a squadron and even in the regiment did try to wear one particular colour since it usually helped to establish identity: for the type of Cossack sabre in the ataman regiment there was no specially ordered pattern.'

21  There were, apparently, no fewer than *four* patterns of three-line rifle, according to its length: infantry, Cossack, dragoon and carbine.

22  The details of Cossack dress and *voisko* colours are shown at Appendix C.

23  The details of the recruiting and mobilization organizations of all hosts are shown in Appendix D.

# 9 The Death of Cossackdom

The 1914 peace establishment of the Russian cavalry and artillery stood at 511 squadrons of cavalry and 327 sotnias of Cossacks, together with 662 batteries of artillery of which only thirty-nine were Cossack. Following the August mobilization the Cossack strength increased to 939 sotnias, of which 360 sotnias and twenty-two batteries came from the Don. But although the strength of the imperial Russian horse exceeded that of the Central Powers and, on paper at least, was truly formidable, this cavalry did not realize the hopes placed on it by the Russian high command and proved to be unsuited to the demands of modern war.

During the First World War the Cossacks were not regarded as being of high fighting value by their foes or by the Russian formation commanders.[1] The Cossack's mount did not show him off to advantage and his lack of discipline and poor turn-out set him apart from the Russian cavalry arm and did not inspire confidence. Like the Russian cavalry the Cossacks were capable of more than holding their own against the troops of the Austro-Hungarian empire, but it is doubtful that they were a match for German mounted troops, who were better trained and incomparably better disciplined. Admittedly the Cossack, particularly if he came from the Don, was more intelligent and had more initiative than most Russian troopers, but it was only too rarely that these qualities were used to advantage. Furthermore the Russian cavalry and its cavalry command were inefficient and suffered from a deep-seated *malaise* of ignorance and prejudice.

Marshal of the Soviet Union Shaposhnikov, the Red Army chief of general staff during much of the Second World War, was the son of a minor civil servant; in 1902 Shaposhnikov had joined a Turkoman rifle regiment, a Russian regiment notwithstanding its name, as a regular army infantry officer, from which he had passed into the general staff college. In 1913 he joined 14 Cavalry Division in Poland as the general staff operations officer, this cavalry division, like many others, being made up of four regiments, hussars, lancers, dragoons and Cossacks. Shaposhnikov, an educated and observant officer, who, for his years, had had a good deal of experience, viewed with a discerning eye the cavalry world in which he had just recently come to live. He subsequently described how Russian cavalry officers of the empire, contrary to popular belief both then and now, for the most part had neither property nor means other than their army pay. Only in the hussars, he said, 'might one find a few darling sons of rich merchants' who, after squandering their patrimonies for two or three years, gave up soldiering and left the regiment. Nor indeed did many line cavalry officers come from the nobility or landed gentry. Yet these officers acted out a part in acquiring an arrogant manner, dandified dress and foppish speech, while remaining virtually ignorant of their profession; too often they were incapable of understanding that the welfare and efficiency of their men and horses were their responsibility and not that of the senior non-commissioned officers, for they believed that the only role demanded of them was that they should lead their men into battle. A great many of the senior cavalry formation commanders were elderly and were similarly prejudiced and ignorant. And, as Baselevich told Knox, 'the guard looked down on everyone, the line cavalry looked down on infantry, while in each cavalry division the hussars despised the lancers who themselves despised the dragoons: and all three despised the Cossacks.'[2] The Cossack officers of the late nineteenth and early twentieth centuries, particularly in the Don host, too often regarded line cavalry as a pattern and adopted many of the mannerisms and faults of the line cavalry officers.

Although on the outbreak of war the number of Cossack divisions, each of four Cossack regiments, had been increased from six to eleven, most regular Cossack regiments were brigaded within cavalry divisions under cavalry commanders, while many of the reserve sotnias and Category 2 and 3 regiments were shared out among the infantry corps and divisions to serve as a reconnaissance and cavalry element. In truth the Cossack regiments were much misused by cavalry and infantry commanders alike in exactly the same fashion as

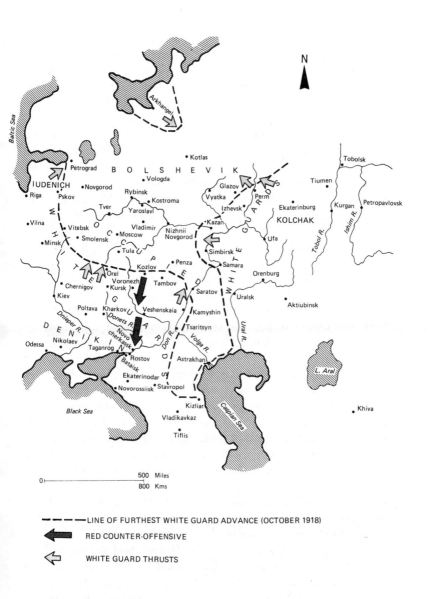

Baltic Sea

Arkhangel

BOLSHEVIK

• Kotlas

Tobolsk

Riga

Petrograd

• Novgorod

• Vologda

Tiumen

IUDENICH

Pskov

Rybinsk

Glazov

Vyatka

Perm

Petropavlovsk

Vilna

Tver

Kostroma

Izhevsk

Ekaterinburg

Kurgan

Vitebsk

Yaroslavl

Nizhnii
Novgorod

Kazan

KOLCHAK

Minsk

Smolensk

Vladimir

Moscow

Ufa

W
H
I
T
E

G
U
A
R
D
S

Tula

Chernigov

Orel

Kozlov

Penza

Simbirsk

Samara

Orenburg

Aktiubinsk

Kiev

Voronezh

Kursk

Tambov

Saratov

Uralsk

Poltava

Kharkov

Veshenskaia

Kamyshin

Novo-
cherkassk

Tsaritsyn

L. Aral

Odessa

Nikolaev

Taganrog

Rostov

Astrakhan

DENIKIN

Bataisk

Ekaterinodar

Stavropol

Novorossiisk

Khiva

Black Sea

Kizliar

Caspian Sea

Vladikavkaz

Tiflis

Dnieper R.

Donets R.

Don R.

Volga R.

Ural R.

Tobol R.

Ishim R.

| 0 | 500 Miles |
|---|---|
| | 800 Kms |

----- LINE OF FURTHEST WHITE GUARD ADVANCE (OCTOBER 1918)

RED COUNTER-OFFENSIVE

WHITE GUARD THRUSTS

15  The Civil War 1918–1919
(The Destruction of the Cossacks)

they had been during the Turkish wars of the preceding century; and no heed had been taken of the official instruction to Russian commanders to rectify this abuse. The Russian generals in the First World War affected to have no higher opinion than their predecessors of Cossack officers and men, and so they split the regiments down to fatigue detachments, to provide escorts, to find gallopers and messengers, sometimes even to furnish the postal service, the pickets and the military police. Cossacks were used to round up stragglers and deserters and provide stop lines to prevent Russian troops withdrawing without orders. It was the Cossacks who carried out the more distasteful duties and chores, from the flogging of soldiers in arrest to the provision of labourers. Many of the commanders of Cossack regiments forming part of Russian divisions saw their units almost completely wasted away by such detachments and fatigue duties.

The Cossack remained the loyal subject of the tsar and the constant supporter of both the military authorities responsible for internal security and of the Russian police; he could still be relied upon to deal with riotous assemblies, whether these were made up of Poles, Ukrainians or Russian workers or peasants, and he would readily charge home against the populace with his flailing nagaika. Before 1914, the Cossack had been less affected than the Russian by the subversive movements that, having taken root in the cities and main towns, were beginning to spread into the countryside, and the reason lay in the closely-knit Cossack stanitsa and village system and, to some extent, in the very strong family ties to be found in most of the Great Russian Cossack hosts, where the young men and their wives worked the family smallholdings or farms as directed by the parents or grandparents. Everyone knew his neighbour and his neighbour's business, and the activities of the agitator or propagandist, who as likely as not would have been a visitor from outside the host, could not go unnoticed by the ataman or the Cossack police.

Conditions changed rapidly, however, during the course of the first two years of the war, since casualties, food shortages, high prices, inflation and government corruption began to tell on a war-weary nation. The empress was unpopular by reputation, even with the rank and file in the army, and the emperor had been so ill-advised as to take over command of the army in the field, leaving the Petrograd (St Petersburg) capital and much of the business of government to the empress while he sojourned in faraway Mogilev, at the *Stavka* general headquarters. Many of the Cossack regiments spent long periods in the line as infantry, sometimes suffering heavy casualties, always a prey to sickness and boredom in time of inaction. Yet, in spite of the privations and the many defeats, the Russian Army in the field and its Cossack component continued to hold together. The seeds of the coming revolution and mutinies were laid not at the front but in the rear areas and, in particular, in the Petrograd garrison among the training and base units, where there were few professional regimental officers and even fewer long-service non-commissioned officers, and where the soldiery in their city barracks and on the streets were vulnerable to the subversion of the revolutionary activists. This propaganda was directed, too, at the Cossack rank and file in and about the capital.

In February 1917 there were strikes and demonstrations in Petrograd against the government, demonstrations that could easily have been dispersed except that the Cossacks, when detailed to support the police, declined to intervene. A training detachment of guard infantry fired upon the crowd when ordered to do so, but then mutinied the next day. The Cossacks, when instructed to move against the mutineers, refused to do so on the pretext that they had insufficient infantry to support them. Then the Don Cossack Regiments 1, 4 and 14, together with a Cossack regiment of the guard, the *Konvoi* (the composite Kuban/Terek imperial escort), went over to the mutineers.[3] The defection of this handful of troops in the capital led to the downfall and abdication of the tsar. Kerensky's provisional government eventually came into being and this was loyally supported by the Petrograd Cossack units with whose help Kerensky succeeded that July in suppressing the armed demonstrations by soldiers and sailors, so forestalling an anarchist and left-wing Bolshevik *coup*. Kerensky had appointed firstly Alekseev and then Brusilov to the commander-in-chief's appointment vacated by the emperor; but then public attention in Russia was drawn to General Kornilov, the former commander of 3 Cavalry Corps, a blunt uncompromising Transbaikal Cossack, half Russian and half Mongol, who demanded the restoration of military discipline with, if necessary, the death penalty for mutineers and deserters. Kornilov became the man of the moment and popular with all classes of Russian society other than those of the political left. Kerensky replaced Brusilov as commander-in-chief by Kornilov.

Petrograd and the empire were in complete disorder with two separate and opposed governments in the capital, Kerensky's provisional government and the Petrograd soviet. Kerensky's only source of power was in the loyalty of the army high command; the only co-ordinated and active strength in the soviet lay in its left wing, and principally in the Bolshevik movement, so that the real opposing forces were at the radical extremes, with Kornilov on the one side and Lenin on the other; both of these men had distinctive Mongolian features, Kornilov from his Buriat mother, and Lenin, according to the current rumour on the lower Volga and Don, from Volga Kalmyk forbears. Kornilov was not in a position to act by himself and was obliged to work hand in hand with Kerensky, or at least to cloak his activity so that it would appear that the provisional government was behind him. Kornilov proposed to be rid of the Bolsheviks by armed force and, in the final outcome, it may be that he intended to do it with or without Kerensky. Kerensky agreed that Kornilov should move 3 Cavalry Corps on the capital as a precaution against the left wing of the soviet, but then, in September, either lost his nerve or regarded Kornilov as a threat to himself. He tried to remove Kornilov from his appointment and openly allied himself with the soviet and the Bolsheviks against the army high command.

Kornilov ordered Krymov's 3 Cavalry Corps, that included Bagration's Caucasian Moslem Cossacks (the Native or Savage Division), into Petrograd against both Kerensky and the soviet; the *coup* failed when it was halted by strikes and obstruction on the part of the railway and telegraph workers and by agitators sent out from the capital to subvert Krymov's troops. Kornilov was arrested on Kerensky's orders and detained with other generals of the high command at Bykhov; Krymov committed suicide and his corps was taken over by Krasnov, a Don Cossack. In October the Bolsheviks decided on armed insurrection against the *bourgeois* provisional government and Kerensky fled for his life, firstly to the army command at Pskov and then abroad. With this second revolution the empire rapidly slid into anarchy, bloodshed and civil war.

The Bolsheviks intended to end Russia's war against the Central Powers immediately and at all costs, for they had promised peace and land to the peasant and independence to the many minorities; they had singled out the officer as the class-enemy of the soldier. The old army, recruited mainly from Russian, Ukrainian and some minority peasantry, disintegrated in a flood of desertion. Many officers went into hiding or began to make their way to the Ukraine or to the territory of the Don Cossacks, the most powerful and the most conservative of the Cossack hosts which, even under the tsars, had preserved a measure of autonomy; during November it became clear that neither the ataman of the Don Cossacks, nor the Ukrainian nationalists, would recognize the authority of the Bolshevik centre. General Dukhonin, the last chief of staff at the Mogilev *Stavka*, aware of the danger in which all officers stood from the new régime, released the five senior generals from Bykhov and advised them to make their way to the Don. These set out for the south-east, joining the throng of the aristocracy, the wealthy, the educated and the conservative, towards what they hoped would be the security of established order.[4] The Don, as the rallying-point of the Old Order, was to prove the Vendée of the Russian revolution.

\* \* \*

Following the February revolution and the abdication of the tsar, there had been a movement among the Don Cossacks to cut themselves off from the splintering empire and reassert the rights that they had once enjoyed before the time of Peter the Great, and this aim was shared by other of the Cossack hosts. There was much talk, though little was achieved, about setting up a Cossack federation that would take in the two powerful hosts in the south, the Don and the Kuban, and may be extend to the Terek, the Astrakhan, the Ural and the Orenburg Cossacks.

The Don province was the most important in population and in resources, and it was from the Don that the lead would have to come. But except in Rostov and in Taganrog, with their factories and shipyards, the Don territories were still mainly rural, their principal exports being livestock, grain, fish and salt. By 1917 a half of the Don territory population was non-Cossack, and although Russian law had done much to equate the *inogorodnie* rights with those of the previously privileged Cossack, the fact remained that the outlanders were the late-comers and were usually much poorer than the registered members of the hosts; for this reason the resentment remained both on the Don and elsewhere. The populations and territory of Rostov and Taganrog had only recently been taken back into the Don province and, in reality, were quite foreign to it, since they held a rich merchant and industrialist population, a flourishing *bourgeoisie* and a very strong working class, all of which were outside the host and had no wish to join it. By 1918 the Bolsheviks were to become very strong on the Don in the few cities and major towns, while the Socialist Revolutionaries had much support from the non-Cossacks living in the country. Townsmen and countrymen outside of the host regarded the Don Cossack with either jealousy or indifference.

In June of 1917 the krug at Novocherkassk had elected Kaledin to be the Don ataman; and when, after the September Kornilov affair, Kerensky had attempted to have Kaledin arrested, the Petrograd orders were ignored on the Don.[5] After the Bolshevik *coup* Kaledin declared that the members of Lenin's government were criminals, and the Don Cossacks took on their new independence.

This independence had, however, been secured at Kaledin's order by the elderly and the very young Cossacks who had been prevented from going to the war by age and who were untainted by revolutionary propaganda. The temper of the host soon changed when the regiments came straggling back from the front, most with, but some without, their officers and all with their soldiers' revolutionary committees; they yearned for peace and harboured no ill-will against the Bolsheviks who were preaching self-determination for the minorities and who had put an end to the war. The Bolsheviks themselves, however, began to move in against the Don from the north Donets and from the industrial area of portside Novorossiisk in the Kuban, establishing close contacts with the proletariat in Rostov and Taganrog. The Socialist Revolutionaries and the Mensheviks opposed any action by the Don host that they judged to be counter-revolutionary, including the disarming of pro-Bolshevik military units. Kaledin could certainly count on no support from the *inogorodnie*, the *bourgeoisie* remained passive, and, with the return of the Cossack field regiments, Kaledin's orders were disregarded throughout the Don territories since they were backed neither by the police nor by the military. The Cossack wanted to remain free from Russia but he did not yet regard the Bolsheviks as a threat to himself, his property or his independence; the newly returned Cossacks did, however, view Kaledin with suspicion since they believed him to be pro-French and pro-Entente and likely to involve them in war against revolutionary Russia or the continuation of hostilities against the Central Powers. Krasnov, the Don Cossack commander of 3 Cavalry Corps that was still in Russia, had tried without success to persuade Kaledin to take more positive action to save the Don. But Kaledin thought that the opportunity, if it had ever existed, had already passed.

Like the Don, the Kuban was stable and quiet in the early days under its ataman Filimonov, who declared the Kuban to be independent and who had the Russian soldiery there disarmed. In the Kuban province there were few large urban or industrial areas except in Novorossiisk, but the *inogorodnie* population in the area was as large as that of the Cossacks. As in the Don the troubles, when they eventually broke out, centred around these outlanders and the Cossacks returning from the front: the port and railway workers soon set up military revolutionary councils, and bands of armed Red workers, guerrillas and banditry attacked the host, this being followed by an invasion of the Kuban by workers and sailors from Novorossiisk. The Bolsheviks had for the moment got the upper hand in Stavropol, and the Terek ataman Karaulov had been killed in the anarchy that was now general on the Caspian. In Astrakhan the Cossacks were shortly to fight a losing battle with the Bolsheviks, although Dutov, the Orenburg ataman, still controlled the railway into Turkestan.

The arrival on the Don of Kornilov and the Bykhov group of generals, followed by Alekseev who came from Moscow, was not pleasing to Kaledin because he knew that the rank and file of the Don Cossacks would not support them; and their efforts to create an anti-Bolshevik Volunteer Army on the Don from non-Cossacks, former army officers, Junkers, cadets, school boys, soldiers and others, would, he thought, merely serve to incite the Bolsheviks to enter the Don lands, particularly since the embryo Volunteer Army had already put down a Bolshevik insurrection in Rostov. So, while giving the Volunteer Army some secret support in the way of funds, he invited it to move south into the Kuban. The Bolshevik bands were, however, already on the move against the Don, heading towards Novocherkassk and Rostov, and a Don Cossack revolutionary military council had been set up in Kamenskaia. Elsewhere the Don Cossacks were unwilling to fight the revolutionaries, and Kaledin, refusing Kornilov's invitation to go south with the Volunteer Army, shot himself. His death caused a stir within the host, and there was much talk of the resistance measures to be taken against a Bolshevik invasion. But it all came to very little, and only 1,500 men joined the newly forming Don Army under Popov. In February 1918 the Volunteer Army, about 4,000 strong, evacuated Rostov on its way south to the Kuban, and the Don Army followed. The new Don host ataman, General Nazarov, refused to leave his post in

Novocherkassk and he, together with his principal officers, was murdered by the Reds on their entry into the capital.

The Volunteer Army moved into the Kuban ill-equipped and ill-supplied, skirmishing as it went; it made an unsuccessful attempt to take Ekaterinodar from the Bolshevik force that had occupied it and there Kornilov was killed. Denikin took over the command, and the decision was made to return to the Don. Although Ekaterinodar had not been taken, the Volunteer Army had begun to recruit Circassians and Kuban Cossacks, many of whom had suffered severely from the arrogance, depredations and atrocities of the mainly city Russian soviets; a Kuban Cossack group under Pokrovskii joined the force. In spite of its lack of weapons the Volunteer Army was of high fighting quality and began to destroy, one by one, the Bolshevik strongholds in Caucasia. Its effectiveness was based largely on its mobility.

The situation on the Don had been changed radically by the Brest Litovsk treaty between the Bolsheviks and the Central Powers, for the conditions included the Russian evacuation of the Ukraine. During March and April the German and Austro-Hungarian troops occupied the Ukraine, driving the Red bands and partisan guerrillas before them, and by early May the German Army occupied Taganrog, Rostov, Bataisk and the Taman peninsula in the Kuban, together with part of the Donets basin, this bringing it to the edge of the Don territories.

The Don Cossack had had ample opportunity to learn that he had nothing in common with the bands of anarchists and criminals and the indisciplined and hostile Red guards who had arrived from the Ukraine or the northern industrial areas, for the Don stanitsas had suffered murder, rape, theft and destruction at their hands. The stanitsas and small outlying villages began to enrol their own home guards that were summoned at the tocsin ringing of the church bell, but volunteers, even for stanitsa defence, were not easy to find at first from among the *frontoviki*, the seasoned warriors that had come back from the war. Fire-arms and ammunition were scarce and horses were now hard to come by, so that the larger part of the Cossacks fought on foot and this curtailed their radius of action. Generally speaking they were ready to defend their own boundaries and would send help to neighbouring stanitsas, but they would not march far afield at any great distance from their homes.

Two Cossack leaders, Denisov and Mamontov, who had remained on the Don, succeeded, however, in raising a standing force of 1,000 horse and 5,000 foot, again mainly from the young, the elderly or the unattached, and this lived out on the steppe. This corps did not suffer from the usual 'Cossack sickness', an unwillingness to stray far from its home stanitsa; on the contrary, in spite of its lack of arms and equipment, it had to be kept on the move and busy raiding and fighting as a safeguard against boredom and desertion. The little force was much superior to its disorganized and indisciplined Bolshevik enemies, so that, by the beginning of May, when the Volunteer Army arrived back, the Don Cossacks had already cleared the Reds from half of the Don territories. Novocherkassk was taken from the enemy with the help of Brozdovskii's 'White' regiment made up of 700 non-Cossack officers and 400 army rank and file that had arrived from the Dniester.

The Don and Kuban Cossacks, and indeed the Cossacks of the other hosts, had always been bedevilled, in times of emergency, by their insistence on meetings and prolonged discussions and arguments that often ended in violence and bloodshed, but without any binding decisions being taken. To this was now added the jealousies and dissensions among the Cossack and White generals and commanders. When Novocherkassk had been cleared a krug was assembled, or more rightly half a krug, since only half of the Don territories were represented, and this came to be known as the 'dumb krug' since the Cossack representatives were strangely inarticulate in the face of Krasnov's fluency and vehemence. Krasnov was elected ataman but he insisted on very firm conditions before he would take up the office. Krasnov required a restoration of discipline, all changes that had been introduced since February 1917 being annulled, with something like dictatorial powers for himself; he had no time for the liberal ideas expressed by Kaledin and, from that time onwards, the *inogorodnie* had to obey the host as the host should see fit. And it was inevitable that Krasnov would not work easily in concert with Denikin or the other Russian generals of the Volunteer and White Armies.

As soon as Novocherkassk had been cleared and even before Krasnov had been elected, the Don Cossacks had been in touch with the German command in Rostov, asking for clarification of German intentions and wanting to know what the Germans were doing in Taganrog and Rostov on Don Cossack soil. The German replies were civil, but unyielding in any particular. For Krasnov, however, the

German occupation of the Ukraine was the salvation of the Don, and Novocherkassk soon entered into a relationship with the German command at Kiev that was close and correct, if not cordial, a relationship that was based on a mutual need—for Krasnov wanted military and technical supplies that the Germans could supply in abundance from captured war stocks, while Berlin needed foodstuffs and some security that a resuscitated and reunited Russian empire was not going to take up arms again on the side of Germany's western enemies. From Russia's former allies Krasnov, for the moment, could expect nothing. By energetic measures Krasnov soon put the Don on to a war footing and before autumn had increased the Don Army to 40,000 men ready for action, with artillery, planes, armoured trains and a river flotilla, and a further 20,000 under training. But, in spite of the restoration of discipline, Krasnov had little confidence that his Cossacks could be relied upon in the event of having to serve away from home for any length of time.

In the early days the Don host was the main supplier of weapons, provisions and cash to the White armies, now at a strength of about 9,000 men, but for this Krasnov received little thanks since Krasnov's transactions with the Germans had earned him angry censure from the Russian generals; some regarded his conduct as treasonable. The Don host was at variance, too, with the Russian generals' avowed intention of restoring a united and indivisible Russia. Since Krasnov was their supplier the Russian generals could impose no restrictions upon him, but the whole made for bad relations between the Cossacks and the Volunteer Army.

In the Kuban the Cossacks were split into a number of factions. Some wanted complete independence. Others of Ukrainian origin wanted to unite with the new hetmanate republic of the Ukraine, an idea that was fiercely opposed by the Volunteer Army since it would, according to the situation at the time, turn the Kuban into another German satellite. Some Kuban Cossacks with Russian or Don Cossack roots wanted federation with the Don or with the larger federation of the South-East Cossacks. The situation was further complicated in that the indigenous Caucasian Cossacks, the Kabards, Ossets, Chechens, Ingush and Daghestanis, had set up their own independent states.

In the early days the Kuban Cossacks were forced to rely largely on the forays of the Volunteer Army that came down from the north, of which fighting force Kuban Cossacks formed a significant part. Later in the year two Kuban Cossack leaders of note came to the fore: a General Shkuro, described by Denikin as 'a brave, rollicking, scatter-brained man of somewhat loose morals', and by the Englishman Williamson as 'a brigand, never without a wolfskin cap and the red, blue and white ribbon of the Volunteer Army on his arm, at the head of a band of 300 or 400 riders all in wolfskin rather than in the traditional Astrakhan wool', who collected funds for their men by barely concealed intimidation; and a General Ulagai, who was said to have been 'honest, ambitious, touchy and a little unbalanced'.

The small Terek host had been all but swamped in a Red Sea of turmoil, and the Astrakhan Cossacks had been scattered by the revolutionaries. In Siberia the situation had been transformed by the Czech expeditionary corps that had stopped up the Trans-Siberian railway, and by the appearance there of Admiral Kolchak who rallied a White force with the support of the Siberian and Orenburg Cossacks and, towards the end of 1918, began a western offensive, scattering the revolutionary forces and taking the city of Perm together with 30,000 prisoners and a great collection of booty. This success drew the attention of the Entente to the possibilities of allied intervention in the Russian Civil War.

The allied victory over the Central Powers and the collapse of the German and Austro-Hungarian empires in November 1918 had led to the removal of the occupying troops from the Ukraine, great areas of which were speedily occupied by the Reds. The western allies now took the place of the Germans in becoming the main supplier to the Don Army and the White armies in the south and north. Two months later, according to Krasnov, the Don Cossacks had 100,000 men under arms, while the Kuban host had 35,000, as against Denikin's White Army strength of under 10,000. Yet Krasnov, at allied insistence, was obliged to step down, his place as ataman being taken by Bogaevskii, and the overall command of the White and Cossack forces went to Denikin. The reasons for Krasnov's removal were not only that he was believed to be pro-German in his sympathies, but that the Russian generals and the western leaders were of the opinion that Krasnov, too, suffered from 'border sickness', a willingness to extend and round off his own borders at the expense of his neigh-bours coupled with a reluctance to engage the enemy beyond his own frontiers; this sickness was common to all the Cossack hosts.

At the end of July 1918 a Don Cossack force under Mamontov had driven in Voroshilov's Red levies west of the Don near the Chir bridge and crossed the shallow and slow moving river. Raiding patrols went whooping eastwards over the steppe, penetrating almost to the Tsaritsyn city outskirts, while others, under Fitskhelaurov, struck north to Kamyshin. Cavalry and armoured trains were used by both Reds and Whites, the fighting taking the form of forced marches and scattered raids, the struggle being fierce and pitiless, wounded and prisoners being done to death by both sides. Tsaritsyn was finally taken and the Cossacks controlled most of Caucasia and the greater part of the Don territories, and there they exacted a terrible vengeance for the fearful atrocities committed by the Reds. Reprisals of an almost indescribable barbarity begat reprisals in their turn. Looting was widespread, not just to eat but to get rich, and this affected Cossack and White morale; the once prosperous territories were reduced to starvation. By February 1919 the Don Cossack Army, advancing northwards beyond its borders, met with reverses and immediately began to melt away so that it numbered barely 15,000 men; it continued to retreat, finally halting beyond the Donets where, according to Denikin, it was saved by the thaw and the spring floods and the presence of the Volunteer Army.

The morale and fighting value of the Don Cossacks varied widely and, so Denikin said, was due to complicated and deep-rooted causes: there was an attachment to the paternal stanitsas, beyond the limits of which many did not wish to fight; at times there glimmered a clearer consciousness of the interests of the Don territory and the Cossack force; and lastly, although this was not very marked, a vague idea of the motherland, embracing Russia as a whole. The men on the Don hated the Bolsheviks, yet they fraternized with Bolshevik Cossacks; they were both valorous and greedy, recklessly gallant yet prone to desertion; had a strong sense of discipline together with a passion for meetings to question their own leadership. This heterogenous compound resulted in extraordinary fluctuations—from lightning successes to total collapse. And that was exactly what befell the Don Cossack front, for, according to Denikin, the Don Cossacks held out through that spring only because of the steadying influence of the Volunteer Army; had this departed, the Cossacks 'would not have remained for a single day.'

Denikin's White force consisted of three armies: on the right Wrangel's Caucasian Army north of the Manych made up largely of Kuban and Caucasian Cossacks; in the centre the field ataman

Sidorin's Don Cossacks to the north of the Don bend; and on the left Mai-Maevsky's Volunteer Army concentrating to the north of Rostov. The White numbers in the south gradually rose between May and October 1919 from 64,000 to 160,000, ranged against the Red strength of Egorev's South Front, estimated that July to be about 178,000 men. In May Ulagai's Kuban Cossacks, moving over the open steppe on the right wing, had defeated the Red cavalry there, and had advanced rapidly up the Volga valley in a movement that had resulted in the taking of Tsaritsyn and Kamyshin.

The Bolshevik plan for a summer counter-offensive had been based on attacking the sector that they believed would be least capable of holding, the centre held by the Don Cossack Army; but their early August offensive was successful only in that it made some ground towards Tsaritsyn and the line of the Khoper; thereafter it was held by bitter resistance from the Don Cossacks. Then came Denikin's grand counter-offensive that began on 12 August. Kiev fell to the Whites at the end of August and Kursk was taken shortly afterwards. Voronezh was occupied by Sidorin's Cossacks. Mamontov with 8,000 mounted Don Cossacks broke deep into the enemy rear, seizing Tambov on 18 August and Kozlov, the headquarters of the Red Army South Front, forcing Trotsky, who happened to be there at the time, to flee for his life. But this operation, that came to be known as the Mamontov raid, traced a great circle behind the enemy front from Tambov, Kozlov, Griazi and Voronezh, and was seen by Denikin as 'an example of brilliant and ineffective prowess'. It certainly destroyed communications and supply depots, cut railway lines, dispersed tens of thousands of mobilized recruits besides creating widespread panic in the Red Army rear. But instead of pushing on to Liskii, according to plan, and striking at the rear of the Eighth and Ninth Soviet Armies, it avoided combat and gave itself over to plunder, filling long columns of wagons with booty and trekking back to the Don stanitsas with thousands of fighting men trailing behind. Soon only 2,000 men were all that remained in the ranks, their horses so encumbered with loot that they looked like pack-mules. Mamontov himself went for a rest to Rostov and Novocherkassk where he was acclaimed a host hero.[6] All in all, Mamontov's raid was without lasting gain and lost the force a strong Don Cossack corps. The Volunteer Army, however, continued its advance and by the end of October stood at Orel, about 180 miles south of Moscow, so that the front lay in a line through Voronezh,

Orel, Chernigov, Kiev and Odessa. Elsewhere Kolchak, having reached a line from Glazov, Buzuluk, Orenburg and Uralsk, mistakenly committed his main effort northwards towards the White Sea instead of to the south to join up with Denikin, a false move that was eventually to cause his retreat and destruction; in the Baltic region, however, Iudenich was rapidly closing on Petrograd, Gatchina being taken on 15 October. But then, between 23 and 25 October 1919, the tide suddenly turned, in that Kolchak and Iudenich were already in retreat, and the Red high command gathered its forces for a massive Soviet counter-blow against Denikin.

Denikin had tried to do too much with too few forces—advance up the Volga, take Moscow and occupy the whole of the Ukraine —and he had failed to make use of his early victories; when the Soviet counter-offensive came he was too dispersed to hold it. Moreover his force was stricken with internal dissension, Cossackdom against Russia, centralist against federalist, Terek against Kuban and Kuban against the Don; the Circassian and Caucasian Cossacks were in dispute among themselves and at logger heads with the Russian hosts; and everywhere the Ukrainians were against the Russians.

The Red Army plan was based on a double blow from the areas of Voronezh and Orel intent on outflanking the Volunteer Army and separating it from the Don Cossacks, it being appreciated that the Cossacks would fall back to their own territories if they felt themselves to be in danger. Voronezh was defended by Shkuro's cavalry, but after a ten-day battle Shkuro gave way, opening a breach through which Budenny's Red cavalry forces advanced and took both Voronezh and Kastornaia, so threatening the right flank of the Volunteer Army. Some Don Cossack formations gave way without a fight. Rebels, that is to say Ukrainian nationalists, anarchists and Bolsheviks, in the rear of the Volunteer Army at Kharkov, Poltava and Ekaterinoslav, were becoming bolder day by day.

The greater and best part of the Don Army was standing on the Khoper, but to move these reserves in a 'non-Cossack' direction, that is to say north-westwards against Budenny's flank was, said Denikin, 'extremely difficult and encountered psychological obstacles and passive resistance;' Denikin resolved to put Wrangel in command of the Volunteer Army together with one Don Cossack corps, hoping that Wrangel might induce the Cossacks to move. When Wrangel met opposition from the Don corps his first step 'in spite of Denikin's warning not to do so' was to place his own man Ulagai, who had been in command of Kuban Cossacks near the Volga, over the Don Cossack corps. Mamontov thereupon, in the middle of the battle, left his corps and returned home, voicing his disgust in telegrams sent to his superiors and to his Don regiments. 'For such an unprecedented breach of discipline' Denikin deprived the absent Mamontov of his command, a command that seems to have been already taken from him. The Don Cossacks, Sidorin and Bogaevskii, took the part of Mamontov. From this time onwards even less reliance could be placed on the Don Cossacks who regarded the White high command as a foreign, almost hostile, body. Mamontov was eventually returned to his former post at the insistence of the Don ataman, but the damage had already been done. Worse was to follow when the Kuban Cossacks, many of whom had become the victims of the propaganda of enemy agitators, took offence at the relegation of Ulagai. In the Kuban itself the Kuban ataman and rada had been removed by a *coup* sponsored by Russian members of the Volunteer Army detachment there. Disillusioned, the Kuban Cossacks left the field and made for home, their morale and discipline destroyed.

Elsewhere there had been a renewal of fighting on the Terek, the Urals and Orenburg (where Dutov, in spite of many reverses repeatedly returned to the battle), in Transbaikal and on the Amur. Gregorii Semenov, a Transbaikal Cossack, ruled part of Eastern Siberia with the support of the Japanese, while other Cossacks, many of them little more than banditry, controlled much of the Siberian railway. Many of these hosts had found troops for Kolchak and they went down in defeat with him.

Denikin's forces finally fell apart; after a forty-day advance Budenny's Red cavalry army reached the Sea of Azov, on 7 January 1920, splitting the White forces between the Crimea and the Caucasus. When the Bolsheviks occupied Caucasia many of the Cossacks took to flight, together with their families, some to Turkey, the others to the Crimea where, in the early months of 1920 they made their last stand, the last of the old order of Cossacks.

\* \* \*

The new Bolshevik government had moved the Russian capital back to Moscow and included 'a Cossack department' in its central executive committee whose principal task it was to subvert the Cossacks in the hosts and bring them over to the side of the

communists. The Bolsheviks formed 'a working Cossack movement', promising the Cossack everything his heart could desire, the
retention of the Cossack way of life, uniform, land, cattle, horses,
churches and freedom: in return, all that the Cossack had to do was
to free himself from the repression of the ataman and his officers and
come over to the Red Army. Numbers of Cossacks did in fact serve
with the Red Army throughout the war; many more who had not
seen communism at first hand or had not suffered from proletariat
occupation, went over to the Red Army only to return to the Whites
when they had had their fill. In order to gain Cossack support,
Budenny, together with his military council (Voroshilov and
Shchadenko, who served as his commissars), decked themselves out
in what they thought to be a form of mounted Cossack dress together
with Cossack-pattern sabres.

A Ukrainian Red Cossack cavalry corps formed part of the Red
Army in these early days. This, however, was merely a sop to
Cossack opinion and to Ukrainian nationalist sentiment, for
Ukrainian Cossack names were simply given to Red detachments of
cavalry that probably included no Cossacks and were not even
predominantly Ukrainian, titles that were as simply removed once
victory had been won. A territorial or national military designation
or name meant as little after the revolution as it had done in the days
of the tsars.

After the White defeat came the Red occupation of the host
territories. As elsewhere, the Bolsheviks divided the population into
the kulaks, those who owned cattle—even though the number might
be only half a dozen or even less, and the poor. All atamans,
starshinas and elders, however petty, were dispossessed and often
shot, and the government authority was delegated to 'committees of
the poor' whose duty it was to govern in the name of the Bolsheviks
and seize their neighbours' grain and cattle in the name of the state.
By this Bolshevik policy, that they called 'looting the looters', com-
munist class-warfare was introduced into the rural stanitsas and
villages.

With communism came the centralization of government and the
suppression of the minorities, a suppression even more draconian
and an autocracy even more absolute than those of Peter the Great
and Nicholas I. In the eyes of the Bolshevik government of Lenin and
his successors all Cossacks were reactionaries and were marked
down for destruction, and so the communists determined to destroy

all trace of the Cossack communities. The hosts, the land rights, even many of the settlements completely disappeared, much of the population being brutally murdered or deported. The singing of Cossack songs and the wearing of Cossack dress were strictly prohibited and Cossacks, as counter-revolutionaries, were banned from conscript call-up for Red Army service, having to serve instead in labour battalions almost penal in their character.

But the troubles of the former Cossacks who had remained and survived as peasants on their ancient homeland were not over. Some of these were 'the poor' who had dispossessed others at the time of the Bolshevik occupation; others were the remnants of the dispossessed who had recovered following the latitude allowed to the peasant smallholder by Lenin's 'New Economic Policy'. But their situation was entirely reversed again by the agrarian reforms that accompanied the introduction of the first of Stalin's Five-Year Plans (1928–32). For these reforms called for the collectivization of all agriculture into state farms and combines. Once again the purges began against the kulak, any man who employed labour, owned livestock, barns or machinery, for these peasants were simply expropriated and denied the right to join the new collectives, and even to work. Only the poorest were given any control in local affairs. Then followed the mass arrests of families who were deported to concentration camps under OGPU guards for heavy labour; and hundreds of thousands were perpetually banished to the north and the east, imprisoned in labour camps for many years under the harshest of conditions, from which death could be their only release.

This was the final death knell of the Cossack populations, particularly on the Don and in the Kuban where collectivization was to be completed in a year. Most had died from the war, the purges or the mass starvation that was to follow, had been deported or imprisoned, or had left the new countryside of the collectives, the great state farms and the machine tractor stations, and had moved into the cities. A few of the remnants on the Don and Terek, in the Kuban, and in the Caucasus and Siberia began to play the part of the outlaws that they already were and took to brigandage, and though their numbers were insignificant, their activities were often sufficient to bring down government reprisals on the heads of any known Cossacks that remained, and so the starvation, beatings, torture, killings and outrages went on sporadically until 1935.

CHAPTER 9 NOTES

1 On the other hand numbers of Cossack officers such as Kornilov, Kaledin, Krasnov and Krymov did reach relatively high rank as army and corps commanders, in command of Russian field formations.

2 Knox was the British general officer accredited to the Russian army in the field (1914–17): Baselevich was his Russian staff officer.

3 The volatile nature of Cossack (and Russian) troops is not easy to explain to the western reader, but the Great Russian in particular was mercurial and unpredictable; he was also primitive, ignorant and easily swayed. Troops that would cheer the tsar until they were hoarse on one day, might open fire on his representative the next; those that might fight to the death today, might surrender without striking a blow tomorrow, and *vice versa*. Cossacks, though less vulnerable than the Russian peasant to subversive agitators, were still very gullible. Moreover three years of war had taken its toll; in 1918 even highly disciplined German troops deserted to their homes and threw over the Kaiser.

4 Kornilov started out at the head of the Bykhov guard unit, the Tekintsi Cossacks, Moslems who had once been the Turkoman horse, but the unit scattered into the Ukraine so that Kornilov arrived on the Don almost alone; Denikin, Markov, Lukomskii and Romanovskii travelled separately and in disguise. Dukhonin remained at his post in Mogilev and was murdered by the Bolsheviks several days later.

5 Kaledin had been an army commander from the South-West Front and had been the former commander of 12 Cavalry Division. Although a disciplinarian, he was taciturn and retiring; married to a Frenchwoman, he was a man of wide education and sterling honesty, and was liberal in his attitude to the *inogorodnie*. From the time of his election he was exhausted and unwell.

6 Earlier during the advance, Cossack carts driven by the old men and the women had come out from the Don territories, and these stripped the Russian countryside bare, taking horses, cattle, livestock, grain, implements, furniture, linen, even the clothing that the unfortunate inhabitants stood up in.

# 10 Epilogue

On 17 March 1936 there was a parade of mounted men in Rostov, a parade that was given wide coverage in the Soviet press at that time, for the men taking part were said to be 'Cossacks of the old sotnias who were showing their willingness to serve their country once more, this time in the ranks of the Red Army'. Who these men were and from where those that were mounted got their horses can only be a matter of conjecture; nothing, however, is spontaneous in the USSR and in all probability these volunteers were serving Red Army men specially got up for the occasion in a Soviet stage-managed demonstration to prepare public opinion for the introduction of Cossack designations into the Red Army and for the conscription of former Cossacks and their descendants into the armed forces. The parade itself was reviewed by Marshal of the Soviet Union Budenny, who was described in the press reports as 'a true son of the Don', by which the uninformed might think that Budenny was a former Don Cossack. This was not the case, for Budenny was the grandson of a serf and his father was born near Voronezh; his mother was a peasant with the Ukrainian name of Emchenko, Budenny being born in 1883 at the *khutor* Koziurin not far from the Platovskaia stanitsa. Budenny had been called up for service on his twentieth birthday in Voronezh as a Russian conscript and, since he had worked as a blacksmith, he was assigned to the Russian line cavalry. Budenny was sent to the Far East during the Russo-Japanese war with other cavalry recruits and was drafted for temporary service with 46 Don Cossack regiment to make up a shortfall in numbers. Within a year these temporary reinforcements were removed and Budenny joined a dragoon regiment in Vladivostok, and he remained with the line cavalry as an extended service non-commissioned officer. In 1914 he went to the west with 18 Severskii dragoon regiment and at the time of the 1917 revolution he was still a sergeant.

Budenny's true origin was unlikely, however, to be known to the man in the street in 1936 or to any of the few scattered Cossack remnants: and the description 'a true son of the Don' was vague enough to admit misinterpretation in Budenny's favour. However that may be, five Red Army conscript line cavalry divisions were set aside and renamed as Cossacks, two Don, one Kuban, the fourth as Kuban-Terek and the fifth had a new designation 'Terek-Stavropol' Cossack; and it was announced, though such an announcement in fact meant very little, that these divisions would henceforth be recruited from the areas from which they got their names. The Soviet government made a particular point of emphasizing that recruiting for these divisions would be open to all classes, without reference to origin, except, however, that the Caucasian hill peoples would not be accepted into the new Cossack formations. Some of the conscripts for these divisions may have come from Cossack lands, but the number of former Cossacks among them would have been small; and in actual fact it was entirely against Soviet policy (as it had once been contrary to the tsarist interest) to raise formations based on ethnic or political minorities or even on purely regional groupings, although this did not preclude the Politburo or tsar giving fictional titles to regiments and to military formations.

These new Cossack divisions were given a distinguishing uniform of a sort, though for the ordinary trooper this did not amount to much. He who was newly named a Don Cossack was issued with a red-banded forage cap with red piping, Cossack shoulder straps and a broad red stripe to be sewn on the outside of the khaki cavalry breeches. For ceremonial occasions or for press photographs some detachments might be given the old-pattern blue forage cap and blue uniform with the Cossack piping and stripes, and in winter the dark sheepskin hat trimmed on the top with fine black or gold braid. Those that were called Kuban and Terek Cossacks might similarly wear a khaki forage cap with a blue cap-band with black piping for the Terek Cossacks and red for the Kuban, the Kuban Cossack wearing the red trouser-stripe while the Terek had the traditional light blue. The *papakha* with a dark grey *cherkesska* with red or blue linings might be worn by some detachments on ceremonial parades, together with the *kinzhal* and old-pattern sword: but for general service the troops of the Kuban and Terek divisions wore the *kubanka*, a newly designed very squat fur or sheepskin round hat, distinctive because it was broader at the crown than at the rim, together with the *burka* cape.

These Soviet Cossacks differed from those of the old hosts in that their saddlery was of general army pattern, with standard buckles and D-pieces: the bridle was still a jointed-snaffle, though the officers had double bridles of the jointed-snaffle and curb-bar and chain type. No lances were carried and the carbine was of the 24/27 army pattern: Cossacks might be armed with the 1914 sabre without the hilt-guard, but more often than not they carried the cavalry pattern 27 sabre with the wooden scabbard covered with leather or canvas. One very important feature that clearly separated the Soviet from the imperial Cossack was that the Red Army man wore spurs and did not carry the nagaika.

Two Soviet Kuban Cossack cavalry corps and one Don Cossack cavalry corps were said to be in existence between 1942 and 1943, and accounts of their exploits, that were made to sound spectacular, were spread abroad for the sake of the western press. At home in the Soviet Union, however, such items of news were toned down and, as Soviet victory became more certain, less and less was said of them. By the war's end, as far as the Soviet public was concerned, Cossacks had almost passed into oblivion, making an appearance only on the occasions of military displays. Red Army cavalry, whether of the line or of the so-called Cossack type, did not have any decisive effect on the course of operations on the Soviet western front in the Second World War, although it did improve the mobility of the Red Army during the great advances of 1944 and 1945.

\* \* \*

In late 1942 German forces had occupied the former Cossack lands of the Don and reached the Volga river at Kamyshin and Stalingrad (Tsaritsyn); they also overran most of the Kuban and the Terek almost to the Caspian. Many Tatars, particularly those in the Crimea, had gone over to the Axis, and the *Wehrmacht* raised and equipped a few Tatar units. On the Don and in the Kuban, however, there was less enthusiasm for the German cause, partly because there were few real Cossacks remaining in the territories and partly because German officialdom at this time was little interested in enlisting Cossack or indeed Russian aid at a time when the war seemed to be going so well for the *Reich*. Nevertheless there was some local recruitment in the forward areas, much of it unofficial, of so-called Cossacks, but this recruitment really extended to any group or nationality—and that included even the Great Russian—that could be of service to Germany. The duties that these local inhabitants undertook might be those connected with local government or administration or as military or labour auxiliaries in the service of the *Wehrmacht*.

By the end of 1942 when it had become apparent that the German thrust to the Volga and the Caucasus might not be successful, the German Army, together with the SS, drew up outline plans for the raising of Cossack units. There was even talk of a project for a Cossack self-governing district in the Kuban, though there never was any intention of granting any Cossack or Russian real autonomy. The SS meanwhile set up a commission to investigate the ethnic origin of 'the Cossack nation' to prove, if such could be done, that Cossacks were neither Russians nor Slavs, since such a proof might have rendered Cossacks more palatable to the German tastes of the time.[1]

Krasnov, the former ataman of the Don Cossacks, had lived in Berlin for some years, and he was encouraged to recruit other former Cossack leaders to his recently formed Cossack nationalist party, enlisting the help of Shkuro and Naumenko in his plans to create 'a Greater Cossackia' based mainly on the former Don territories. These plans came to nothing, however, since the Germans had already fallen back from the Volga and were losing ground everywhere in the Kuban and on the Don. But as the German reverses mounted so did the need to raise more troops from the occupied territories and from among prisoners of war held in Germany. The auxiliaries that had been raised on the Kuban, Terek and Don withdrew with the German forces into the Ukraine, but these alone had little military value and their indiscipline was such as to make for many difficulties in their use and control.

A German Cossack division was eventually formed in Poland under a German officer von Pannwitz, this being equipped and organized in German fashion, horses, saddlery, accoutrements and weapons being mainly German: only the style of uniform was Cossack, even the nagaika being restored. The recruits for this formation were found partly from the prisoner of war camps, although Russians and others who said they had Cossack connections were added to their number. In reality many of the rank and file had no claim to being Cossacks and many on arriving with this cavalry formation did not know how to ride. The officer cadre contained a large number of Germans. Krasnov was appointed as 'the principal Cossack' responsible to the German high command.

It was probably the lack of German confidence in these new Cossacks that caused them to be deployed mainly in the west and south, where the risk of subversion and desertion was reckoned to be less than it might have been in Russia. These so-called Cossack troops had grown in numbers to about 20,000, and they included a wide variety of ethnic groups that were employed mainly in North Italy and the northern Balkans, and these were eventually disarmed in the area of Lienz.[2] Their fate was certainly an unenviable one, for many of their leaders and some of the troops were handed over as prisoners to the Soviet Union. Krasnov, the former Don ataman, Shkuro and von Pannwitz, none of them former Soviet citizens, were executed in Moscow in 1947.

Krasnov and Shkuro, and some of the more elderly of the leaders, certainly had been Cossacks, but the mass of the rank and file in the German service had no more claim to being Cossacks than their fellow countrymen in the Red Army cavalry that wore Cossack colours and insignia. Sometimes, indeed, they were one and the same, having passed from the Russian to the German service through the prisoner of war camps.

True Cossackdom died in 1920 and its legitimate heirs, or what was left of them, were the aging remnants that were spread over the globe, from France to the Americas and from the Middle East to China.

CHAPTER 10 NOTES

1 A 'numbered copy' report *Das Kosakentum* was eventually produced by the SS Institute at Wannsee in Berlin; although it was not particularly well-informed it was sufficiently honest to give a fairly balanced and correct conclusion as to Cossack origins.
2 In Italy they formed part of what was known as the German 'Turkoman division'; in the Balkans 1 Cossack Division formed part of LXIX (German) Corps.

# APPENDICES

## The Cossack Asiatic Hordes (1200–1800)

| Lithuania | Russia and the Ukraine | | | | Caucasus | |
|---|---|---|---|---|---|---|
| | | | | | Caucasians | |
| | | | Nogai | | | |
| | Budzhak | Edisan | Tauride | Azov | | N.Caucasu |
| Lithuanian Tatar | | | | | | |
| | | | Crimea | Kazan | | Astrakha |
| | | | Kasimov | | | |

1300—

1400—

1500—

1600—

1700—

1800—

NOTES:

1　These hordes were all Mongol, Mongol-Turkic or Turkic, although they assimilated or controlled in addition other non-Turkic races.

2　The Caucasian peoples, although at one time subject to the Golden Horde, were ethnically neither Mongol nor Turkic.

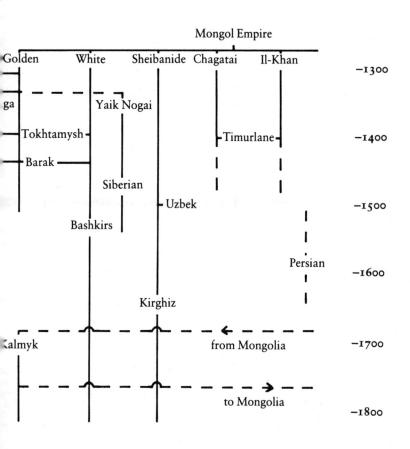

Asia

3  The Mongol Kalmyks came to the Caucasus in the 17th C., and returned
   to Dzungaria in the late 18th C., leaving one-third of their numbers on
   the Don and the Volga.

## The Cossack Hosts in Europe and Asia (1500–1914)

| Lithuania | Ukraine | Russia |
|---|---|---|

1500—  Lithuanian Tatar

Zaporozhian

Ukrainian

Don

1st Volga

1600—

Slobodsk

1700—  Polish

2nd Volga

Bug—Ekaterinoslav

1800—  Ust Dunaisk /Banat    Budzhak

Black Sea

Cauca...

Stavropol   Khop...

Kavkaz  Kuban  Labin...

Danube

Azov

New Russian

Kuban

1900—

Caucasus                                    Siberia

−1500

Terek

Yaik                    1st Siberian

Grebensk
Terek                                       −1600
Agrakhansk
Kizliar

−1700

Siberian

Orenburg

Ural                                        −1800

ne
olga     Mozdok     Semein
adikavkaz  Sunzha  /Kizliar           Transbaikal
         Terek                              Amur
                    Semirechie
                                            Ussuri
                                            −1900

## Russian Cossack Uniform

All mounted Cossacks wore loose trousers and leather knee boots without spurs (except in the guard) and carried the nagaika.

In the late nineteenth and twentieth centuries Cossack hosts, except the Kuban and Terek, wore the greyish brown Russian greatcoat and the army tunic and forage cap. A lambswool, sheepskin or fur *shapka* with a coloured top was worn in winter. The host colours were displayed on the top of the fur headdress or round the band of the forage cap, on the shoulder straps and belt, and on the stripe on the outer edge of the trousers.

The host colours were:

|  | Cap band or top | Shoulder strap | Trouser stripe | Belt |
|---|---|---|---|---|
| *Don* | red | blue red piping | red | light blue |
| *Astrakhan* | yellow piping | yellow | yellow | yellow |
| *Ural* | crimson piping | crimson | crimson | crimson |
| *Orenburg* | blue yellow piping | blue yellow piping | yellow | yellow |
| *Siberian* | scarlet | scarlet | scarlet | scarlet |
| *Semirechie* | crimson | crimson | crimson | crimson |
| *Transbaikal* | yellow | yellow | yellow | yellow |
| *Amur* | yellow piping | green yellow piping | yellow | yellow |
| *Ussuri* | yellow | yellow green piping | yellow | yellow |

The Kuban and Terek Cossacks wore neither the forage cap nor the greatcoat, but had the *papakha* headdress and *burka* instead. A knee-length open frock-coat *cherkesska* (usually black) with cartridge pockets was worn (instead of the tunic) over a coloured *beshmet* waistcoat. The Circassian fur *papakha* top and the shoulder straps were crimson for the Kuban host and light blue for the Terek.

# Russian Cossack Recruiting and Mobilization 1886

## DON

### Guard
There were two Don Cossack guard regiments, the Emperor's and the Tsarevich-Ataman; the former (that belonged to the old guard) recruited principally from the area of the Novocherkassk capital and the latter (new guard) mainly from the Ust Medvedinskaia district, though they also took recruits from elsewhere.

### Line Cossack
The host had forty-five line regiments and thirty independent sotnias, and their numbers, location and recruiting districts were as follows:

| Recruiting District | District HQ | 1st Categ. Regiments | 2nd Categ. Regiments | 3rd Categ. Regiments |
|---|---|---|---|---|
| 1st | Novocherkassk | 7, 8, 9 | 22, 23, 24 | 37, 38, 39 |
| 2nd | Kamenskaia | 10, 11, 12 | 25, 26, 27 | 40, 41, 42 |
| 3rd | Nizhne Chirskaia | 2, 5, 6 | 17, 20, 21 | 32, 35, 36 |
| 4th | Ust Medvedinskaia | 3, 4, 15 | 18, 19, 30 | 33, 34, 45 |
| 5th | Uriupinskaia | 1, 13, 14 | 16, 28, 29 | 31, 43, 44 |

Only regiments of the 1st Category existed in peacetime.

## KUBAN

### Guard
There were two guard squadrons that, together with two squadrons of Terek Cossacks and a Crimean Tatar detachment, formed the imperial escort regiment (the *Konvoi*) of the new guard.

### Line Cossack
Ten regiments were maintained in peace, four being recruited from the

Uman district and three each from the Ekaterinodar and Maikop recruiting districts; a further twenty regiments could be raised in war. The ten peacetime regiments bore distinctive names—e.g. 1st Khoper: and the 2nd and the 3rd Khoper were the 2nd and 3rd Category regiments. The names of the ten regiments and their depots were as follows:

| | |
|---|---|
| Khoper | Batalpashinsk |
| Kuban | Prochno Okopskaia |
| Taman | Slavianskaia |
| Poltava | Medvedovskaia |
| Eisk | Umanskaia |
| Uman | Umanskaia |
| Ekaterinodar | Ekaterinodar (host capital) |
| Kavkaz | Tifliskaia |
| Laba | Labinskaia |
| Urup | Maikop |

*Cossack Infantry*
In 1886 there were only two *plastun* battalions in peace numbered 1 and 2 and based on Ekaterinodar and Maikop

## TEREK

*Guard*
There were two guard squadrons forming part of the *Konvoi*.

*Line Cossack*
The host had four regiments in peace and twelve in war, the 2nd and 3rd Category regiments (like the Kuban Cossacks) taking their names from the 1st Category. The regiments and depots were:

| | |
|---|---|
| Kizliar-Grebensk | Kizliar |
| Gorsko-Mozdok | Mozdok |
| Volga | Vladikavkaz |
| Sunzha-Vladikavkaz | Vladikavkaz (host capital) |

## ASTRAKHAN

The host had one line Cossack regiment in peace, increased to three in war; it had two recruiting districts, one at Enotaevsk and the other at Kamyshin. The host capital was Astrakhan.

## URAL

*Guard*
One squadron only formed an independent guard squadron.

*Line Cossack*
There were three recruiting districts at Uralsk, Guriev and Kalmykov each of which raised a regiment in peace. In war this was raised to eight regiments, the regiments being numbered consecutively as on the Don. The host capital was at Uralsk.

## ORENBURG

There were three recruiting districts—at Orenburg (the host capital), Verkhne Uralsk and Troitsk, each maintaining two regiments and one independent sotnia: in war this was increased to twelve regiments and thirty independent sotnias. The regiments were numbered consecutively throughout as on the Don.

## SIBERIAN

The three recruiting districts were at Kokchetavsk (host capital), Omsk and Ust Kamenogorsk, maintaining three regiments in peace and nine in war. All were numbered as on the Don except that the 1st had an additional honorary title the 'Ermak Timofeev'.

## SEMIRECHIE

The host had one regiment and three in war, recruited from its headquarters district at Vernyi.

## TRANSBAIKAL

*Line Cossack*
The host had two recruiting districts for horse, Troitskosavsk and Aksha, and it maintained one regiment in peace and three regiments in war. The host capital was at Chita.

*Cossack Infantry*
Two battalions were recruited at Nerchinsk in peace and six in war.

## AMUR

Only one half regiment of cavalry and two half battalions of foot were recruited in peace, the horse being expanded to a full regiment in war; one of these detachments was later to become the Ussuri host. The Amur capital was at Blagoveshchensk.

## LATER CHANGES

There were some minor changes between 1886 and 1914 insofar as the Ussuri Cossacks came into being and all of the hosts, except the Don, Kuban and Terek, furnished small detachments to a new 'combined' or 'composite' guard Cossack regiment of the new guard.

The 1914 peace and war establishments of the principal hosts were as follows:

|  | Peace Regiments | War Regiments |
|---|---|---|
| Don | 19 | 54 |
| Kuban | 11 | 33 |
| Terek | 4 | 12 |
| Ural | 3 | 9 |
| Orenburg | 6 | 18 |
| Siberian | 3 | 9 |
| Transbaikal | 4 | 9 |

The total 1914 Cossack war strength stood at 152 regiments and 57 independent sotnias.

By 1914 all the hosts had given up their line infantry except in the Kuban where the number of *plastun* battalions had been increased to six in peace and eighteen in war.

# Select Bibliography

ACKERMANN, R., *Characteristic Portraits of the Various Tribes of Cossacks*. Ackermann, London 1820

ALLEN, W.E.D., and MURATOFF, P., *Caucasian Battlefields*. Cambridge University Press 1953

D'ALMEIDA, P.C. and DE JONGH, F., *L'Armée Russe d'après photographies instantanées exécutées par de Jongh frères*. Imprimeries Lemercier, Paris 1896

AMBURGER, E., *Geschichte der Behördenorganisation Russlands vom Peter dem Grossen bis 1917*. Brill, Leiden 1966

ANTONOVICH, V. B., *Korotka Istoriia Kazachchyny*. Kolomiia 1912

BRETT-JAMES, A., *The Hundred Days*. Macmillan, London 1964 *"1812"*. Macmillan, London 1966

CANTACUZENE, PRINCESS, *Revolutionary Days 1914–1917*. Small, Maynard & Company, Boston 1919

CAULAINCOURT, A. A. L., *Memoirs of General de Caulaincourt, Duke of Vincenze*, two volumes. Cassell, London 1935–8 (editor/translator, Jean Hanoteau)

CAUNTER, J. H., *The Oriental Annual – Lives of the Moghul Emperors*. Charles Tilt, London 1837

CHERNIAVSKY, M., (ed.), *The Structure of Russian History*. Random House, New York 1970

CHEVALIER, P., *Histoire de la Guerre des Cosaques contre la Pologne*. Librairie A. Franck, Paris 1859

*Chteniya v Imperatorskom Obshchestv*. Moscow University, 1863

CRESSON, W. P., *The Cossacks – Their History and Their Country*. Brentano's, New York 1919

CURTISS, J. S., *The Russian Army under Nicholas I 1825–1855*. Duke University Press, Durham N.C. 1965

*Entsiklopedicheskii Slovar'*. Brockhaus/Efron, St Petersburg 1893–1903

ERCKERT, R. VON, *Der Ursprung der Kasaken*. Harrwitz und Gossmann, Berlin 1882

FEDEROV-DAVYDOV, G. A., *Obshchestvennyi stroi Zolotoi Ordy.* Moscow 1973

GAJECKY, G., *The Cossack Administration of the Hetmanate,* two volumes. Harvard University Press, 1978

GAWRONSKI, F., *Kozaczyzna ukrainna w Rzeczyrospolitej Polskiej.* Warsaw 1922

GOLOBUTSKII, V. A., *Chernomorskoe Kazachestvo.* Kiev 1956 *Osvoboditel'naia Voina Ukrainskogo Naroda.* Moscow 1954 *Zaporozhskoe Kazachestvo.* Kiev 1957

GOLUBYKH, M., *Kazach'ia Derevnia.* Moscow 1930

GORDEEV, A. A., *Istoriia Kazakov,* four volumes. Paris 1968–71

GREKOV, I. B., *Vostochnaia Evropa i upadok Zolotoi Ordy.* Moscow 1975

GROUSSET, R., *L'Empire des Steppes.* Payot, Paris 1939

GROVE, F. C., *The Frosty Caucasus.* Longmans Green & Co., London 1875

HARCAVE, S., *Russia – A History.* J. P. Lippincott Company, New York 1959

HINDUS, M., *The Cossacks.* Doubleday, Doran & Company Inc., New York 1945

HOLDERNESS, M., *New Russia.* Sherwood Jones & Co., London 1823

HOUSSAYE, H., *"1815",* four volumes. La Librairie Perrin, Paris 1888

HOWORTH, H. H., *History of the Mongols,* five volumes. London 1876 *Istoricheskoe opisanie zemli voyska Donskago.* Donskoi Vestnik 1867 *Istoricheskii Vestnik'.* St Petersburg 1902

KARGALOV, V. V., *Mongolo-tatarskoe nashestvie na Rus'.* Moscow 1966

KLUBANOV, A. I., *Istoriia Religioznogo Sektantstva v Rossii.* Moscow 1965

KNOX, A. W. F., *Within the Russian Army 1914–17.* Hutchinson & Co., London 1921

KORNMAYR, E., *Les Cosaques de Hitler.* Paris 1964

LONGWORTH, P., *The Cossacks.* Constable, London 1969

MACKIE, J. M., *Life of Schamyl and the Circassian War of Independence against Russia.* J. P. Jewett & Company, Boston 1856

MARKOV, E. L., *Ocherki Kavkaza.* St Petersburg 1904

AL MUFTI, SHAUKET, *Heroes and Emperors in Circassian History.* Librairie du Liban, Beirut 1972

NORMAN, H., *All the Russias.* Heinemann, London 1902

PARES, B., *A History of Russia.* Alfred Knopf, New York 1964

PARKER, E. H., *A Thousand Years of the Tatars.* Alfred A. Knopf, New York 1926

*Piat'desiat Let Sovetskikh Vooruzhennykh Sil Fotodokumenty.* Moscow 1967

POPOV, M. I., *Azovskoe Sidenie.* Moscow 1961

RIASANOVSKY, N. V., *A History of Russia.* Oxford University Press, New York 1963

ROZNER, I. G., *Kazachestvo v Krestiianskoi Voine 1773–75.* Lvov 1966

SAUNDERS, J. J., *The History of the Mongol Conquests*. Routledge & Kegan Paul, London 1971

SAVANT, J., *Les Cosaques*. Editions Balzac, 1944

SETON-WATSON, H., *The Russian Empire 1801–1917*. Oxford University Press, London 1967

SHCHERBINA, F. A., *Istoriia Kubanskago Kazach'iago Voiska*, two volumes. Ekaterinodar 1913

SHOLOKHOV, M., *And Quiet Flows the Don*, four volumes. Progress Publishers, Moscow 1959–74
*Virgin Soil Upturned*, two volumes. Progress Publishers, Moscow. 1961

SPÜLER, B., *Die Goldene Horde – Die Mongolen in Russland 1223–1502*. Otto Harrassowitz, Wiesbaden 1965

STEBLAU, E. L. VON, *The Diary of Erich Lassota von Steblau 1594*. Ukrainian Academic Press, 1975

STÖKL, G., *Die Entstehung des Kosakentums*. Isar Verlag, Munich 1953

LE SUR, C. L., *Histoire des Cosaques*. Nicolle, Paris 1814

TETTAU, FRHR VON, *Die Kasaken Heere*. Verlag der Liebelschen Buchhandlung, Berlin S. W. 1892

TOLSTOY, L. N., *The Cossacks* and *The Raid*. Walter Scott, London 1888

*Ukraine – A Concise Encyclopaedia*. University of Toronto Press

VATEISHVILI, D. L., *Russkaia Obshchestvennaia Mysl' i Pechat' na Kavkaze*. Moscow 1973

VERNADSKY, G., *A History of Russia*. Yale University Press, 1944

VISKOVATOV, (ed.), *Istoricheskoe opisanie odezhdy i vooruzhenniya rossiyskikh voysk*. St Petersburg 1841–8

VODOVOZOVA, N. V., *Skazanie o tsarstve Kazanskom*. Moscow 1959

WAGNER, M., *Travels in Persia*, three volumes. Hurst & Blackett, London 1856

ZASEDATELEVA, L. B., *Terskie Kazaki*. Moscow 1974

# Index & Glossary